To my wonderful mom,

thank you for always being there.

I love you with all my heart,

Jenn

Praise for *Don't Mind Me, I'm Just Having a Bad Life*

"Such a joy to read Lewis's fluid writing! Wonderful vibrant dialogue and images. His is a vivid and very honest voice. Bravo!

— Martin Moran, author of *The Tricky Part* and *All the Rage*

"Incredibly strong... riveting."

— John Kazlauskas, TV writer

"Deeply raw and revealing, and I imagine, freeing all at once. It's a fast read because it's so compelling. In a world so superfluous, it's refreshingly honest. Reads like *Catcher in the Rye.*"

— Dave Earick

"Lewis brings forth so many incredible challenges and visions of a world that teeters just on the edge of stereotypical normalcy, yet then descends into incredible challenge... Crazy powerful."

— Ray Robinson, Dog Ear Publishing

"Nice storytelling... really authentic and homespun.

— Flynn Falcone, Author

About the Author

Lewis Kempfer grew up in Denver where he began his writing, singing, and acting careers. He attended college in Phoenix, studying print journalism at Arizona State University while working at the city's largest public relations firm. When offered a development deal to be a country recording artist, he relocated to Nashville in 1995 where he earned his bachelor's degree from Trevecca Nazarene University. Then, in 2000, he co-founded the Boiler Room Theatre. While directing and producing at the Boiler Room, he wrote book and lyrics for two original musicals, *That '60s Christmas Show* and *Billy Bob's Holiday Hoedown,* both of which played to enthusiastic, standing-room-only houses. His six-year body of work at the Boiler Room led to a dream job with a major entertainment company in L.A. Lewis also created an award-winning, self-promotional short film, *From Concept to Completion,* in 2007. After three roller-coaster decades, he returned to Denver where he lives with his best canine mate, Marty McPug.

www.LewisKempfer.com
Blog and Book-Related Photo Gallery

Don't Mind Me,

I'm Just Having A Bad Life

– a memoir –

LEWIS KEMPFER

FIRST EDITION

* * *

LK PUBLISHING
DENVER, COLORADO

This is a work of nonfiction and everything that happened is true. Certain names, locations, and identifying details have been altered for sake of clarity and to honor the privacy of individuals.

ISBN: 978-1-54397-075-3

ISBN e-Book: 978-1-54397-076-0

Library of Congress Control Number: 2019904549

www.LewisKempfer.com

Cover Design by Kenny Holcomb

Author Photo by Martin Bentsen

Printed in the United States of America

Contents

For Mom.
I love you with all my heart forever.

Introduction

I've always been a historian and archivist. Whether it was publishing the 5th grade newsletter, serving as my high school's yearbook editor for two years, writing a weekly column for the *Broomfield Enterprise* newspaper, working in public relations, or marketing and documenting the theater I co-founded, I've always been known to be the one with a mind "like a steel trap." Well, before that trap starts to get too rusty, I need to tell my story. It's not a typical memoir that focuses on one event, nor is it an autobiography, chiefly because I'm not a celebrity. But I believe my story must be told and that someone out there desperately needs to hear the message of hope that's woven through it.

Don't let the title throw you; this is not fifty-two chapters of woe-is-me hard-luck tales. I believe you'll find plenty of humor however dark and self-deprecating. It was sometimes my bizarre sense of humor that got me through.

I started writing this book shortly after my brother's suicide in 2014. That event and its aftermath are not included in this memoir but will be the subject of this book's sequel. Part of what's taken me more than five years to write and revise this book has been my wavering conviction. I started the memoir as a testimony to Christ saving me from myself. Then, influenced by social media and the advice I received from an agent's seminar, I decided to make the book less Christian-y and step up the snappy repartee to appeal to the LGBTQ community, my target audience. Still, it didn't feel right. I figured some church-minded person would accuse me of trying to further the "gay agenda," although I don't know what that is. By the fourth revision, I decided to go for the broadest, most commercial angle possible appealing to a large swath of readers; I was going to publish a bestseller!

Then God brought me, once again, to my knees. I was humbled by physical and mental challenges as I crept at a snail's pace through draft five. I was reminded that the only reason I had any story to tell was because of God's grace. Who was I to be so arrogant to decide how many people should read the thing? If God deemed that I should spend five years writing a book for one person to read, who was I to be so selfish to withhold my story?

This was going to be a Christian book for an audience of believers. But I've been continually reminded that it's not the saved believer who needs to read my story. So, the dilemma I've faced has been to either homogenize my story for the Christian reader, or tell it with the shocking grit that reflects the events as they happened. Make no mistake, there's adult language in this book. I have tried to limit my use of expletives to within dialogue and my italicized thoughts. There are many uncomfortable scenes, but they are true. They all happened, and they played key roles in my faith journey. It's sad that the Christian faith wants the soul without the story. Perhaps church attendance wouldn't decline if there was less judgment on what a person went through to become a believer.

My path to salvation was wickedly twisted. I was a hard sell for God. I was defiant and believed I was self-sufficient—until I wasn't.

Coming to know Christ didn't magically take away the gay part of me, although I wish it had. Instead, it left me searching for answers about the way I should live as a redeemed child of God. I still haven't gotten that part right, but thankfully, we have a kind gentle, and loving yet powerful Father in Heaven, who, like a shepherd, watches carefully over his flock.

I can imagine what you're thinking, "Oh great, another book about sheep and shepherds and getting saved." Stick with me. Be a sheep for a while. In essence, that's what the Lord told me. "Stay with me. Become a sheep. If this doesn't work for you, your old ways are eagerly waiting for you."

Join me on my rough-and-tumble journey, and see where it leads you. If nothing else, I hope you find my story entertaining.

He lifted me out of the slimy pit,

out of the mud and mire;

He set my feet on a rock

and gave me a firm place to stand.

Psalm 40:2 (NIV)

* * *

In the day of my trouble,

I will call upon You

and You will answer me.

Psalm 86:7 (NKJV)

Part One

DARK CLOUDS GATHER

Prelude

Death Wish
HOLLYWOOD, CALIFORNIA: 2008

Spinning out of control.

My head was spinning, and my stomach was churning, doing somersaults between violent bouts of vomiting.

Dying.

Was this how dying felt?

My limbs were heavy, too heavy to move. I couldn't hold my head up. I couldn't focus my eyes. I was sure I was going crazy. Or dying. Probably, maybe, hopefully both.

Was that a demon that just popped out from behind the drapes? And what was the creature that just disappeared into the closet?

No, I didn't want to die—at least not this way. Naked, except for the leather restraints on my wrists and ankles, I found myself sliding around in my own bodily fluids on the filthy floor of an infamous gay drug motel in east Hollywood.

I had been throwing up for what felt like hours since I dragged myself from the nasty, flea-ridden mattress to the toilet.

No, I hadn't been kidnapped. I had rented the motel room. I had bought the drugs. And from my ad on Craigslist, I had carefully

9

selected and hired a mean-looking, tattooed Mexican gangbanger to tie me down and rough me up. In our online chat, I pushed for a name only because the front desk would require one. He said his name was Miguel. I didn't care.

My arms were already bruised and bloody from my own attempts to slam before he arrived at my motel room and made it worse with his multiple stabbing attempts of finding a decent vein.

Once I was sufficiently high, he clicked the padlocks on the restraints and made me drink a tall glass of Diet Coke mixed with GHB. The "G" was to facilitate the scene I had devised: knock me out, and bring your buddies over to use me, rape me, kick my head in, whatever. I didn't care.

I don't think the scene unfolded the way I had scripted. Apparently, the dose of GHB was near lethal, and he told me he'd shot me up with more meth in an attempt to revive me. He said he didn't want to be stuck with a dead fag. So, once I was awake, he unlocked the restraints and was gone.

Usually, I hooked up to feel wanted, attractive, special, or for some measure of validation. This time, I wanted to be higher than I'd ever been and severely beaten. This time, I wanted to punish myself for every mistake I'd ever made in my life, including becoming addicted to anonymous sex and crystal meth. I wanted to show the world how much I hated myself. This time, I thought I had a death wish.

But there, on my knees, naked, drugged nearly to death, and helplessly alone, I called upon the God I'd never known and had always pushed away.

I prayed, "Dear God, dear Jesus, dear whoever's up there, please don't let me die this way. Not here. Not today. Please."

As I slipped in and out of consciousness, I was certain a flock of demons were crowding around me.

Then I blacked out.

1

Worthless Kid
AURORA, COLORADO: 1970

I have a dirty secret. Not a little secret, but a huge elephant-in-the-room secret. This secret has been far more debilitating than if I had gone through life missing a limb, or an eye, or my hearing. I hate myself. I believe I've always hated myself. This deficit of self-love has been the force that has propelled me into countless traumatic situations and negative experiences.

But just how and when did it begin?

* * *

I was four years old when I moved to Colorado with my parents. It was the second of two big moves; this time from Omaha, Nebraska, due to my biological father's job as an engineer at Western Electric. I never knew exactly what he did for work, but I figured it had something to do with trains.

We lived in Aurora in a small apartment while our new house was being built. Mom called it a ranch, and I incorrectly imagined a place with cowboys and horses. Turns out she meant ranch-style house, the one-level flavor.

Every weekend, my father would pile Mom and me into the

new 1970 turquoise Chevrolet Nova and make a sort of weekly pilgrimage to the construction site. It was at the bottom of a steep cul-de-sac called Chambers Road Circle, and it felt like an amusement park ride when the car went down the hill. It made something deep inside my stomach sort of tickle, like the time I went on the Tilt-a-Whirl. He would march us over uneven dirt mounds and around piles of lumber scraps, as he inspected each nail and screw, every pipe and board, making sure he got every cent of value out of the seventeen grand he'd paid Melody Homes.

One day the ranch was finished. In it I had my own room with a twin bed and a scratchy, orange and brown plaid bedspread. On the yellow wall next to my bed, Mom hung a set of cardboard cut-outs of dozens of Disney characters. I loved looking at them because they looked exactly like their pictures in my Disney books. But Mary Poppins was my favorite because she made me feel safe. Despite her ability to fly, she was the cutout whose Scotch-tape attachment often failed under the added weight of her umbrella and carpet bag. Frequently, in the middle of the night, she'd come sliding and scraping down the wall.

Nice move, Poppins. You were supposed to be my protector, but instead, you scared the crap out of me.

Mike Leak lived in the house to our right. He was the cool kid, the one who made catching a football look easy, the one who was always in charge. He had a dog and a sister and the biggest Big Wheel bike, the likes of which I had only ever seen in the Sears Christmas catalog. I adored him. As an only child, I wished I had a brother like Mike. He lived uphill by one address, and there was a great grassy slope between us that served as the stage for many afternoon

14

adventures. Often, our mothers would pin bath towels to our shirts, and we'd run up and down the hill as superheroes. I was always Robin to his Batman; it was, perhaps, the first layer of my less-than foundation. He was always the boss and always the one who decided when, where, and what we would play.

On hot afternoons, he wanted to run through the sprinkler in my backyard. Sometimes he would bring his Slip 'N Slide. My contribution was a toy called the Water Wiggle. Basically, it was a yellow, phallus-shaped mushroom cup head with a stupid face and a sprout of black yarn for hair. When hooked to the hose, the Water Wiggle would jump, spin, and cavort uncontrollably, thoroughly soaking everything within one-hundred feet. Mom hated the thing because it would spray her freshly Windexed windows. My father had been in the Air Force and expected his home to be spotless, going so far as wearing a white glove from his military uniform when he checked for dust. Mom worked hard to please him. She always tried to make everyone happy.

And I liked making Mike happy. I also liked touching Mike—nothing sexual, of course. I was only four going on five and had no idea what the thing between my legs—that thing Mom called a "dinglebottle"—was used for other than making pee-pee. But I liked to touch Mike on his arm or on his shoulder. When I would try to hug him, he'd push me away saying something like, "You're gross."

Then, one day, I was no longer allowed to play with Mike. His big bull of a father had made it clear to my father—who, from this point forward, I will only refer to as Dennis—that I was no longer allowed to play with Mike. (At that point in my life, I was the junior to my father's senior and was called Denny instead.) Dennis yelled at me because Mike's dad had yelled at him. I didn't know what I had done wrong, but Dennis told me I was punished and had to stay in my bedroom with the door closed. I wasn't allowed to look at my books or play with any toys. I was to sit quietly and think about what I had done to make Mike's dad so angry.

I tried to obey, to be still, but my eyes were hot and wet, and I felt like I couldn't breathe. I didn't know what had happened, but it must have been very bad, and I screamed and cried because I could no longer be Mike's friend. I was so mad at myself that I beat my forehead against my wooden headboard. It must have helped because I stopped crying and just sat on the bed, hanging my head. Dennis called that behavior pouting, something a spoiled-rotten kid did when he didn't get his way. But it wasn't that at all. It was just a hollow, empty feeling. It may have been my first experience with depression.

But is it even possible to be depressed when you're only four years old? Perhaps. The feeling didn't have a name, at least not any that I knew. Rather, it just felt like a gloomy, rainy day despite the hot Colorado sun overhead. It wasn't the sad feeling; no, sad felt and tasted differently. Sad was its own thing.

And when I felt this way, nothing could make me smile. Not a new toy, or a new book, or a new record. Mom would try to get me to play a game with her or listen to her tell a story, but I just wanted to be alone. I just wanted to hide under my bed where I felt safe. There, behind the scratchy bedspread that hung all the way to the mustard-colored carpet; there, with my Geronimo action figure; there, I felt somewhat safe. Maybe safe isn't even the correct word, but rather, out of sight, especially if Dennis was home. Because if he couldn't find me, he couldn't yell at me, and if he couldn't yell at me, he couldn't hit me in the face like he did when I spilled a little cup of strawberry shake from McDonald's in the back seat of the new car.

I felt safe when I was with Mike. He was slightly older and slightly taller and was good at everything. But now that was over. Sure, there were other kids on the cul-de-sac. There was Bossy Deborah next door, who, unprovoked, had hit me in the head with a stick. There was the older, supposedly retarded son of the German couple across from my house who would spin in circles on his front lawn. And there was Mindy and Her Pew, a bizarre kid who always carried a wad of tin foil with something stinky wrapped inside. She called it her "pew" and protected the thing like an injured baby bird. The pickings were slim on the cul-de-sac.

Many nights, I would lie in bed crying softly, bemoaning my existence.

Why does everyone hate me? What did I do? What's wrong with me?

That was around the time the little voice in my head made its debut, providing answers, "Because you're different from real boys. You can't catch a ball. You still ride a tricycle. You'd rather do girl things, like look at your stupid books when you should be playing outside."

The little voice never had anything nice to say. Over the years, the voice took on different characters. When I first tried to locate the voice, I imagined the little devil and little angel who appeared over each of Fred Flintstone's shoulders, always whispering conflicting advice.

Then, on a rerun of *The Mickey Mouse Club*, Jiminy Cricket

would sing, "and always let your conscience be your guide." I asked Mom who or what the conscience was, and she tried to explain that it was the part of me that told me whether something was good or bad.

Sometimes the voice sounded like Dennis. Later, it was a gym teacher or a psychiatrist or ex-boyfriend. But the messaging never wavered from its steady stream of condemnation.

The little voice was an asshole.

* * *

On Saturday nights, Dennis and Mom entertained some of his friends from work. They would come over to play cards or Monopoly and partake in the weekly quota of Pepsi. Dennis didn't drink liquor and wouldn't tolerate others drinking in his presence. Even soft drinks were something to approach cautiously; he would allow Mom only a half-bottle of Pepsi per week and only on Saturday nights. It's not that soft drinks were necessarily evil, it's that they cost precious pennies. The rest of the week it was water or watered-down Kool-Aid. Dennis was proud of his pennies and had a big, glass Miracle Whip jar filled with them that he kept on the kitchen counter.

I was afraid of Dennis and dreaded being alone with him. But I felt safe when he had his work friends over. Like George. George was the husband of one of the married couples who came over every week. George was easy-going, soft spoken, and friendly with immensely kind eyes. He was never upset or angry like Dennis. He would call me over while the grown-ups sat in the living room, drinking black coffee and talking about boring things. George would invite me into his lap and tousle my hair, as he pressed Brach's butterscotch candies into my hand.

I wished George were my father. I couldn't imagine him ever being mad and breaking things. I wanted to sneak away with George and his wife one night when they were putting on their coats and collecting their Monopoly game.

Maybe no one would even notice or care I was gone.

Dennis was always mad, always yelling, and it seemed to get worse after we were in the new house. He was a strict taskmaster with a relentless drive for perfection that frequently manifested as an angry and destructive temper. I didn't understand at the time what it meant when Mom said he would "lose his temper." I just knew that it rhymed with our last name and that he threw things whenever he couldn't find "his temper."

A Wisconsin native, Dennis loved his Green Bay Packers with a dangerous passion. When the Packers were playing, Mom and I knew to never disturb him. If they were winning, well, things were good. But when they were losing, as they frequently were in 1970, well, Hell hath no fury like a man whose football team was trailing at half-time.

It was after one of those games when Dennis couldn't find his temper. Mom was sitting quietly on our fuzzy, chocolate-brown plank of a sofa making yarn daisies for her never-to-be finished, field-of-daisies afghan. I was playing on the floor with my Matchbox cars. The Packers had just lost. (It was their final game of a disappointing 6-and-8 season.) Dennis, who had been sitting on the edge of his seat in the orange swivel chair, leapt to his feet, picked up the spindly-legged coffee table, and hurled it across the living room, nearly knocking out the picture window. The coffee table landed noisily in a broken heap as it seemed to ask, "Now what did I do to deserve this?" Mom knew better than to gasp in astonishment and kept me still and silent. I think she was afraid we could be next.

I never understood how a little kid like me could make Dennis so angry. It just seemed I could never do anything to please him. My toys were never straight enough on my shelf, or I would forget to put my tennis shoes at the end of my bed. I loved my collection of books, but sometimes, I would get sleepy and leave some books on the floor. I was a fairly quick learner and loved looking at my collection of Little Golden Books. I hadn't yet learned to read but was fascinated by words and the way the letters looked with their fancy little squiggles and tails.

It happened on a Saturday afternoon. I didn't know the days of the week but I knew Saturday very well because it was the day Dennis mowed the grass so it would look nice for his friends. I was playing in the front yard while Dennis used the clippers to finish the lawn.

Ever the budding young wordsmith, I was playing with my Matchbox cars and sounding out words that rhymed. "Duck, truck, yuck." Then it just came out. "Fuck." I have no idea why I said the word and certainly didn't know what it meant but was sure I'd heard someone say it.

Dennis, the outwardly devout church-goer who never drank, smoked, or cussed (except when the Packers lost, of course), was livid when he heard me.

"WHAT did you just say?" he yelled, as he pulled me violently by the left arm and knocked me face first into the lawn.

"Nothing," I replied, tongue thick with terror and grass clippings.

"No, you said SOMETHING. Now what was it?"

"I said 'buck.'"

"Buck?!"

"Yes, like what donkeys do, I guess."

"Well, that's not what I heard," Dennis said, as he loosened his thick, black leather belt.

He started my public humiliation by hitting my bare legs. Then, right there in the front yard with Mike and the other neighbor kids watching, Dennis ripped off my play shorts and whipped my bare behind with a vengeance that far exceeded the small sin I had committed. I cried and screamed and begged him to stop until finally he pushed me aside and called me a worthless kid.

I was learning that a father was someone to be feared, and that a father harshly punished his children.

* * *

Dennis's pursuit of perfection became everyone else's pursuit, as well. Mom was expected to keep a perfectly clean, clutter-free home at all times. She was only allowed to have one knick-knack at any given time on an end or coffee table, that is, when we had a coffee table. Sheets were to be ironed. Towels were to be folded into perfect squares. Kids were to be raised to exceed expectations, to excel, and to never disappoint.

We were in the ranch house for only one Christmas, I think— the year that I asked Santa for a big boy bike. I couldn't fall asleep that night before Christmas, and I laid awake chanting to myself, "Please let me get a bike, please let me get a bike, please let me get a bike." I don't know if I was asking Santa or God or if I was just throwing it out there to the Cosmos.

Once I heard the *scuff-scuff-scuff* of Mom's slippers in the kitchen, I knew it was safe to go to the living room. And there, next to the sparsely decorated and dimly lit tree, was a purple metallic Huffy with a banana seat, shiny streamers coming out of the handles, and little wheels on the back that made the bike look like a bigger version of my tricycle.

I loved my bike, and the training wheels gave me the confidence to ride up the street to the top of the cul-de-sac. I don't think I was allowed to go that far, but I did so anyway. I don't think Dennis cared because I wasn't bothering him. Turns out he had noticed, and he took the joy out of riding my bike when he used it against me.

"Don't think I haven't seen you riding all the way up the street when I told you not to," Dennis said. "Well, since you're a big enough boy to ride that far, then you're a big enough boy to learn to ride without the training wheels."

The warning scared me so much that I hid the bike in the backyard, hoping Dennis would forget about his threat and that no one would ever ask me about the thing.

But on an unseasonably warm Saturday morning in February, Dennis told me to get dressed. It was the day I would learn to ride like a big boy. I was petrified. I hadn't yet eaten breakfast or brushed my teeth when Dennis took me and the bike to the high school's vacant parking lot. As soon as we reached the Hinkley High School lot, Dennis produced a wrench, and in moments, the training wheels were off.

"Today, you learn to ride."

I cursed myself for wishing for the bike. "I can't Daddy. I can't without the little wheels."

"Yes, you can. You wanted a bike, so now you're going to ride it like a big boy," said the always-angry voice.

I got on the bike while Dennis held it in place, and I attempted to balance myself. With feet barely on the pedals, he let go, and I was down with the first knee scrape of the day.

"Get back on."

Dennis held the bike steady until I began to pedal, pushing down hard with my right foot, then again with my left, hearing the tires crunch on the gravel hardscape of the parking lot. One complete wobbly revolution. Then another. Then Dennis let go, and I immediately tipped over, bike crashing down on me. This time, the bike suffered its first injury.

"Get back on. Now."

I set the bike back up straight, mounted, pedaled, and crashed. We did it again. And again. And again.

The sun grew hot, and I wanted something to drink. My stomach growled and hurt. I had to pee, and I was afraid I was going to wet my shorts. I wasn't making any progress because I just couldn't keep my balance, but we kept trying. Rather, Dennis kept barking commands, and I kept failing miserably.

"Daddy, I've got to go number one."

"Too bad. Get on the bike."

The lesson continued into late afternoon as the February sun was starting to sink behind the peaks of the Rockies, the air becoming chilly. I was making a hint of progress but not nearly enough for Dennis.

I started crying.

Somewhere a few blocks away, Mom was worrying but finally got brave and walked up to the high school with a sandwich for me in hand. She confronted Dennis.

"What are you doing to my son?"

"Teaching him to ride a bike like a man."

"Dennis, he's four years old, and you've had him out here since eight-o-clock this morning without any food or water."

"It's good for him. Toughen him up."

Mom draped a jacket around me. "And look. He's shivering."

Dennis backed down, giving up his quest for that day.

Back home, he re-attached the training wheels, torquing the bolts so hard and tight that they were stripped. "He wants training wheels? Fine. He's got training wheels. Now they're on for good," he said, as he threw the wrench across the garage making a hole in the still-fresh drywall.

2

Learning to Sink

SOUTH LONGMONT, COLORADO: 1971

Dennis was Mom's high-school sweetheart and was a wickedly handsome teetotaler with porkchop sideburns and slicked-back black hair. They both grew up in Madison, Wisconsin. He went to East High; Mom went to Central. He was a bit older and was already out of school when Mom graduated in 1962. Dennis idolized Elvis Presley and had a wild side that scared Mom. He drove a Jeep and on one of their dates, Dennis drove recklessly on a country road and flipped it over, pinning Mom under the vehicle. He blamed the accident on Mom distracting him and was far more concerned about the Jeep's condition than hers. Mom limped to a farmhouse to use the bathroom and clean the blood off her face while Dennis inspected the Jeep.

* * *

We didn't stay long in Aurora. I didn't know why, but another new house was being built for us, this time in Longmont, a place that sounded a long way away. I didn't know how often people changed houses, but it seemed like since things had become bad at the bottom of the cul-de-sac, it was time for a new house. We moved into the new split-level house on Ashcroft Drive when I was halfway through

25

kindergarten, which was probably as good a time as any to stick me in a different school. I didn't have any friends anyway.

The storms began soon after we moved into the new house in Southmoor Park. The other homes around and behind us were still in various stages of construction, with piles of two-by-fours and stacks of plywood sheets everywhere. Across the street was an open dirt field that had yet to be excavated for its quota of tract homes.

It seemed wherever the Kempfers moved, trouble followed. The first—and only—spring season in the house came with some pretty nasty weather, as record-breaking destructive winds blew into south Longmont.

Perhaps it had been that same week, but Mom had just had her custom draperies installed in the living and dining rooms. Her new white velvet sofa with gold velvet piping stood proudly atop the greenish-gold shag carpeting, framed by the harvest-gold drapes and cream-colored sheers, in the on-trend Mediterranean-style front room. Everything smelled so clean and new.

I was in my upstairs bedroom when the power went out. I had just watched *The Wizard of Oz* on TV the week before the storm, so with a frightening cyclone sequence fresh in my mind, I was afraid— or maybe secretly hoping—that our house would be airlifted to some strange location.

Alone in the dark, I yelled for Mom. Always angry, always yelling it seemed, Dennis rushed up the stairs with his heavy military flashlight, more concerned about finding the breaker box than his own kid.

The winds were so loud that I could barely hear Dennis's voice ordering me downstairs. He pushed me in the direction of the dining room where Mom was huddled under the ornate dining room table. There, in the dining room, he continued to make giant Xs out of brown packing tape on the windows. But before he could finish, a sheet of plywood came sailing through, shattering the glass and ripping the drapes. He shooed me to the family room, as he enlisted Mom to help nail the rogue plywood over the window frame.

Alone in the family room, I sat in my black beanbag chair that was right up against the glass patio doors. Not a smart place to camp out, but what did I know? I studied the wheels of a Matchbox car, trying to be brave. Another window blew. I sprang from the beanbag and screamed for Mom. Within seconds, the wind hurled a piece of wood through the sliding door, spraying shards of glass everywhere, which sliced through the beanbag, and gouged the linoleum floor.

By the time the storm subsided, we had lost nearly every window on the back of the house. Everything was ruined, with an inch-thick coating of dirt on every surface. Miraculously, the beloved white couch was unscathed. Mom loved that couch more than life, I think. Having grown up with an alcoholic father, bouncing from various apartments, that white couch was the first nice piece of furniture she'd ever had.

* * *

After the cleanup of the storm damage was complete, the sod for the front and back yards was delivered. Again, the ever-diligent servant of exterior landscaping, Dennis painstakingly laid out the rolls of freshly grown grass. A couple of his work buddies came over to help tamp down the newly installed strips with a thing that looked like a barrel attached to a lawnmower. I was hoping to see George, but he wasn't there.

Overnight, the backyard became a thick green carpet, another perfect location for afternoon adventures. Even so, I preferred my private adventures across the street on the dirt hills that had been formed by the excavation of basements yet to come. The grass may have been "greener" in my own backyard, but I preferred the dirt. Typical for a kid, yet also a harbinger of my adult life.

Dennis had brought my little plastic pool to the new backyard, and miraculously, yet quite unfortunately, it had survived the storm. Summer wasn't the same without Mike, and I still missed him. Mom would fill the pool and try to get me to splash around while she tanned her legs, but I wasn't interested. And, I was deathly afraid of water.

One afternoon, Mom went with a neighbor to shop at Safeway, leaving me alone with Dennis. He filled the wading pool then told me to change into my swimming shorts as he changed into his square-cut, 1960s beach-party style trunks, displaying a massive bulge of the thing he once made me touch after a bath together.

"Today, you're going to learn to swim," he announced.

"Um, OK," I said, wondering if there was even enough water in the little pool for that to happen.

The plastic pool was filled to the brim, which, at the most, probably made it a foot deep. The hose remained draped over the side of the pool, providing a steady flow of water.

"OK, get in."

"It looks deep."

"Get in," Dennis ordered. Then, a moment of tenderness. "I'll get in with you."

He got in with me, as gallons of the cold water sloshed out, soaking the grass and exposing the seams of the recently planted sod.

Determined to teach me to float, Dennis had me lie on my back across his lap.

At first, I felt safe, draped across his lap, the cool water lapping against my little pasty-white body. His large, strong hands supported my head, and I felt like I was drifting into sleep. It was a relaxing feeling, being held by my dad, skin against skin. But just when I was relaxed enough to float on my own, he quickly pulled out his hands, and my head went under. He held me underwater a few seconds until I began to panic and flail about. I've always wondered if, in that moment, Dennis had the great temptation to drown me, the great disappointment of a kid.

He released my head, and I darted up out of the water, gasping for breath, and pushing the water out of my eyes.

"You were supposed to just lie still and float."

"You didn't tell me."

"Well, let's try again."

"Daddy, no, please. I can't," I begged.

I stretched across his lap, but my body was rigid with fear and anticipation.

"Relax, Denny. Relax."

"I'm trying." But of course, the more I tried, the less successful I was.

Frustrated, he declared that swimming was done for the day, making it clear in his body language that I had, yet again, failed him.

"No boy of mine gives up that quickly," he said, as he threw a towel around my shoulders and spanked me into the house. "Might as well take your bath and put you to bed, you pathetic baby."

"Why do I have to go to bed so early?"

"Because that's what we do with babies."

He ran the warm bath water, stripped off both our pairs of trunks, and deposited us in the tub. Unlike previous baths, there was no Mr. Bubble, no rubber ducks, no toy boats, and no touching his dinglebottle. Just a quick rinse. The warm bath water felt soothing, calming after the ordeal of having my head held under water. I decided I liked water but only to an extent—and only on my terms.

We emerged from the tub, and Dennis dried my back so hard with the towel that it hurt.

"Ow. Daddy, that hurts."

"You think that hurts?" He spun me around and slapped me hard across the face, his wedding band cutting my lip.

By this point, I was crying for Mom. He rushed me into my footie pajamas and tucked me into bed in the middle of a sunny Saturday afternoon.

"Now go to sleep, stupid baby," Dennis yelled, as he slammed my door shut.

I think Mom was surprised to find me in bed so early. Dennis told her we had a swimming lesson and that I had started to feel sick. Then the voices were muffled, and I could no longer understand the words.

I cried myself to sleep.

I had learned that fathers could not be trusted, that fathers were unrelenting taskmasters, and that they were mean.

3

And the people said "Almond"

During the short time we lived on Ashcroft Drive, there were rare moments of appearing and functioning like a normal family. Plenty of trips to the zoo (always zoos) and museums, and of course, public parks, because they were, after all, free.

Then there was church.

Westview Presbyterian Church was located one boring car ride north on Hover Road. In the early 1970s, new Protestant churches were constructed in modern, abstract, and downright bizarre architectural styles. Our church reminded me of the big top tent at the Ringling Bros. circus I had visited in Baraboo, Wisconsin, but instead of a red peak on the big top, it was non-descript brown. Two smaller, attached structures that looked like miniature circus tents flanked the big top—rather, the main sanctuary—building.

The church was so new that it had yet to acquire traditional pews. Instead, it had the most uncomfortable, unforgiving gray metal folding chairs, complete with Bible and hymnal slots soldered to the back of each chair. The chairs were placed in semi-circular rows atop the bluish-brown carpeting. At the front of the sanctuary, there was a stage that spanned the width of the building, with two choir riser steps leading up to the sacred zone of the pastor.

Westview didn't offer a traditional Sunday school. Instead, there was a children's message wedged in the middle of the worship service. That's when a bunch of confused and crying kids were invited (or pushed, as the case may be) forward to sit with the pastor in front of the congregation.

Akin to Mister Rogers, our pastor always had some type of visual with him that he would use to illustrate his kiddie sermons. We would sit Indian style, squirmy and ill-focused, but the pastor was like a master magician and knew how to recapture our attention. Once, during an Adam and Eve lesson, he tossed a rubber snake at us and terrified one little girl so much that she took a whiz and had to be dragged off to some nether region of the building. After a quick singing of "Jesus loves me / this I know / for the Bible tells me so…" we were prodded and herded back to our seats by several of the volunteer church ladies, who smelled like mothballs and flowery perfume, and had stomach-churning, stinky breath.

And then the pastor would start the adult sermon and drone on for what felt like hours, as I busied myself doodling on the back of the bulletin with a pen from Mom's purse. I tuned it all out and prayed for the stupid ordeal to end.

Fortunately, Presbyterians are clock-watchers. One could always sense the hour mark approaching when the congregation began wiggling papers, making exaggerated looks at watches, and snapping purses closed. These were all little cues for the pastor to wrap it up. There's coffee to drink, by God! After the sermon, the organist would play the introductory strains of the "Doxology," which would prompt a louder rustling, the audible waking of sleepy children, and the relieved stirrings of grateful adults as they jumped to their feet, knowing the service was almost over (thank God), and coffee would be served (praise the Lord).

Praise God, from Whom all blessings flow;

Praise Him, all creatures here below;

Praise Him above, ye heavenly host;

Praise Father, Son, and Holy Ghost.

Amen.

Then I would add, under my breath of course, "and now let's get the hell out of here and drink coffee. *Almond!*" It was just the beginning of what would become a lifelong pastime of watching people and making up dialogue. I would wonder, *why do they say "almond" after every single thing?* You see, I thought that the church people were saying and singing "almond," rather than "amen." At least that's what I heard. And the frequent mentioning of the Holy Ghost was confusing. I pictured Charlie Brown in his hole-riddled bedsheet in the Peanuts Halloween special.

Church made little sense, and I had no one to help me understand it. It just seemed like a bunch of stuffy women who showed up once a week to show off their new dress and for obnoxious men who sold insurance or cars or something to exchange business cards. And, of course, to drink coffee. Oh, yes. Always coffee. I dreaded going to church and found no redeeming value in it whatsoever, especially since I was too young to imbibe the holy caffeinated elixir.

In the backseat of the Nova on the way home from the weekly Sunday service, I would play with my fingers, forming the "sad, empty church" and the "happy, populated church." First, I would clasp my hands together, fingers laced over the top, with my two index fingers vertical to form a steeple.

"Here's the church. Here's the steeple. Open the doors, and where's all the people?" I would say, as I spread open my palms, fingers still entwined. Fascinating stuff.

But then came the real clincher. Fingers were rearranged to point down, hidden between palms, again with the customary steeple position of the index fingers.

"Now *here's* the church, and *here's* the steeple. Open the doors, and see *all* the people," I said in a sing-song voice, as I wiggled my entwined fingers together, making up conversations inspired by those I overheard every week.

"Oh, my! What a—er, ah—*lovely* dress!"

"Where's your husband today?"

"Oh, I don't know. Who cares? Did you see that foxy man over there?"

"Hey, we're out of coffee. Isn't someone going to make more, for God's sake?"

"I just *love* your hair. How *do* you manage to pile it all up on your head that way, dear? It looks simply, um, *fabulous.*"

And so on.

I never heard anyone talk about godly stuff, mulling over the deeper meaning of the week's message. It was just stand up, sit down, sing a little ditty, repeat as needed, followed by the exodus to the fellowship hall for an hour of gossip. If there had been talk about God's commandments, righteous living, or becoming more like Jesus, it certainly didn't register with me. Church was just a dull exercise in boredom. It made an indelible mark and formed an impregnable perception of church; I wanted nothing to do with it, thank you very much.

* * *

In the summer of 1971, the locusts came.

Alright, so technically, they were grasshoppers. "Locusts" just sounds so much more dramatic and biblical. In any case, my neighborhood was hit with a grasshopper infestation. The bugs were so thickly blanketed on the windows that it made the house dark inside during the daytime. And they were noisy. Occasionally, a brave grasshopper would fly recklessly away from the swarm before making a sort-of suicidal Kamikaze dive against the glass.

Those that weren't on the windows or glass doors formed a moving carpet on the front porch, and it made a sickening crunch when you stepped on them. It was nearly impossible to get in or out of the house without being attacked by the grasshoppers. They scared Mom so badly that she would scream when one jumped at her.

I was in that bug-collecting phase of childhood and felt bad when Dennis would kill them with his shoe. I was inspired by a character in one of my books who caught fireflies and kept them in a jar. I couldn't find an empty jar, so I improvised with a coffee can. I poked holes in the plastic lid and kept a dozen or so grasshoppers in the can next to my bed. At night, I would hear them jumping inside the metal can.

Eventually Mom found my hoard of grasshoppers and, in abject horror, made Dennis take them away. I was sad and stoic as Dennis took them. It wasn't that I wanted to touch or play with the bugs, I just felt bad for them and, I suppose, wanted to protect them.

Especially after losing Puffy.

Puffy was my first dog, a basset hound puppy that I named Puffy, presumably because I was missing my two front teeth and couldn't pronounce words correctly. Still, "Puppy" would have been a highly unimaginative name for a puppy.

Puffy wasn't with us for long. She was difficult to house train (and there was the whole white couch and newly replaced carpet thing) and spent most of her short life in the backyard. One night, she gnawed off a piece of the roof of her wooden doghouse, choked to death, and fell into the window well on the north side of the house. I was the lucky one that found her and cried for a week. I wasn't batting 1,000 with pets.

It was during that summer that Dennis started going out at night to look for paint—or at least that was the story he told Mom. Now, why a complete tightwad—a man who unabashedly lugged a heavy jar of pennies to fairs and zoos—was suddenly interested in home improvement was a mystery, especially since the house on Ashcroft was less than a year old. The house didn't need any paint work with the possible exception of around the damaged window frames, and Melody Homes had already taken care of that. And 1972 was many years away from the advent of stores like Home Depot that sells paint after 6 p.m.

As it turned out, Dennis was actually going out to see a woman from work. Her name was Sharon, and it was the name I would hear hundreds of times in countless stories of heartbreak: Sharon, the woman who stole Dennis away; Sharon, the cheap hussy who left his son fatherless; Sharon, the whore of Western Electric. She had a bad reputation, bleach-blonde hair, and big boobs.

It wasn't his first transgression, Mom would tell me many years later. The day President Kennedy was assassinated, Dennis received his orders to report to Goose Bay, Labrador, less than a year after he married Mom. Goose Bay is a frigid place; perhaps that's why he sought warmth in the presumably hairy arms of an Eskimo woman. It still evokes an odd image of Dennis in his Air Force uniform being pulled into an igloo by a toothless (but quite hospitable), aroused, fur-clad arctic wench.

Back to Sharon. One night (bad things usually happened after dark, it seemed), Dennis came home and announced to Mom he was in love with a woman named Sharon and wanted a divorce. With an ear to my bedroom door, I heard the muffled sounds of Dennis yelling and Mom crying and begging in the living room.

Mom was completely devastated. Dennis, the high-school sweetheart, the clean-cut guy from the good school across the tracks, the seemingly religious non-drinker had a piece on the side.

After ten years of outwardly wedded bliss, Mom's whole world came crashing down in one fell swoop. The night of his confession, Dennis grabbed some clothes, threw them in the trunk of Sharon's car, and sped off into her waiting arms, leaving his wife and six-year-old kid in the construction dust of Ashcroft Drive.

He didn't even bother to say goodbye to me, his own flesh and blood.

4

The Almighty Potluck
LONGMONT AND MADISON, WISCONSIN: 1972

I was sitting alone among my packed boxes of toys and books. All I knew was that my dad was gone, and I was absolutely convinced it was entirely my fault.

If I could have ridden the bike. If I could have learned to swim. If I could have caught the ball. If I could have been the boy he wanted.

But I couldn't, and I wasn't.

Dennis officially moved out shortly after Christmas. The artificial tree was still up, and Mom was tasked with the formidable chore of plucking the 127 "life-like" branches out of the tree's center pole and stuffing them back into its cardboard storage box. Mom loved Christmas as much as I did and took great care in packing up our many Christmas decorations. Dennis had made it clear he didn't want any of it.

Among the decorations were a punch-out-and-put-it-together cardboard nativity set and a little plastic manger scene. I loved them both, and they were a treasured part of Christmas for me. I think I understood we were celebrating Jesus' birthday, but I didn't know why, nor did I understand who He was. He was just the innocent baby lying in the cardboard hay.

Then, a few months later, around Easter, I saw a portrait of Jesus dying on the cross. The kiddie pastor attempted to connect the dots between the manger and the crucifixion, but it didn't add up. Somehow, the little baby in the manger had grown up in just a matter of months and died a horrible death, and I was absolutely sure that was my fault too. I hated Easter because of that picture of baby Jesus as a grown man hanging from a tree. To further confuse the issue, the stinky old church ladies would point to the picture and condemn me. "He died for you, you disgusting sinner."

Without the benefit of Sunday school, I never learned about the Gospel message. I tried piecing it together by reading Mom's old King James Bible. Not a word of it made sense to me. I prayed for my dad to come back, which probably seems like an odd thing to do since I was so afraid of him, but I just wanted Mom to stop crying. When I realized he wasn't coming back, though, I started to figure that God wasn't there, didn't hear me, or simply didn't care.

* * *

Mom soldiered on and continued to attend the same church that looked like circus tents. But her efforts to remain in the church were quashed by the pastor, who taught his congregation to shun divorced women with children. Hard looks down Presbyterian noses prompted Mom to seat us in the back row, then scoot us out before the coffee-and-gossip hour.

On one occasion, the pastor invited Mom to an adult prayer meeting at his home, making it clear that children were not welcome. When Mom couldn't secure a babysitter for the night, she brought me along, much to the chagrin of the pastor and his cronies. She tried to explain the situation, emphasizing that I was a quiet kid. Nevertheless, we were told to leave, making Mom feel ashamed and embarrassed.

Mom wasn't ready to give up on church, so we landed in a non-denominational Universalist or Unitarian or Uni-something church. The First Congregational "Universal-itarian" Church of North Longmont. Or something. Again, Mom felt out of place and unwelcome. I wasn't a part of the already-formed Sunday school groups and had nothing to contribute in the way of either biblical knowledge or social skills.

But there were potlucks. An absurd number of potlucks. Not knowing what this church was for or against, at least one thing was clear: they believed in the almighty potluck. I hated the potlucks as much as I dreaded going to church. Mom was a great cook, and I didn't want to eat anyone else's food, unless, of course, someone had brought a thing of Jell-O cubes and whipped cream.

Mom always brought a big casserole dish of her favorite recipe, a concoction she called "hot dish." I hated hot dish. It's not that it had anything particularly gross in it like fish; it was just hamburger meat, tomato sauce, and elbow macaroni, but it would join a long folding potluck table covered with pans of other stuff that looked exactly like hot dish—eight not-so-delicious feet of bowls and pots and glass dishes all caked around their rims with crusty, meaty, tomato-saucy rings of nastiness. Hot dish reminded me of church, and I begged Mom to stop making it.

Mom finally gave up on organized religion but still made me recite my nightly prayer:

Now I lay me down to sleep.

I pray The Lord my soul to keep.

If I should die before I wake,

I pray The Lord my soul to take.

Honestly, the "if I should die before I wake" part always scared the crap out of me. I had no understanding of what it meant for the Lord to take my soul, so it remained a scary and vague concept.

Although I tried to pray on a semi-regular, but mostly as-needed, basis during my teen and adult years, I had no solid idea to what or to whom I was praying. The name "God" conjured pop-culture images of George Burns playing the titular role in the 1977 film, *Oh, God!* Terms like "Father in Heaven" made me think of Dennis and that put an even larger wedge between the Almighty and me. Prayers, especially as spiritual confusion infiltrated my twenties, often began, "Dear God, Dear Jesus, Dear Whoever might be up there listening..." They were essentially Hail Marys, like a football quarterback in the final seconds of a game throwing the ball to anyone who might catch it.

* * *

One day, we were living in a nice house on a nice street in a nice neighborhood, attending a seemingly nice church. Not quite 1950s sitcom family perfection, but it could have looked that way to outsiders. Then, in a flash, Mom and I were out on our own in a dizzying *tour de force* of ugly rental homes with nasty shag carpeting. These were the only spaces that a single mother could afford, spaces that signaled a rapid decline down the economic food chain.

Mom got to keep the car, but she gave up the house in the divorce settlement. She could have taken Dennis for all he had, had she been less naive and frightened. Mom would lament for years her giving up the Ashcroft house and its nice custom drapes. (Seriously, though, what was it with couches and drapes?) It had a mere $140 mortgage payment, which in 1972, could have been manageable for a working woman with Mom's secretarial skills. But fear of the unknown grabbed hold of Mom in the worst way and never let go.

We spent the first year after the divorce moving between Longmont and Madison, Wisconsin. Five round-trips, at least. And each time with the sacred white couch. Five times I had to put my books in boxes and be without them for weeks. Five complete moves between sunny (but depressing) Colorado and dreary (but depressing) Wisconsin. If Mom was trying to bury her sorrow, Wisconsin in the winter was definitely not the place to do it.

The divorce agreement stipulated that Dennis drive us in the Nova back to Madison while our stuff was *en route* via North American Van Lines. Mind you, he was only required to help with the first move. This was just the beginning of the many days and weeks I spent living in the backseat of that turquoise, two-door Chevy. Dennis was at the wheel, blaring Elvis on every AM radio station across an infinite landscape of corn and cows. Driving straight through at ninety miles per hour with no stopping for food or bathroom breaks, Nebraska and Iowa were a blurred frenzy of farms. Without speaking a word to either of us, Dennis left us in Madison at the airport and, without so much as a goodbye, hopped on the first flight back to Sharon.

Dumped into the gloomy, gray winter night, there we were—Mom, me, and the Nova. Mom wasn't an experienced driver, yet she was brave and picked her way through the ice-covered sheets of asphalt, winding her way to Grandma's split-level apartment on East Dayton Street.

Grandma took us in, reluctantly, I think. Being the tough, old, wonderful, independent bird that she was, Grandma didn't have the time or patience for Mom's ceaseless bawling over Dennis. She told Mom repeatedly to "wash her face, put on a smile, and get back out there." This advice, this mandate, would stay with me throughout my life, and in some of my worst moments, I often sought counsel from the memory of Grandma, asking myself, "Now, what would Grandma do?"

5

Key to the Zoo
MADISON: 1972

Evelyn Lucille Zimmerman Jewell was a firecracker of a woman. Born June 16, 1911 in Osakis, Minnesota, Evelyn—Mom's mother—was the embodiment of independence. From strong Dutch-German ancestry, Evelyn was as tough as a Midwest winter. During the 1930s, she and my grandfather travelled the country, opening new Walgreens soda fountains, overseeing the installation of the equipment and fixtures, and hiring and training the staff before moving on to the next city.

Mom was born in 1944 when the Jewells settled in Chicago. Mom's father, William, was an alcoholic with a violent temper. At some point during Mom's young years in Chicago, William (Billy) developed tuberculosis and required treatment that was only available at the veteran's hospital in Madison.

The Jewells moved to Madison where both Evelyn and Billy continued to work in the restaurant industry. Grandma became a waitress at an upscale steak house called Rohde's. Billy had been a cook while serving in the Navy and found work as a chef at the Edgewater Hotel. Then, after he was fired for drinking on the job, Rohde's took him on, where he worked alongside Grandma until he died.

Like me, Mom grew up with a pretty warped sense of what a father should or could be. Annually, she regales stories of her Dad coming home drunk on Christmas Eves, falling into and under the Christmas tree, or just knocking the whole thing over. While other kids eagerly awaited Santa, leaving glasses of milk and plates of cookies, Mom dreaded Christmas Eve. And for her Santa, she learned to set out a can of Old Milwaukee and a bowl of peanuts.

Grandma wasn't a heavy drinker, but she did enjoy her brandy. During the one Christmas we lived in the Ashcroft house, Grandma came to visit. We were in the midst of a typically unpredictable Colorado winter, and when Grandma arrived, the temperature was in the low 70s. She had been expecting the same bitter cold she had just left in Wisconsin and looked silly standing on our front porch all bundled up in her purple coat with a fur collar and her snow boots on the wrong feet. Grandma didn't like to fly on airplanes and always "boozed it up" (her words) to endure the flight. By the time the plane reached Denver's Stapleton Airport, Grandma was plastered and had hurriedly shoved her boots back on, albeit on the wrong feet. As she stood on the porch, cigarette in hand, hair ratted high and tucked safely inside a polyester scarf, she was quite the sight.

After Billy died in the V.A. hospital from self-inflicted wounds, Grandma swore off getting re-married and wanted nothing to do with men. As I've said, she was a tough old bird, always capable of providing for herself, Mom, and Mom's brother David. She treasured her freedom, her independence, and her space.

Years later, after Mom remarried, we would come for an annual summer visit. She reluctantly offered to let us stay with her, although upon seeing all the luggage and two Coleman coolers piled into her tiny entryway, she'd remark, "Oh! How long were you planning to stay?" No doubt she was wondering, *"Did you bring that stupid white couch, too?"*

After a few days of our visits, there always came a morning when we would find Grandma seated at her Formica-topped kitchen dinette, hair wrapped in protective toilet paper, coffee cup in one hand, Kent cigarette in the other, with her back positioned squarely to the door. No words were needed; Grandma's body language told us it was time to leave.

So, I think she, at best, tolerated it when Mom and I landed back in Madison after the divorce. We temporarily moved into Grandma's two-bedroom apartment, but she made it patently clear that Mom was to find her own place and a job immediately.

Mom rented a shabby-yet-spacious apartment in Grandma's neighborhood, not surprisingly identical to the one on Pawling Street where she and Dennis lived after they married. It was in that apartment that I was finally conceived after three years of failed attempts and specialist visits. Mom must have been the one who wanted a child because he sure didn't care much about me.

Mom would spend the next several years trying to rebuild and recreate what she *believed* she had with Dennis—a stable family unit.

The apartment was built during the post-Depression era, a four-unit cracker box of a building. We had the upper left unit, amazingly, coincidentally, the same placement she had had on Pawling Street, but this unit was dreary and depressing. Unlike Pawling, there wasn't a jovial neighbor lady downstairs banging out "Hello, Dolly!" on an out-of-tune spinet piano.

I was deposited into an empty bedroom, miserably sick with my bi-monthly bronchitis flare-up. I laid shivering under a thin blanket on the semi-clean, blue carpet while my toys, bed, and books were still packed somewhere on a moving truck. Mom had her best girlfriend Carol over to help line the kitchen cupboards with floral contact paper. Mom cried, Carol cut, and I tried to show interest in the plastic dump truck she brought me from Woolworths.

I remained sick most of the time we lived in Madison, and other than walks with Grandma to the corner store—a tiny Mom-and-Pop grocery called Ullsvik's—there wasn't much to be joyful about. There was, however, the bookmobile, a rolling children's library that would materialize every week in the Piggly Wiggly parking lot. No matter how badly my throat hurt or how awful I knew my chest would feel walking in the bitter cold, I always begged Mom to take me. Stepping into the bookmobile was like entering an enchanted kingdom. It had an intoxicating, musty smell that I've encountered every now and then as an adult, and each time, I'm stopped cold to inhale deep draughts of the scent. (The stairwell to Grandma's second-floor apartment had that same, wonderful smell.) By this time, I had learned to read simple books and could recognize some of the words on the spines. My favorite books were *Harold and the Purple Crayon* and *Where the Wild Things Are*, and I would check them out as often as possible. I loved the sound of the bindings crackling as I opened a new book. Reading opened up a new world of semi-imaginary friends who didn't tease me and didn't care that my front teeth stuck out.

But books weren't actual friends. Elementary school is usually a crucial time for a kid to forge friendships and develop social skills, but I was never in one place long enough to do so. My first couple of school years were a dizzying, not-so-merry-go-round of moving vans and apartments that all looked the same.

When Mom and I were in Colorado, I continued to attend Burlington Elementary, the same school I attended for the latter half of kindergarten. In those days—and this may have changed—kids only went for half days. I was a morning-session kid in a class taught by a likable young woman named Miss Fox. Then, at some point, Miss Fox disappeared for a while to get married. She came back as Mrs. Wolfe. I kid you not, she went from Fox to Wolfe and, in the process, became less kind, less gentle, and a lot less patient with her snotty-nosed charges.

In the large, open multi-purpose room that served as the kindergarten wing, I was among the twenty-five other brats who spent their half days making things with (and no doubt eating) that wonderful school paste that came in glass jars. We colored, we sang, and we sat in circles playing games, such as "Duck, Duck, Goose." Then, after *that* excitement waned, we napped on bathroom towels on the hard floor for twenty minutes toward the end of each half-day session. The sterner, newly married Mrs. Wolfe had morphed into a strict disciplinarian and demanded we keep our eyes tightly closed during the entire duration of naptime. I could hear her rustling around the room, collecting papers and probably snacking on a little paste herself.

After what seemed like hours, one lucky kid (hint: it was never me) was tapped on the shoulder by Mrs. Wolfe and was handed the coveted wake-up wand. Then, the blessed, chosen one who had received the honor of playing the non-gender-specific role of

Wake-Up Fairy got to go around to all the other twenty-four kids and, with the magic tap of the wand (complete with a tin-foil star and a painted dowel handle), decided who got to get up and in what order. It was an excruciating, early version of the yet-to-come drill of picking teams in PE. More often than not, I was the last kid selected to wake up, which meant I had to lie still with my eyes tightly closed, while all the others picked up their towels and gleefully stepped over me.

I hated being me—stupid, friendless, ugly me.

My confidence level plummeted as I started first grade in Madison. Emerson Elementary had already been in session for a couple of weeks, so I was the awkward, late-to-the-party kid with the funny front teeth who got assigned to the last available desk—the broken one. The school was old and smelly and different from what I had known in Colorado. In Longmont, the schools were bright, modern, and embraced the trend of open-space classrooms with modern heating and cooling. At Emerson, there were three cold and menacing floors of individual classrooms, each with its own antique steam radiator.

I had no friends in Madison (or anywhere, for that matter), and I rarely spoke. I spent a lot of school hours gazing out the drafty windows that overlooked a bleak and gray Madison winterscape of timeworn houses, cars buried under dirty snow, and icicles weighing down ancient tree limbs. Wisconsin in the winter was enough to make anyone suicidal, let alone depressed.

My classroom was on the second level and had cracked floor tiles and peeling yellow paint on the walls. It was on the back side of the school and offered a premium view of the dumpsters near the cafeteria's loading dock. At least, I assume there was a cafeteria. We were instructed to bring our lunches in brown paper bags. Lunchboxes were prohibited because there was no place to store them. At lunchtime, we marched in a single-file line to the cloak room to retrieve our lunch bags. The sacks, and consequently, the food inside, were usually damp, courtesy of an old pipe that spent each morning taking a leak on lunch.

With our lunches, we marched single file to the front of the classroom where we sat in a big circle next to our friends, well, assuming one had friends. Each day, maybe an hour or so prior to lunch, a metal crate of half-pint milk cartons was delivered and placed on top of the radiator, an odd location for a cold beverage. Then in the lunch "pow-wow" circle, we were each issued a carton of warm milk and a paper straw. Ah yes, someone's brilliant invention: the paper straw. One good sip, and the straw was toast.

Depending on the day, I suppose, either Mom or Grandma would pack my lunch. I could tell who had prepared it by the way the sandwich was wrapped. Grandma used a solid sheet of wax paper and folded a perfect little pocket around my peanut-butter-and-jelly on white. Mom was a modernist and employed the plastic Baggie brand sandwich bag. Alas, neither method was an effective barrier from the faulty plumbing. Probably in a rush, Grandma would throw in an apple or a box of raisins. Mom would give me a snack-sized bag of Cheetos, a snack-sized Hunt's tapioca pudding cup, and sometimes, a raspberry Zinger.

I would sit alone at the outermost perimeter of the circle and make up conversations with my animal key. Allow me to explain.

One summer, on a trip back to Madison to see Grandma,

Dennis (and the jar of pennies) took us to the Circus World Zoo in Baraboo. I had one souvenir from the zoo trip: a red, plastic key shaped like an elephant. Grandma picked it out, which made it special. Young zoo enthusiasts could insert his or her animal key into a special box at each animal's exhibit and hear a story about the creature. The animal keys were free, but the "interactive audio experience" (as Disney might call it today) required a ten-cent fee. But since there were no dimes in Dennis's colossal jar of pennies, I had to make up my own stories for each animal. Nevertheless, I loved the little plastic elephant. He was like a friend I could carry in my pocket. When I felt scared or sad, I could reach for the key and think about seeing Grandma at the end of the day.

I carried the animal key every day to school and protected it with my life. Every day except the nightmarish day we had to make sculptures.

On that day, the old battleax of a teacher scooped a big clump of sawdust and paste onto each of our desks. We were also issued small pieces of wood for our masterpieces to sit upon. I was afraid to put my hands in the glop. Worse still, I was terrified because I didn't know what to make. All the other kids were busy, happily making dinosaurs or race cars or snowmen. After Mrs. Battleax scolded me a few times for not participating, I was red-faced and ashamed of myself and dived in with both hands, angrily squeezing the mess, and ended up making something that looked like a stepped-on pile of dog poop. When we were asked to stand and describe our masterpieces, all I could manage to say was, "It's nothing. It's just a stupid, ugly, nothing thing. Just like me."

And so, it was on that traumatic day that in one not-so-brilliant moment of absent-mindedness, I placed the key inside my lunch bag while I was eating. Then the bell rang signaling it was time to stand, form our single-file line, and march past a big trash can to deposit the remains of our lunch on our way to the restrooms.

As the other kids were proudly taking home their art pieces when school was dismissed, I grabbed mine and threw it as hard as I could in the trash can then hit my head on the wall. I had my cardboard school box tucked under my arm as I reached for my animal key. I dug in my left pants pocket for the elephant. Nothing. Right pocket. Not there. Back pockets? Nope. Jacket pockets were empty except for a ratty Kleenex Mom had deposited there, much like the ones she often pulled from her purse that emitted a mushroom cloud of linty dust particles.

What had I done? How stupid could I possibly be? I threw the key away with my lunch, I figured. Frantic, I ran back inside to find my teacher, but the classroom was dark, and Mrs. Whatever-Her-Name-Was had already left, probably rushing home to line up her own brood in perfectly straight, single-file lines.

I ran—slid, rather—down the freshly mopped industrial-tiled hallway. The acrid odor of ammonia made my eyes sting and burn. I saw the janitor, a young and handsome guy who was probably some lucky kid's dad. Exasperated, I spilled my story about the lost key. I think he thought it was a real key, which probably explains the authority and urgency with which he took on the task of jumping into the dumpster.

Tossing lunch bag after stinky lunch bag out onto the frozen pavement, we proceeded to scour the soggy bags for my precious key. It was the oddest of bonding moments, but for that bit of time,

I felt like I had a friend and wished he could be my dad—or my brother or my uncle or my best friend.

After digging through what seemed like hundreds of bags, the search was called off as the sky darkened and a light snow started to fall. I never saw my little red elephant again.

6

Wishing and Moping
SOUTH LONGMONT: 1973

One of the best traits I inherited from Mom was her strong, Midwestern, post-Depression era work ethic, a quality that could easily be traced to Grandma. Mom believed, deep down, that she could fix any situation/man/home/problem by applying hard work and an equally large dose of worry.

While Mom was frantically trying to forget Dennis, I sought solitude in my room. I was bored with my books and had no desire for any new toys. I moved my little orange-painted desk into the middle of my bedroom and built a sort of fort around it, essentially creating my first home office. I would sit at my desk stapling papers together, making gibberish notes on a Big Chief pad, and pretend I was working. Like Mom, I suppose.

Mom gave me her old Smith-Corona typewriter that she received one Christmas as a kid, and although the layout of the keys made no sense, I figured it out and created a one-finger typing method. I didn't know what to write, so I just tapped out words I knew. I was fast, too—well, as fast as anyone who might be typing with a lone index finger—and used great force to make solid, black impressions on the paper. Sometimes, that powerful finger would slip between the keys and jam down hard on the metal levers, bending my fingernail backwards or creating a painful cut.

Often the quiet desperation of loneliness became such a deafening roar that I would bang my head on the wall, on my headboard, on the big storybook from Grandma, or on my desk to stop the noise. When I made a typing mistake, I would punish myself by breaking one of my toys. Then I would be sad about the toy and hide under my desk. Worse still, I would pick up the typewriter (it was the lightweight, portable "Skyriter" model) and slam it against my forehead until I felt dizzy and sleepy. For years, hundreds of well-meaning people have admonished me saying I was too hard on myself. They had no idea.

* * *

Mom and I were back in Colorado in a rental townhome in our old neighborhood. Still reeling from the sudden divorce, Mom was trying hard to find a new husband for companionship, for financial security, and to step into the vacant role of father.

Mom joined a supposedly helpful group called Parents Without Partners (PWP), a support group or social club for single, divorced, and widowed parents. It didn't take long for her to learn that it was essentially a meat market for horny single men (or men pretending to be single) to hook up with lonely women. "Mom was lonely and naïve, two qualities that rarely make a great combination." This I know all too well.

Mom's nights were filled with extra clerical work (she had, by this time, returned to the working world as a stenographer) and dates with men from PWP. I was never left alone without a babysitter. Often, I had the same inept teenage girl who would lock me in my bedroom while she had different boyfriends over to play Monopoly. At least, that's what she told me. Whenever she was my sitter, the living room was smoky and smelled like a skunk.

I could have saved Mom the babysitter money. I didn't want to leave my room and would stare out my second-floor bedroom window, craning my neck to look down the street for Mom's car.

I was frequently in the throes of a full anxiety attack on those nights, as I cried for Mom. I was terrified that she wouldn't come back for me. I tried to console myself by remembering a poem from one of my schoolbooks. Simply entitled "Waiting," the poem was accompanied by an illustration of a kid staring out a rainy window, waiting for the storm to pass so he could go outside and play baseball. The only line I knew was "waiting is the hardest thing to do." There was some kind of positive payoff at the end of the kiddie poem, probably the cliché message about the good things in store for those who wait.

When the act of waiting became exhausting, I would eventually cry myself to sleep, often still perched on the window ledge looking out on my own stormy night.

Even when Mom was home, I dreaded going to bed, not because I had to stop playing—I had no interest in it around the time Dennis left—but because going to bed meant lying for hours staring at an ugly popcorn ceiling. Sometimes I would cry in frustration, but mostly, I was mad at myself for, well, everything that I couldn't do, which included falling asleep. Sometimes I would get up and hit my head on the window frame so hard that my vision became blurry and I collapsed into bed, finally asleep. And every night I wished with all my might that I would never wake up.

7

Alley Brats

After the 1972 World Series of Moving (I think we lost, by the way), Mom and I finally settled in a duplex on South Bowen Street in the same general area as the Ashcroft house, but still a couple of notches closer to the bottom of the rental-home food chain. The place was clean, had the latest kitchen appliances, new carpet, and nice drapes. The drapes even had a set of sheers and that was the tipping point for Mom; she's very particular about her window coverings.

Mom told me that we had to stay in the duplex and that we had to make it work. I think she was talking more to herself than to me. Moving was no longer an option, as Mom had given the vast majority of the money she had received in the divorce settlement to North American Van Lines. They were the real winners, and we landed perilously close to being on welfare or on the street. But no matter how tight things became, Mom held fast and vowed she would never take government handouts, such as welfare or food stamps. And she valiantly kept that vow.

Mom had been the top typist in her high school class and won a prestigious award. During the first stay in Madison, Mom dusted off her typing, stenography, and shorthand skills and got a job with the City of Madison. Impeccable in her appearance and presentation, Mom got every job for which she interviewed.

Back in Colorado, Mom's work experience and skills also served her well. She landed a position in the City of Longmont's finance department, then worked as a switchboard operator while she waited for a better job. Mom's diligence reaped blessings when she was offered a permanent position as secretary for the Parks and Recreation department. Although far from glamorous—she was handing out basketballs and collecting sweaty towels—it continued to secure her future with the City.

The pay was still pitifully low and not enough, so Mom took on evening work capturing, in her flawless shorthand, the breathtaking and exhilarating minutes of truly exciting City groups and associations, like the Golf Board, the Water and Sewer Task Force, and the Long-Range Planning and Zoning Commission.

Between the additional income and the great deal Mom got on the rent for the Bowen duplex, she successfully avoided government assistance. Dennis haphazardly made monthly alimony and child support payments, and Mom learned to not rely on that income. The alimony stopped first, then later, the $110 he paid in child support went away. I knew the amount because Mom spoke so frequently of not receiving it and how worried she was about money. My takeaway from it was that I wasn't even worth a hundred bucks per month.

Mom worked small miracles with money; she was never late with rent or utilities, and she always had food on the table. Sure, there were nights when we only had scrambled eggs and pancakes for dinner, but I loved breakfast and thought it was neat.

Often, after a long work day, the sadness would grab a firm

hold on Mom, as she walked into our rented duplex and cranked up Tammy Wynette on the record player. Accompanied by Tammy wailing about a thing spelled D-I-V-O-R-C-E, Mom would bemoan her fate asking, "What did I do wrong? Why did Dennis leave me? How long can I keep going? I can't be alone; I'll never make it alone." My heart broke for her, and I offered to sell all my toys if it would make her stop crying.

* * *

I was only in second grade, but I had become a latch-key kid, which, as it turns out, would become a defining hallmark of my generation, a generation greatly affected by broken families, deadbeat dads, and kids left to their own non-electronic devices in the hours between school letting out and the adult workday ending. I walked home alone but knew if I needed help, I could stop at one of the "helping hand" houses. Perhaps as some sort of neighborhood-watch program, these homes had a black-on-white construction paper cut-out of an open palm displayed in the front window.

Once home, I would tend to the list of chores Mom had left for me, which was usually about dusting, and I usually completed the list. Usually. But not always.

It was on one of those unstructured afternoons when Mom was working late when Denise, a little Mexican girl from down the street, caught up with me as I was walking home. We were both in second grade, but she had a different teacher, so I didn't know her. Denise asked if I wanted to play after we got home. I was elated that someone wanted to be my friend. I said I had to check my chores list first but couldn't find one, so I followed her out to the alley behind my duplex.

She informed me that the people in the adjoining unit were out of town.

"So? Who cares?" I asked.

"Let's break in and steal their food!" Denise answered.

"Why would we do that?"

"For fun. *¿Cuál es el problema? ¿Es tu caco?*" She repeated to herself, this time in English. "What's your deal? You a chicken? *¿Un pollo?*"

"I'm not a chicken." *This is a bad thing*, I thought. I tried the doorknob to the back door. "It's locked. Oh well."

Denise shoved a metal garbage can under the kitchen window, hopped onto the can, and ripped the window screen off.

She's done this before.

Behind the screen, the sliding window was standing open about an inch or two. She jumped down and egged me on.

"I did the hard part, *bicho.*"

Reluctantly, I took her place on the garbage can, slid the window open all the way, and, with Denise's goading, climbed in through the window, feet landing in the harvest-gold porcelain sink.

"Now unlock the door, *bicho.*" I didn't understand the word she kept calling me but would later learn it was vulgar Spanish slang for penis.

I climbed down off the counter and unlocked the door. Denise pushed her way in and went straight to the pantry. She started to throw to the floor boxes of Kraft Macaroni and Cheese, Kellogg's Frosted Flakes, and Duncan-Hines yellow cake mix.

"Um, I thought you were hungry and just wanted some food," I reminded her.

"First, we gotta trash the place. Help me."

"Why? What are you—?"

She ripped open a bag of flour and shook it all over the kitchen, then threw a fistful at me. Next, she tore open a box of Rice Krispies and added them to the mess. Then some ketchup. I had been taught not to steal and to respect other people's things. I started to leave.

"Nuh uh, *bicho*. Take some food."

"I don't want to steal anything. We should go."

"Take something, or I'll tell *tu mamá* this was all your idea."

I was trapped. I grabbed a box of lime Jell-O and dashed for the door. Denise followed me out empty-handed, ripping the box out of my hands and shoving it in her shorts.

"Hey, we should clean up this mess," she said. I thought she was finally coming to her senses.

"Yeah, we did a bad thing. How do we clean all this up?"

"Grab that hose." A garden hose was attached to the duplex's spigot in the small patch of semi-divided backyard. "Stick it through the window."

"Um, what? Why?" The hose sprang to life in my hand and sputtered water into the sink. Denise had turned on the water and continued to increase the flow. She grabbed the hose from me and, cackling with glee, sprayed the walls, the cupboards, the glass-topped kitchen table, and what I later learned was a newly carpeted floor.

As the water flooded my neighbors' home, Denise ran as fast as she could down the alley. I ran the opposite way, around the block, and then attempted to walk casually inside and to my bedroom. I was relieved Mom wasn't home yet. I grabbed the dust rag and frantically started to clean. (Cleaning has always been my go-to activity when I'm stressed, scared, or nervous.)

The neighbors arrived home the next day, and the landlord came to assess the extensive water damage. I assume the hose ran all night. Mom asked if I had seen or heard anything, and I lied that I had been busy vacuuming.

I didn't want to play with Denise again, but one Saturday afternoon, a few weeks later, loneliness caused me to give in when she came to the back door and lured me outside to the alley. The twisted window screen from the recently flooded unit was tossed atop a pile of soaked carpeting, baseboards, and the big pantry cupboard that didn't survive. I felt sick with guilt, yet there I was with Denise, fashioning the debris into a little fort, right there at the scene of the crime below the neighbors' kitchen window.

"Finish building the fort, and I will show you my *ho-ho*."

I thought she said "yo-yo," and that sounded like a fun thing to do. I had a yo-yo, but like most other physical activities, I had no skill or coordination. I imagined I was building a super-secret hideout for yo-yo champions to share their tricks. Ideas for a sign started to form in my overactive brain.

Once the fort was complete (it wasn't much of a structure; the outer wall was the window screen), she said it was time to move in and play "house." Playing along, I said I'd be the dad and go out and mow the yard. This didn't fit into her script, and she ordered me to stay in the fort with her. She lifted her dirty T-shirt over her head, exposing the two lumps on her chest that would one day become breasts.

"Now you take off your shirt, *bicho*."

Being a hot day, I complied. Then, in a flash, her shorts were off, and I was overwhelmed by a stench that smelled like poop, dead cat, and rotten mayonnaise. She was sitting bare-ass naked in the fort on a dirty, wet piece of carpet. Before I knew what was happening, Denise used both of her hands, scraping my skin with her little nails, to yank my shorts down and touch my penis, coaxing it to become erect. Somehow, it did. In those days, I was hard most of the time anyway, especially at school, having to hide it behind a book or my lunchbox. But here I was, naked with an evil little Mexican girl in a filthy garbage heap in the alley.

"*Bicho*. Put it in my ho-ho. Stick it in my *caja*." Another Spanish slang term I didn't know but later learned it was a bad word for the vagina. I didn't—and still don't—know what a ho-ho was, but it definitely wasn't made by Duncan.

I had no idea what was happening. She pulled me toward her and attempted to guide my penis into her stinky hole. Perhaps it was the odor or nerves or both, but my ever-hard wiener deflated like a popped balloon. I fully expected it to curl backwards, like the feet of the Wicked Witch of the East. Clearly peeved, she slapped it hard and yelled something at me in Spanish, as she pulled on her clothes and scurried down the alley. I was left there, naked, in a stupid see-through fort with a rank smell hanging in the air—a cloud of nauseating stink I was sure I would never wash off. Thank God she didn't take my clothes. I dressed as fast as I could, kicked over the fort, and ran inside to the bathroom and threw up. Mom asked if I was alright. I lied and told her that a bug flew in my mouth and I'd swallowed it.

Unbelievably, this wasn't the last of I'd see of Denise.

One afternoon she cornered me on the school playground and wanted to play. I insisted that I had to go home right away, but she didn't believe me.

The playground was an odd assortment of huge cement cylinders, tubes, and a teepee-igloo-like thing, which were all supposed to encourage creative and imaginative play in a cold, apocalyptic setting.

Denise pulled me down inside the largest structure, the igloo thing, which could only be accessed from the top. To get out, one had to scale the inside using a couple of rebar handles. Child safety wasn't on anyone's radar in 1973.

"Let's play house," she said.

Of course. House. Always house.

Sitting on the dirt floor of the concrete bunker, Denise whipped up her skirt, kicked off her panties, and grabbed the waistband of my rust-colored corduroys. *Oh no, not again*, I thought, as her filthy hands tried to reach inside my pants, with that horrible smell from her privates flooding my nostrils.

"Um, I have to go home right away," I lied as I climbed my way out, leaving her sitting in the dirt. A trail of Spanish expletives echoed from within the cement teepee, as I ran the trail along St. Vrain Creek, past the giant Japanese pagoda, and out of sight.

Maybe her family moved, but I never saw Denise again at school nor did she ever come looking for me. But in the short time I knew Denise, she had turned me into a thief, a liar, and a fornicator. Perfect. Three commandments broken by the age of seven. The Devil had my number.

8

Almost, Kind of, Sort of Every Other Weekend
SOUTH LONGMONT AND DENVER: 1973

The every-other-weekend visits with Dennis began during the first year of the two years we lived in the Bowen Street duplex. And "every other weekend" is being generous.

As part of the divorce agreement, Dennis was granted joint custody and, in theory, a fifty-percent split of my time. I can't imagine that Dennis was in support of this arrangement since he left so quickly and couldn't remember my birthday, but Mom, in her desperate attempts to provide a male role model for me, insisted on the equal time split. She always worried that if she made any misstep as a mother, Dennis would take me away.

Her fears were unfounded as Dennis's interest in seeing me was flimsy at best. Sometimes he would call Mom with some excuse for a delay or a flat-out cancellation. I would often be dressed and ready to go with him for some to-be-determined weekend adventure. Sitting in the orange velvet chair, with my overnight bag packed and at my feet, I waited patiently for Dennis, anxious for a change of scenery, yet still a bit afraid to leave home. I suppose I felt some level of disappointment when he didn't show.

"I'm sorry, Denny," Mom would say, emerging from the

avocado-green kitchen where she had been vigorously scrubbing the stove or disinfecting the refrigerator's vegetable bin. "Dennis just called and can't take you this weekend. I'm sorry. You should go unpack, so your shirts don't get wrinkled."

If anything, Mom probably experienced the greater disappointment, as now she had a seven-year-old to keep occupied for the weekend. More than once, she had to cancel evening plans due to no babysitters being available on short notice. I knew she was mad and frustrated because she would slam the cupboard doors as she yelled and cried. I already blamed myself for pushing Dennis away; now, it was my fault that I ruined her life.

Some weekends, Dennis didn't even bother to call; he just didn't show. After sitting in the ugly orange chair for three or more hours, Mom would pronounce that Dennis wasn't coming. I knew the routine well: go to my room, unpack, and try to find something to do. It was during this time that I learned that people—men, in particular—disappoint and abandon. Surely, it hurt at first, but after a few cancellations and no-shows, the wound healed over with tougher skin, and I began to approach life with an attitude of "expect nothing and be pleasantly surprised."

Dennis's no-shows further sculpted my definition of fathers. A father was not someone I could depend on. A father did not keep his word. A father didn't care about his kid.

* * *

After marrying Sharon, Dennis moved into her run-down house in Lakewood, a suburb of southwest Denver. Sharon had three obnoxious children from her previous marriage: Sonny, who was about a year older than me; Susan, who was my age; and Sammy, who was four.

The new Kempfer house had two tiny bedrooms—one for Dennis and Sharon, and one for the three kids. When I was added to the mix for a sleepover, Susan would bunk with her mom and new stepdad, leaving Sonny, Sammy, and me to share Susan's girly bed that was covered with a frilly canopy that looked like a wedding dress. I couldn't figure out their usual sleeping configuration when I wasn't there, but I guessed that the three step-kids slept together under the glittery fabric.

I liked the kids well enough and envied them in a couple of ways. First, they had each other and always had a playmate. Second, they had a big, round trampoline in their backyard.

Like most kids who grew up in the early '70s, we idolized and emulated our television heroes. Sometimes, we were the *Zoom* kids, singing and dancing about zoom-ah-zoom-ah-zoom-ah zooming. Sometimes, we were the highly forgettable kids from *The Electric Company*. But more often than not, we were the Brady kids.

I was gifted with a vivid imagination—perhaps too much so. As I was inventing scenarios for us to play out, I was also strengthening the same mental muscle that would ultimately help me envision a wide assortment of negative outcomes for every situation. My what-if skills were consistently skewed to imagine all the ways good things could quickly morph into abrupt, unhappy endings. Later, this would become my trademark, being a sort of Devil's advocate meets martyr meets total pessimist.

We would re-enact favorite *Brady Bunch* episodes until Dennis and Sharon loaded us into the Chevy station wagon and hauled us off on culinary quests to places like Burger Chef, The Yum-Yum Tree (a cheap forerunner to the mall food court), and, on special occasions, a treasured trip to Casa Bonita.

Anyone who grew up in Denver has probably been to, or at least has heard of, Casa Bonita, the bona fide Disneyland of Mexican restaurants. Complete with cascading waterfalls, cliff divers, and countless caves in which one could eat an endless supply of sloppy cheese enchiladas and honey-filled *sopapillas*, it was a kid's dream come true at its tackiest. Truthfully, the food sucked and was supposedly peppered with cockroach carcasses, but as with most dinner-and-a-show type experiences, you were paying for the entertainment, not the cuisine. It also wasn't necessarily cheap, and with four kids and a wife to feed, it's a wonder that Dennis even took us. But Sharon had quite the influence over Dennis, so much so that the dusty wallet would creak open for rare splurges to Casa Bonita, which were usually for one of Sharon's kids' birthdays.

Other weekend visits with Dennis included an assortment of cheap or free activities, such as combing flea markets for 45-RPM records (cheap), swimming at the public pool (free), and drive-in movies (cheap because admission was by the carload).

One of the first Friday night sleepovers was unforgettable. Young Sammy was sleeping on the left side of the bed, Sonny was in the middle, and I was on the right side. It was a lot of stinky boyhood in one frilly bed.

After Sammy was asleep, Sonny rolled toward me.

"Let's do something fun," he said.

Always up for an adventure, my mind started to spin on the possibilities. Maybe he wanted to play a prank on Sammy or act like ghosts to scare Susan in the next room. Or maybe we would raid the freezer for Otter Pops.

"OK, like what?" I asked with breathless anticipation.

"Let's get naked."

What was it with always wanting to get naked? First, it was Denise in the alley, and now, it was Sonny in the princess bed.

Because he was older, stronger, and a bit on the forceful side, I complied. We both kicked off our pajamas. It felt weird, although not altogether unpleasant, when Sonny started to rub against me, naked young skin against naked young skin. I was still in my always-hard phase, so it didn't take much to sport wood.

We laid face-to-face. When Sonny reached down and felt my hard member, he quickly flipped so his back was against my front.

"Let's try something fun," he whispered over his shoulder.

"Um, OK."

"Stick your thing in my hole."

"What?! Wait—why?"

"'Cause it's fun to do."

"I don't think it's supposed to go in there," I said, perhaps uttering the most profound words spoken in my lifetime.

"Sure, you'll see. It's fun. My dad and I do it."

I wonder to this day to which father he was referring. Did Dennis do such things with him? Was it his biological dad? Or did he just make it up?

I wished my penis wasn't hard. My mind flashed to Denise, and thankfully, the thing deflated. But not before it touched a sticky, warm place between the ghostly white half-moons of his freckled butt. It was gross, and it didn't feel right.

"It won't go in," I announced.

"Flip over. I'll try it with you."

"That's OK, really."

"Nah, c'mon. Don't be a chicken."

Always wanting to please my stepbrother, I did as I was told. Soon, I felt him push against my butt. I giggled out loud.

"See it's fun, huh?"

I laughed more, perhaps at the ridiculousness of the situation and the embarrassment of doing something that felt wrong. A light snapped on in the hallway and heavy footsteps approached.

"Knock it off in there and go to sleep," Dennis yelled.

"Yes, sir," Sonny called to his stepdad, as he put his hand over my mouth to keep me quiet. "Hold still 'til he goes away," he warned.

The act didn't take long, but it did happen. And it happened again on other overnights. I didn't know if it was acceptable to do what Sonny wanted. I didn't enjoy what we did, and it hurt, but I liked making him happy. As much as I could never please my real dad, it was something—I suppose—to make my stepbrother smile.

9

I Only Have Ears for You
ANAHEIM, CALIFORNIA: 1973

Early on during the "every-other" visits, it was announced that the newly formed Kempfer clan was going to Disneyland. And it was arranged—at Mom's behest—that I would come along. I looked forward to the two-week vacation away from boredom and babysitters. I had no idea what to expect, and the combination of excitement and anxiety kept me awake many nights prior to the trip.

As with all visits with Dennis, he would pick me up in Longmont in his Chevy Caprice. He never brought Sharon or the kids along, stating he wanted the time alone with me. It was early July, and I was wearing shorts. Although the Caprice had air conditioning, Dennis was loath to use it, as it increased his fuel consumption. His effort to cool the car was limited to rolling down all the windows and blowing warm air through the vents. To protect the precious navy-blue vinyl seats, he had (in the front seat only) a pair of scratchy, hard nylon mesh seat covers that, in theory, were supposed to not only protect the seats but keep the car's occupants' backsides cool. Someone was overpaid for the invention because all the seat covers accomplished was making you feel more uncomfortable while leaving a stylish crisscross imprint over the back of your thighs.

After loading my suitcase into the trunk, we took our respective places in the front seat. When we were a few blocks away from the duplex, he slipped his right hand over onto my left thigh and sort of caressed it.

"You know, I've missed you a lot, Denny."

"Really?" I asked in mock excitement. *Yeah, and Mom sure has missed those child support payments,* I thought.

"We're going to spend a lot of time together this summer on this vacation. I really want you to get to know Sharon and your new stepbrothers and sister. We're your family, and you belong with us."

Bet you don't know how well I already know Sonny.

"Um, OK," I said, not completely grasping the scenario Dennis was laying out.

"And I really want you and Sharon to get close. Wouldn't you like to have Sharon as your mother?"

"I already have a great mother, the best mother—"

"Alright. Sure, sure," he said with a dismissive leg pat.

"We're taking Sharon's station wagon and a pop-up camper. That way we get to sleep out under the stars."

Not quite the vacation I imagined. Holiday Inn was already more my style.

"That sounds fun, I guess."

"And this summer, you're finally going to learn to swim. Your mother tells me you don't like the swimming lessons on Saturdays at the recreation center. That's understandable. You need to be taught in a special way, don't you?" Dennis said with another thigh squeeze.

"Um, how so?"

"By an expert like me. Anyway, we'll get you swimming like a pro, and by the time we get to the ocean, you'll be ready to swim with Sonny—like a big boy."

I knew there was a catch. Why was I going on this trip again?

The next morning, we all piled into the iconic American summer vacation-mobile: a dark blue 1969 Chevrolet Kingswood Estate station wagon, with quintessential faux-wood side panels. It was a beast of a car that had three bench seats, although the third one, the furthest toward the back, was folded down and piled high with a Coleman cooler, jugs of water, Sharon's hefty make-up case, and several brown paper grocery bags filled with Wonder Bread and store-brand peanut butter. As such, the four of us kids got to share the second-row seat, shoved in like sweaty sardines without the benefit of oil. Thankfully, once in a while, Susan would climb into the front seat and snuggle between her mother and Dennis. This made room for more boyish buffoonery in the backseat, including Sonny's armpit fart noises, Sammy's loud burps, and my exclamations of "You're gross!"

The rattletrap car filled with Dennis and Sharon, kids, sweat, and farts dragged along a Starcraft trailer that purported, in fancy advertising script on its side, that it "sleeps four comfortably." Well, there were six of us, so I deduced that at least two people would *not* be sleeping so comfortably.

When we stopped for the first night somewhere in middle-of-nowhere Utah, Dennis cranked up the Starcraft to erect the flimsy metal framework of the poor man's RV and zipped up the fabric panels to complete the strangest-looking contraption I'd ever seen. The sleeping arrangements were akin to those at the Kempfer house: the adults and Susan shared one sleeping berth, and the three boys got the other.

The second day was longer, hotter, and smellier, as we rumbled across Utah into Nevada on our way to Las Vegas, an unlikely vacation spot for a tightwad dad with a car full of kids. Plus, it was 1973, and Vegas had yet to evolve into the family-friendly city that it strives to be today. Meaning, there were no themed hotels with elaborate roller coasters, pirate ship shows, or indoor boat rides. Why we even stopped and stayed on the Vegas Strip remains a mystery. But I can proudly state that I spent two nights in a mildewed pop-up camper at the now long-gone Camperland RV lot behind the now-demolished Stardust Casino. Also, the city's only drive-in theater that showed new movies was situated behind the Stardust, so that was probably a selling point. RV parking, pool use, and free drive-in movies were all included in the campground fee of one dollar per day. Such a deal.

During the day, we all walked from Camperland like a bunch of hobos to the Stardust's Big Dipper pool. Sharon positioned herself on a lawn chair with a tattered, thrift-store Harlequin Romance novel while Dennis got down to business getting us kids ready to swim. Actually, the stepkids were already in the pool, merrily splashing under the scorching Nevada sun. I'm sure it was a welcome relief from the car and the camper. I was afraid to go near the water but tentatively made my way to the edge and put my feet in. Dennis was in the water and swam over to me.

"Get in the pool, Denny."

"I don't feel so good. Can I just sit here?"

"And make us all look like fools?"

"Honest. I don't feel good enough to swim."

"You mean you don't *want* to swim. There's a difference."

I held my stomach and tried feigning illness.

"What kid wouldn't want to be in this great pool?" Dennis continued.

This kid, you jerk, I thought. "Maybe later, please?"

"There won't be a later," he said, as he pulled me by the legs into the water. I started to panic and splash around like I was going to drown. "I've got you," Dennis said, pulling me roughly to his smooth chest.

I tried to relax but couldn't. He must have sensed it and, in his usual cruel taskmaster manner, decided to teach me a lesson.

"Oops, I slipped," he said, as he let go of me. I bobbed under the water, struggled my way to the surface, and gasped for air just as Dennis dunked my head under again. By this time, Sonny and Sammy were there, egging him on and laughing at me. Chlorine burned the inside of my nose as I coughed up water.

Some father.

And this man wanted me to come live with him? First of all, why? He clearly didn't care a lick about me. And second, he seemed to have so much more pride in Sharon's kids. I couldn't imagine why he would even entertain the thought of getting custody of me, if that was ever his true intention. I suddenly missed Mom and wanted to cry.

Late in the afternoon, Dennis and Sharon parked us on the sidewalk outside the casino while they went in to gamble. Perhaps Sharon was the impetus. After all, Dennis wouldn't splurge on a bottle of Pepsi more than once a week, plus there was the TP-rationing thing. Although it's not in my memory bank, Mom tells me how Dennis used to dole out toilet paper: one square for number one, three squares for number two. Heaven forbid one had diarrhea.

And there we were, four snot-nosed ragamuffins hanging out in front of the automatic sliding glass doors of the Stardust like we were begging for food. During one of our stops, I had purchased a slot machine key ring with a little plastic handle that actually spun the three dials. It was a welcome distraction as we killed time sitting on the grimy sidewalk as gamblers and drunks stepped over us. Sonny wanted to play with it, but I was afraid he'd break it.

Eventually, well after sundown, Sharon and Dennis emerged from the casino. Dennis seemed to be in a particularly bad mood; perhaps Sharon had foolishly blown the week's Camperland savings on a roulette wheel. Or maybe they stopped getting free Pepsis when they stopped playing the nickel slots.

Despite the pool ordeal, I have good memories of staying at the Stardust. Ironically, the once-iconic hotel and casino was imploded on March 13, 2007, the same day I learned I was HIV positive. When I heard the news out of Vegas shortly after I received my own life-demolishing news, I thought, *Well, there goes that.*

After another long day's drive, we arrived in Anaheim, California. Dennis had already located another bargain RV lot in the Good Sam campground-finder guide. I guess Vacationland, the overnight RV parking lot at the Disneyland Hotel, was too expensive, so we stayed at the affordable Trailerland lot at the corner of Harbor Boulevard and Ball Road, which was inevitably another victim of the wrecking ball.

After an exhausting walk over the Santa Ana (Interstate 5) Freeway and another dozen or more blocks south on Harbor, us Kempfers made our not-so triumphant entry into the Magic Kingdom. From the moment I saw the glimmering, gigantic Disneyland marquee, I was ecstatic. The word Disneyland was carved out of elegant, Olde-World plastic and looked just like the logo on my large collection of Disney book and record sets. There was just something awe-inspiring about the massive sign. If the marquee looked this great, who knew what wonders awaited me inside the park?

In 1973, all of Disneyland's rides and attractions required ride coupons that could be purchased in books (the famous A through E tickets) or individually at the themed ticket huts in each land. Dennis opted, of course, for the individual tickets and was choosy about the rides he deemed "worth the money." Maybe it was Sharon who pointed out the cost effectiveness of purchasing a stack of multi-ticket books, but suddenly, Disneyland opened its arms to us.

We got to ride everything in Fantasyland: the Mad Tea Party tea cups, Dumbo the Flying Elephant, Casey Jr. Circus Train, "it's a small world," Peter Pan's Flight, Mr. Toad's Wild Ride, and the Skyway tram. But the two attractions that made the deepest impression on me were the Carousel of Progress in Tomorrowland and the Haunted Mansion in New Orleans Square.

I was fascinated with the audio-animatronic figures in both attractions and how amazingly real they seemed. I was especially taken with the Haunted Mansion, although parts of it scared the crap out of me. One of the few souvenirs I could afford to purchase at Disneyland was a long string of postcards with scenes from the Mansion that folded down neatly into a little envelope pouch. After I got back home, the postcards were one of my favorite possessions that I proudly displayed in my room during the day. They seemed to glow in the dark, so at night, I hid them in a drawer to prevent nightmares.

Later, when I had a backyard of my own in north Longmont, I erected an elaborate Haunted Mansion fashioned out of two refrigerator boxes. It was a one-of-a-kind "crawl-through" experience that I was determined would be the highlight of my own backyard theme park, Kempferland. But, alas, Kempferland never got off the ground, even though I added a three-hole miniature-golf course with a semi-animatronic witch and a petting farm featuring my pet turtle. I charged 10 cents for admission, but my only paying customer—my only visitor—was Mom, who refused to crawl through the boxes and claimed that touching the turtle would give her warts.

It was at some point during the visit to Disneyland that I decided I wanted to work there one day. Doing what, I had no clue. *Maybe something to do with the Haunted Mansion*, I thought. Or even sweeping trash—anything just to be there.

Toward the end of our second day at Disneyland, we made a final pass through Fantasyland and into the Mad Hatter shop. Given Mom's financial situation, she didn't have a lot of money to give me for the trip, maybe twenty bucks that I had to budget for the entire two weeks. But between snacks here and there, the little slot machine toy, the postcards at Disneyland, and the purchase of a second ride through the Mansion, I was nearly broke.

Sonny, Susan, and Sammy all decided they wanted Mickey Mouse ear hats with their names beautifully embroidered on the back in yellow Disney script. As Dennis gave their orders to the clerk, I handed an ear hat to him for myself. I assumed we were all getting them.

"Do you have enough money for this, Denny?" he asked.

Digging deep in the pockets of my shorts, I was able to produce a crumpled dollar bill and a few pennies.

"Oh, that doesn't appear to be enough money for one of these hats, Denny. Maybe you should choose something else."

Dejected, embarrassed, and singled out, I sheepishly put the Mickey ears back on the shelf and found a Donald Duck hat on a bottom markdown shelf. Constructed like a baseball cap with Donald's bill as the bill of the hat, it was on clearance because the squeaker didn't work.

Who needs a hat that squeaks anyway?

I decided on the Donald hat for economic reasons, but later realized it was the perfect choice for me; I was different from the other kids, and for most of my life, I saw that as a bad thing. It wouldn't have broken the bank for Dennis to include me in the hat purchase. I certainly didn't see Sharon's kids coughing up their own dough for souvenirs.

It was a hard slap in the face that reinforced exactly what I was to my biological father: a loser, a failure, worthless, an embarrassment. That single moment, there in the Mad Hatter shop in Disneyland, was permanently etched on my brain, and everything that happened after that point—post-Ear Hat trauma—was through that lens, through the filter of the negative, less-than feelings he instilled that day.

Before the Ear Hat, there was always the hope that I might please Dennis, but after, I knew without a doubt that I was all those things he called me.

The rest of the trip was mostly uneventful, unless you count being thrown in the ocean in one final attempt to see if I would "sink or swim." For the record, I sunk. A wave crested over my head and pulled me down in its undertow. To be clear, it was a lifeguard—not my own father—who rescued me from drowning, pulled me onto the sand, and pushed on my stomach to get me to vomit the salty Pacific water. I looked up to see Dennis shaking his head in disgust.

"You're worthless," he said, as he went to collect Sharon and her kids.

I couldn't wait to get back home to Mom. Dennis drove me alone to Longmont, and without so much as a "so long" or "screw you, kid," he dumped me in front of the Bowen Street duplex and sped away. At least a year passed before we heard from him again. Then, like the child support payments, one day, he just disappeared.

10

Day Careless

I got back from Disneyland to find that I would spend the rest of my summer days at a daycare home. Half of those days would be spent at a tortuous little place called Vacation Bible School, along with the other daycare detainees.

Now, why a family that already had eleven kids wanted to bring more snot-nosed little heathens into their already busting-at-the-seams, run-down home remains a mystery. Perhaps it was an odd paradox; they had so many kids that they couldn't afford to feed them without bringing in more kids, hence, more income. Single moms, like mine, forked over the cash to have someone—anyone—watch their kids while they were out struggling to put food on their own tables.

A stern, by-the-book Catholic woman, the matriarch of the two-bedroom ranch house, always wore thread-bare housecoats and mismatched slippers. She had a pair of horn-rimmed glasses dangling around her skinny neck from a hefty safety cable, as if they once attempted to escape. Papa Catholic just looked worn out (rightly so) and wore frumpy, ill-fitting cardigans with slacks two inches too short for his lanky frame.

A large, imposing picnic table constructed of rough-hewn boards and two equally rickety bench seats occupied most of the kitchen. There, in shifts, the kids (both biological and income-producing), were positioned neatly on the two long benches, in order of height and, of course, separated by gender. Mama Catholic sat on a metal kitchen stool at the end of the table, an arm's reach within the black-crusted burners of the electric range. Mama had a sawed-off wooden yardstick with which she could reach down the length of the table to slap a wrist should its behavior warrant. Perhaps it was a Catholic belief, but she believed that any child who used his or her left hand to hold an eating utensil was Satan's spawn. Thankfully, I was right-handed, but other kids weren't so blessed.

At one of the meals of watered-down macaroni and cheese, a new intake sitting next to me picked up his fork with his left hand and proceeded to shovel cheese sauce into his face.

Thwack!

The yardstick appeared as if out of nowhere and slammed down on the kid's hand, sending limp macaroni flying and anemic cheese sauce splattering across the faces of those in striking range. I felt the heat of the slap as the kid yelped in pain, clutching his southpaw to his chest, cradling it as he moaned. The yardstick left its trademark red welt.

"That's what you get for using the Devil's hand," Mama Catholic crooned. Then, addressing the larger congregation of children, she preached, "Children! You are *never* to use your left hand. If you do, it's an unmistakable, immutable sign that you are of the Devil, a true child of Satan who belongs in Hell. Unless this describes you, you are never, ever to use your left hand."

I snickered silently, as I imagined a bunch of kids going through life with left arms and hands hanging uselessly, limply at their sides. *"Use both hands to catch that dodge ball!"* I imagined some physical education teacher yelling. *"I can't! Mama won't let me use my left hand for anything,"* came the imagined reply.

Before each of these bountiful meals, we were strictly reminded to fold our hands, bow our heads, and recite the Lord's Prayer. One day, Mama gave us some backstory.

"Children! Listen up. Does anyone know why we say the Lord's Prayer?"

Yeah, to give thanks for this crappy, food-stamps slop, you ugly witch, said the smart-ass voice in my head.

A wave of confused looks appeared down one bench and up the other.

"Because all good things come from the Lord..."

Makes sense. I'm with you, lady.

"...and the Lord is your Father in Heaven, who is just like your *real* father."

And now you've lost me. Just like my real father? You mean, everyone has an angry, mean, bad-tempered, abandoning father just like mine?

It was, perhaps, the first connection I'd made between earthly fathers and our God, and it was not a healthy association. It was a life-altering moment in which I vowed to myself that if God was anything like Dennis, I wanted nothing to do with Him.

Mama C. had eight sons in her litter of little Catholics. Three of them were younger than me and registered barely a blip on my radar. But the eldest five brothers adopted me to become one of their camper buddies. The son closest to my age was Vincent. He was a decently cool kid, despite his chunky Buddy Holly glasses and questionable hygiene. He was the one bright, however geeky, spot in this gloomy house of horrors. Then, one afternoon at Vincent's suggestion, I was invited into (cue ominous music) the camper.

The family had an old camper shell plopped onto the bed of an even older pickup truck that lived on the stretch of dead grass parallel to their driveway. It seemed like a fun, new adventure. Maybe we would play G.I. Joes or Matchbox cars. (Clueless idiot, party of one…Clueless idiot? Oh, there you are. Right this way.)

As soon as we had crammed inside and the camper door was securely locked behind us, the oldest brother, Greg, whipped out a deck of cards from under one of the seat cushions around the camper table.

"Strip-dare-poker time!" he gleefully announced.

This was a new game for me. As I would discover, it explained why the brothers were wearing winter coats, hats, and scarves on a hot August day. I didn't know how to play cards, unless Old Maid or Go Fish counted, and I certainly didn't know how to play strip-dare-poker.

Rules were vaguely laid out as cards were dealt. First one naked (that would be the loser) had to perform a dare of the group's choosing while totally naked. It was sick. Twisted. But somehow, it made something beneath my shorts stir in anticipation. It didn't take me long to figure out that, between my lack of poker knowledge and single layer of clothing, I was heading straight toward being the loser.

Sitting there in the camper with nothing left to lose but my

J.C. Penney Townscraft briefs, Vincent looked at my cards and whispered almost apologetically, "Shoot, you lost. You gotta take off your undershorts."

In total embarrassment, I started to peel down my briefs and, as if on cue, my penis sprung to full attention, garnering a round of hearty laughs from the brothers. In a moment of stupid inspiration, I turned the humiliation to my advantage, as I made my wiener bounce wildly to their shocked amusement.

"Far out!" said Vincent.

Thinking I had succeeded (and mightily so), I started to put on my underwear.

"No way, man," bellowed Greg. "You still have to do a dare."

A chorus of brothers echoed his instructions, then huddled together to concoct a fitting dare for the naked newbie.

"Run around the camper nude."

That didn't seem too hard, as we pretty much occupied all available real estate inside the creaking RV shell. I sort of ran in place before reaching for my underwear.

"Outside," said Greg. "Run around the outside of the camper—naked."

Before I knew it, the camper door was unlocked and flung open, and I was pushed out onto the dead grass, partially shielded by a bit of backyard fence and row of garbage cans. The brothers took their spectator positions on the open driveway and egged me on.

"Do it now!"

"Run! Run!"

"Run, or you'll have to do something worse!"

Praying it would be over quickly and that no one would see me, I performed my lap around the truck, hands locked over my privates in fig-leaf position, then scurried back inside the musty camper, out of breath and totally humiliated.

"Wow! He actually did it!"

"I can't believe it!"

"What a boner!"

"What?! What do you mean?" I asked.

"You didn't really have to do the whole thing, you know," said a middle brother.

Um, no, I didn't know.

"But it's super cool that you did," Greg beamed. "Everyone else get naked now." In a flash, a flurry of sweaty boy clothes flung in all directions. "Now that we're already naked, we play to the dare."

Was getting naked the only thing to do for fun in 1973?

As cards were shuffled and dealt, it felt exciting and dangerous to be sitting naked with a bunch of other boys.

I lost again. Trying to be a good sport and still riding the wave of adrenaline from my streaking spree, I boldly asked, "OK, so what do I have to do?"

"Holy smokes. He's an eager one, huh?" one of the older middle brothers exclaimed.

Greg had the dare ready. "Get on your knees, and put your mouth around Vincent's wiener. If your tongue touches it, you have to do it to all of us."

I saw no way out of my predicament but was determined to end my humiliation, and as such, followed instructions perfectly. Before I could claim the accolades for achievement, a startled voice emerged from behind the camper's side curtains.

"Oh, shit! Mom's coming," one of the younger brothers warned, as we scrambled back into our clothes. We assembled ourselves around the tiny camper table as if in the middle of our card game.

"Now! All you boys! Get out of the camper now!" Mama Catholic yelled in a high-pitched drawl that hinted at a Southern upbringing. "Get in the house NOW!"

As I stumbled down the hallway toward the lone bathroom at Camp Catholic, I saw the large statue of Jesus nailed to the cross. His eyes were horribly sad, as they appeared to beam down on me in total disappointment, staring right into my sin-stained soul.

Inside the dirty pink-and-yellow bathroom, I pulled down my shorts to pee. I stared at the pink-shag tank cover and coordinating pee-encrusted rug as I tried to get the flow started. It was then I looked down and realized I was using my *right* hand to hold my member. *Well, at least I can't be* all *bad.*

* * *

The next summer, I was parked at a new daycare home that backed up to the alfalfa field behind Mountain View Cemetery on Main Street. Although it may sound like the perfect setting for a horror movie, it was a fun, if irreverent, setting for many afternoon adventures. The alfalfa field was a zillion different stages for a kid with a big imagination. Sometimes, it was the poppy field in *The Wizard of Oz,* as we trudged merrily to the Emerald City, which was between the Civil War graves and the new multiplex mausoleum. Sometimes, it was the jungle where G.I. Joe was on a secret mission. Still, other times, it was the village from *Planet of the Apes*.

But sometimes, the fun was inside the daycare mother's home. Her name was Charlene, and she had two boys of her own. The younger boy, Mark, was about my age. His older brother, Christopher, was already in high school and drove a bright blue '65 Mustang. A high-school stud, he always had a bunch of stupid girls hanging on his every word and broad shoulders. He had a hairy chest and loved to show it off to his many admirers, which, I have to admit, included me.

One afternoon, after our fun in the cemetery had died down, Mark and I were hanging out in the basement. It was an older house, and the cellar had a dirt embankment that led from the top of a short retaining wall to the house's foundation. On this particular day, older brother Christopher came lumbering down the wooden basement stairs after closing and locking the basement door. He approached with a cocky, confident swagger.

"Let's have some fun," Christopher announced. "But keep your voices down."

"You gonna play G.I. Joes with us?" I asked.

"Nah, that's baby stuff," said Mark, suddenly having outgrown action figures.

Mark tossed his brother a cautionary look, which was met with a returned head nod, stating "it's cool."

Christopher pulled his shirt over his head, exposing his hairy armpits and chest. He ran his hand over his chest as I watched, perhaps too intently.

"This is what a *man* looks like," Christopher snorted as if he was a prize bull.

In a flash, he pulled me toward him and roughly covered my mouth with his left hand, as he pushed his brother's face toward his crotch.

"Don't make a sound, Denny. Mark, you know what to do. Show Denny how it's done." Then, looking me square in the eyes, said, "Pay attention. You're next."

I felt an odd sense of excitement co-mingled with a tinge of fear. But Mark was enjoying this game, and no doubt Christopher was, too. Was I forced? No. I was just wired to please from an early age, plus I didn't know if what we were doing was right or wrong. It happened a few more times that summer. I even asked Mark—probably too often—if his brother was going to play with us.

Truly, this must have been what bored kids did in the 1970s. After all, we didn't have smartphones or Snapchat.

11

It's a Beautiful Gay in the Neighborhood
NORTH LONGMONT: 1975

At first, Ruben seemed promising. He made good money managing the Ford dealership parts department on south Main Street and took Mom and me out to eat a couple of nights each week. Mom seemed happier and would often be singing "Tiny Bubbles" or "The Happiest Girl in the Whole U.S.A." as she dusted and polished the behemoth Mediterranean furniture. Still, Ruben was odd. If you've ever wondered just who bought and wore those hideously ugly leisure suits of the 1970s, it was Ruben. He had a forest of chest hair that climbed over the v-neck collar of the blue velour shirt he so frequently wore. He always had a lit cigarette in his hand and reeked of smoke. Ruben rarely spoke to me, rather just stared at me like I was some circus oddity.

One day, Mom announced, "Denny, you're going to have a new father."

I was hoping she meant Norm, a tall, good-looking cop who Mom had dated.

"No, it's Ruben. I'm marrying Ruben."

"Oh. That's nice, I guess."

After just a few short months of dating, Mom married Ruben. Sometime in January of 1975, they had a thrown-together wedding ceremony at a Vegas-style, rent-it-by-the-hour wedding chapel in Loveland, Colorado. Mom's co-worker, Jodi, coordinated the event. Mom wore a floor-length, turquoise satin dress, and Ruben wore a tacky mint-green tux with a ruffled-yellow shirt that matched his yellow teeth and nicotine-stained fingers.

Shortly after the wedding, we moved to the outskirts of north Longmont to a 1960s-era ranch on 19th Avenue. A white-bricked tract house, it had a big unfinished basement and a fenced-in backyard lined with tall Cypress trees. I had my own room with a bookshelf on the wall that I filled with my growing collection of chapter books I got through the Scholastic Book program at school. My new school, Northridge Elementary, was just down the block, at the end of our street. I was even allowed to keep the goldfish I won at a ring-toss booth on Spring back-to-school night. Things were looking up.

The house was in a middle-class neighborhood nestled among a cluster of street names that would portend my future. The main north-south thoroughfare was boldly named Gay Street. It intersected with Queens Avenue, Duchess Drive, Princess Promenade, and Countess Court. As a kid, it seemed boring to have an address on a numbered street, but as an adult, I was happy I didn't have to state that I lived on Gay Street.

It was the autumn of 1975, and I was in fourth grade at my new school. It was during this time that I began to envy and obsess over other boys, boys who had nice fathers, boys who were more masculine than me, boys who were better looking, boys who were good at sports, boys who had hordes of friends, boys who were boys.

I just wanted one of them to be my friend, to not be ashamed to be seen with me, to make time for me, to drape a strong arm around my skinny shoulders and say, "You're alright, Denny. I like you just the way you are." As I matured, I began to overlay this desire on guys in a romantic way.

Scott Douglas was my first boyhood crush and first attempt to fill the aching, empty hole inside myself.

Scott had it all: an unbroken family, a brother, a dog, and a huge aquarium filled with tropical fish. His bedroom was fourth-grade perfection. Over his neatly made twin bed with its super-cool *Star Trek* bedspread was an entire wall of bookshelves filled with all the books in the *Hardy Boys* series, all fifty-six blue spines lined up in perfect numerical order. On the shelf below, there were several dozen *Star Trek* and other science fiction novels, each with a crisp, uncracked spine. Scott took great care of his books and toys. There was just something totally unblemished about Scott.

Scott, was, of course, fantastic looking, with sandy brown hair and a huge toothy grin that stretched across his tan, freckled face. He never seemed to have a care in the world, unlike me, who, despite the fresh start afforded by a new school and neighborhood, always appeared to be carrying the weight of the world on my young, skinny shoulders.

Everyone liked Scott, and he liked everyone back.

Scott was the number one draft pick when teams were formed on the playground in outdoor Phys Ed. I was not only the last to be picked, but the team captains would argue over who would be stuck with "Bucktooth," the charming nickname I was given thanks to the overbite that developed when my adult front teeth grew in crookedly.

Scott could run the fifty-yard dash in seven seconds. It took me almost a minute if you count my tripping and falling.

Scott could climb the damn yellow rope all the way to the ceiling in record time in gym class. I could never climb the frigging thing. And in what would become a signature trait, in sheer frustration, I would run to the side of the gym and beat my head against the hard cinder block wall until I was dismissed from class. At least once, I drew blood. But no one cared; it was just loser Bucktooth being his loser self. On more than one occasion, the school counselor mandated a sit-down discussion with herself and Mom to discuss my head banging.

Scott lived two streets behind me on Duchess Drive. I'm not sure how I won his friendship, but I was thankful for it. He must have seen me hit my head but never mentioned it. Maybe I was a pity friendship. Whatever the case, it felt like pure magic when I was in his confident, 100-percent boyish presence. He mattered, and I wanted to matter to him. Perhaps I did, to some extent, at least until I fell out of favor for more popular and athletic friends—friends who didn't publicly harm themselves out of frustration.

I still had my collection of G.I. Joes, all veterans of the construction zones on Ashcroft Drive and the alley filth of Bowen Street. I had also acquired an impressive collection of cool accessories for my Joes.

Scott was into the "Big Jim" line of manly action figures. I don't know on what or whom Big Jim was based, but the character, much like Scott himself, somehow seemed smarter and worldlier than his military counterpart. Well-matched to Scott, Big Jim was ruggedly handsome, with nice chiseled-in-plastic pecs and rippled-in-rubber abs under his snap-up flannel shirt. Being the outdoorsy, butch kind of action figure that he was, the most coveted deluxe accessory in the Big Jim merchandise line-up that a kid could score was the Big Jim Camper. Scott, of course, had one, as well as every piece and part and accessory imaginable to go with it. Inside the RV, Scott had neatly stuffed all of Big Jim's cool gear, including the rubbery-plastic camp-fire, coffee grate and coffee pot, coils of plastic rope, plastic fishing poles and hunting rifles, and the deluxe pop-up tent for those away-from-the-camper excursions.

So maybe our friendship began because I lived close by or maybe because of my complementary set of G.I. Joes and gear; I was just grateful—awestruck, really—to be selected as a friend by this god-man of boyhood perfection.

Scott caught up with me one day after school.

"Hey, Denny. Wait up!" he called out. "Let's have a big campout for Big Jim and G.I. Joe!"

Plans were made for Friday night, permission had been obtained from parents, and I started packing all of my Joe gear into his semi-official foot locker. I didn't have the official one, so I impro-vised with a Buster Brown shoebox colored with dark green crayon. I made lists of my inventory, stressing over and sorting gear. I could hardly sleep for the anticipation of a real, live sleepover at Scott's. He told me it would be a sleepover for *us* as well, instructing me to pack my PJs and toothbrush for what I probably prayed would be a night filled with adventure in the blissful glow of being with Scott.

Nothing about Scott ever registered as sexual attraction. How could it have? I was only nine years old, albeit, a sexually-experienced nine. I spent two days obsessing over the sleeping arrangements. Since

Scott only had one twin bed in his room, I wasn't sure where I would bunk for the night. But I knew I desperately wanted to be snuggled up close to Scott, to sleep in the protective peace of his company.

"So, um, Scott, where am I gonna sleep?" I asked almost immediately upon arrival. As would become a well-embedded pattern for me, I jumped right to worrying about details of how the night would play out.

"You thinking 'bout sleep already, bud?" Scott scolded. "We've got a whole night ahead of us."

Magical words for a lost kid who would have followed Scott to the ends of the earth and back.

"Yeah, OK, we'll figure that out later," I said, ever the little event planner. I always needed to know what came next, and in this case, how long I would be granted my stay in paradise.

As it turned out, I never got to spend the night.

About mid-way through the super-colossal "Big Jim and G.I. Joe Campout of 1975," Scott started heaving. Perhaps he'd eaten too many of the buttercream-frosted graham crackers Mom had sent with me. Or maybe it was just my company.

"I'm sorry, Denny, but Scott is very sick with a fever," announced his perfectly coiffed and manicured mother. "You'll need to pack up your toys and go home."

Her words hung in the air, as my world came crashing down. There was no mention of re-scheduling.

I went home and cried myself to sleep.

I spent a miserable weekend alone in my room, counting the minutes until school on Monday morning, hoping upon hope I would see Scott. I imagined him feeling better, seeking me out first thing, and expressing his heartfelt regret for our beautiful evening cut short. I imagined him running up to me, breathless, talking about when we could try it again.

Monday morning came, and I could hardly wait to get to school. That, actually, was typical for me. Not that school offered anything better than home life did, but at least it meant a change of scenery for seven hours, five days a week, out from under Ruben's hateful gaze.

I sat nervously in class, anxiously looking around, watching the door for Scott's broad shoulders and broader smile to come barreling in and brightening the room. The bell rang and still no Scott. I asked around and learned he was still sick and had to stay home, probably all week. The words were a sucker punch deep in my gut.

As soon as the 3:15 p.m. bell rang and school was dismissed, I sprinted home, jumped on my red ten-speed, and peddled as fast as I could to Scott's. I pulled my bike into Scott's driveway, pushed the kickstand down with my trembling right foot, and prayed Scott would be home.

He was.

Scott was in his green flannel pajamas, working at his desk, finishing another *Star Trek* model kit. He had previously assembled and perfectly painted a scale replica of the Starship Enterprise's bridge. I once tried building the same model and only ended up with a glop of glue and gray plastic.

"So, how are you feeling?" I asked tentatively, my foot drawing shapes in his bedroom's shag carpet. "Your mom said it was OK for me to come back and say hi, 'cause you're not contagious." Not that I would have cared if he got me sick. It would have been *his* germs, after all.

"I have something called Fifth Disease," Scott said, as he hiked up his flannel pajama shirt to show me the red rash that was covering his chest, arms, and back.

"What's a *fisk* disease?" I asked.

"No, it's FIFTH Disease."

He explained that it was called such because it was the most recently discovered and yet unnamed childhood disease, joining the other four rash-based ailments, including measles, scarlet fever, rubella (German measles) and chicken pox. He spoke like a studied expert on the subject. With a physician for a father, Scott had a knack for the family trade.

"How on earth did you get *that*?"

"I dunno. It doesn't hurt or itch or anything. And I can *prolly* go back to school after this week," he explained. "It's kind of super far-out 'cause I get to stay home and play but don't have to stay in bed."

"Wow. Can I get it from you?" I desperately wanted his disease to feel closer to him.

"Nah, you'd have had it by now if you were going to get it. But why would you want it?"

"Well, if I also had it, I could stay home with you and keep you company. And we could play G.I. Joes and stuff."

"Oh, wow, super neat idea!" Scott exclaimed, handing me the blanket from his bed. "Here, rub this on you. I've been sleeping with this blanket since I got sick. Maybe it still has germs on it."

I thought this was about the best offer I'd ever received: a chance to get Scott Douglas's germs *and* to rub his scent all over me. I was over-the-moon happy with this new scheme, this delicious plot twist.

Because the blanket was too big for me to smuggle out of Scott's bedroom, he gave me one of his flannel pajama shirts he had worn the day before. Like manna from Heaven, like winning the lottery, like finding the proverbial pot of gold at the end of some twisted rainbow, like—well, you get the idea—I carefully tucked the rolled-up shirt under my arm and rode home, as the sun was setting west of Gay Street.

But alas, the miracle didn't happen. Although I tried to fake my own version of Fifth Disease by rubbing the flannel shirt against my chest until it was raw and red, it didn't fool Mom. Worse still, I had to return the flannel shirt to Scott and face Ruben, who by now had stepped into the vacant role of "angry father."

"Ain't right for a boy to be sleeping with another boy's shirt like a sissy rag doll," Ruben so eloquently explained. "No kid of mine is gonna be a faggot."

12

The Absolute Worst Day of the Week
NORTH LONGMONT: 1976–1977

Sundays have always been the hardest day of the week for me, both as a kid and as an adult. As a kid, Sundays meant an especially lonely day with endless hours to fill. Not that Saturdays were much better, but there were options. Even a kid with no friends could usually glom onto some poor soul in the neighborhood in the spirit of killing time. Later, I realized that that poor soul was actually me, and no one was coming around.

Most people in my area still observed Sunday as a holy day and took their brood to church. Friends (or more aptly stated, acquaintances) were stuffed into Sunday School classes by their stuffy pew-warming parents. The streets of north Longmont were virtually deserted and eerily quiet on Sunday mornings. Sure, there was the occasional buzz of a neighbor's lawn mower and the rumble of a car, but not much happened anywhere until after one in the afternoon. After church, after fellowship coffee and all those mindless potlucks, after long lunches with parents at Village Inn were complete, then handfuls of kids might take to the streets on bikes or toss a football in their front yard while the adults busied themselves with preparations for the "big game" that afternoon. (No matter the sports season, no matter the team, every game was always the "big game" and was revered as an event at least as holy as church.)

Only a few stores were open on Sundays, but those that were didn't flip over their "open" sign until one o'clock and promptly flipped it back to "closed" by five. For a few precious hours, I would ride my bike to any possible oasis—that is, an open store—in which I could pass time. Anything to feel like I was doing something, and absolutely any reason to be out of the house and away from Ruben.

My favorite way to fill a Sunday afternoon was in the Waldenbooks store in the Horizon Park Mall. I must have known by heart their rack arrangements and available stock at any given moment. I think it was there that I fell in love with books: the look, the feel, the smell of the ink, the crack of the pristine virgin bindings, and the infinite wisdom and adventures contained between the covers. Books such as *The Hobbit, Watership Down,* and Narnia's *Prince Caspian* topped my list of favorites. Other kids—normal kids—spent their allowances on candy or ice cream, but mine went to the book store.

At closing time, I pedaled home slowly as the sun was starting to sink behind the Front Range of the Rockies. Slowly enough to kill a few more minutes, but cognizant enough of time that I wouldn't miss *Walt Disney's Wonderful World of Color.* I felt a special thrill every time the music from "When You Wish Upon A Star" swelled, and the image of the Disneyland castle filled our Magnavox screen. I had, after all, walked across that same drawbridge.

Television served both as my best friend and electronic babysitter (the latter function was quite common for my generation). I longed to be part of a family like the one I saw on *Little House on the Prairie.* I was drawn to the simplicity of 1800s pioneer life and had read all of the Laura Ingalls Wilder books to the chagrin of my male classmates.

I was also drawn to Matthew Laborteaux.

Matthew played the fictional character Albert, an orphaned kid adopted by the Ingalls family, ostensibly as part of some plot-furthering device. I wanted Albert to adopt me as his best friend, his brother, his stable boy, really any role that would place me into his world and out of mine. I was still in that slightly delusional 10-year-old's headspace in which the lines between TV fantasy and mundane reality co-mingled. If only Albert/Matthew could meet me, he'd be my friend. I was sure of it. But how to meet *him*?

I was a subscriber to the Scholastic Book Club magazine *Dynamite,* and in one of the issues, *Little House* was featured on the cover. Inside, at the end of the feature article, there was an open invitation to write to the stars via NBC TV. I was in! I found my way to Albert/Matthew!

So, I wrote a sugary love letter to the guy. I'd be mortified today if I were to read the actual letter, but to poor Matthew—if the letter even reached him—it probably read like a bad scene from an alternate-universe show called *Little House on the* Fairy:

◆ ◆ ◆

Dear Matthew,

I am a lonely ten-year-old mama's boy with no friends and no male role model in my life. My real dad abandoned me and my mom, and now my new stepfather calls me names, like Bookworm, Matilda, and Nellie, but

I'm not at all mean like your Nellie. And he hits me all the time. You look like a nice guy. Can I come live with you? I think I love you.

Love,

Denny Kempfer

◆ ◆ ◆

I never received a response from Matthew Laborteaux. Not even one of those mass-produced autographed headshots.

Although the whole Albert/Matthew thing turned out to be just another disappointment in my growing list of disappointments, I continued to watch *Little House* religiously, which, perhaps, is an interesting adverb choice for a kid who knew next to nothing about church, religion, or God. And for most of my adult life, I considered those three terms—church, religion, and God—to be as much of an inseparable trinity as the Father, the Son, and the Holy Ghost.

The three-in-one Holy Trinity was already mightily confusing: the old, tiny-print King James Bible I had was impossible to comprehend, even for a voracious reader like I was. The imagery in the Bible was hard to understand for a kid—hell, for a non-Christian adult even—who had little-to-no exposure to Sunday school and certainly no biblical teachings at home. What little exposure I did have to the Bible left me with a mental mish-mash of images of sheep, people eating Jesus' flesh and drinking His blood, shepherds, fig trees, mustard seeds, more sheep, sowing, reaping, crosses, and winepresses— metaphorically none of which are easy for a kid to grasp. How could Jesus be God and the Holy Ghost at the same time? And, as a kid with a runaway imagination, the term "Holy Ghost" only managed to conjure images from the haunted house specials I adored on PBS.

Then, in what seemed like every other episode of *Little House*, the townsfolk of Walnut Grove were in church singing the same old hymn. As a kid who was raised outside the church, I wholeheartedly believed they were singing, "bringing in the cheese, bringing in the cheese, we shall go rejoicing, bringing in the cheese."

Why are they always singing about cheese? And why do they always have to bring it in? Did they leave it outside by mistake?

I later learned the word was "sheaves" not cheese. Oops.

Church and all things religious remained a mystery as I grew older. In fact, Christianity seemed to be a big party to which I wasn't invited and certainly wasn't welcome.

* * *

As horribly boring as most of my Sundays were, there was another type of Sunday that I dreaded and feared, which eventually became the stuff of my nightmares: fishing in the mountains.

Ruben wasn't much of a sports fan, so missing the "big game" was never an issue for him. And because he wasn't much of a sports guy (or much of a stepfather), I was spared from being forced to join school sports teams or having to endure long sessions of playing catch in the backyard.

On fishing Sundays, he would pack Mom, me, and a ton of stinky fishing gear into his green, four-door Ford Granada. We would head up Highway 66 to the tiny town of Lyons, always with the obligatory stop at the fish farm with the giant fisherman sign to pay twenty-five cents to feed overfed carp. Then, we would continue further up toward Estes Park and the Big Thompson River area, all on a quest for rainbow trout. Or carp. Or basically whatever Ruben could pull from the water. Sometimes it was fishing in a river; sometimes it was fishing in a reservoir; sometimes it was fishing in an actual lake. No matter the body of water, it was always terrible.

Ruben would sit for hours with his fishing tackle, a pole or three in the water, and a cigarette dangling from his mouth. Always smoking. There was rarely a time when there wasn't a nasty Merit menthol wedged between his dirty, yellowed teeth. And on fishing days, he didn't bother to bathe, so he reeked of fish, body odor, and smoke. (To be fair, he actually didn't bathe often on non-fishing days either.) His greasy, pageboy hairdo would flip in the mountain breeze, adding yet another unpleasant aroma to the once-fresh mountain air.

Mom couldn't have cared less about fishing but was always a good sport in the ongoing quest to please her man. By this time, she had become a world-class actress in her own life, happily agreeing to do whatever Ruben wanted, despite her true feelings. Her one escape, especially on fishing trips, was sunbathing. As long as Ruben was upwind of her folding banana lounger, and as long as she could anoint herself with suntan oil, all was good in her world.

Then, there was me. As with baseball, I couldn't catch a fish to save my life. Ruben was an equally demanding taskmaster as Dennis but with drunken belligerence thrown in for variety. As where Dennis would have kept me at the lake re-baiting and re-casting my line for hours, Ruben's style was a little more to the point. "Either you catch a fish, or you walk home." Considering we were at least two hours from home via treacherous, winding mountain roads in the middle of nowhere, his threats were well heeded.

I tried to embrace fishing by intellectualizing it and researching techniques at the school library. This didn't mean I enjoyed fishing or would ever aspire to enjoy the sport, but I somehow made it slightly more palatable because I had made the personal investment of time, took a fain interest in the sport, and worked to apply myself to achieve success. This, along with constant worry, anxiety, and self-berating would become my trademark formula for approaching life.

Truth is I hated fish. Didn't want to touch them and certainly didn't want to eat them. Maybe that's another reason that so much of the Gospel fell on deaf ears. In what I had been exposed to thus far, Jesus was always talking about fish, fishing, fishermen, and the like. I deduced in my ten-year-old brain that if following Jesus meant enduring fishing excursions like the ones with Ruben, I had no further interest, thank you very much.

But I *could* bait the hook. That part I could do. I could actually touch a worm or the squishy red salmon eggs that came in the cute little jars and impale the slippery suckers on the barbed hook.

Casting the line was problematic for me, so with Ruben's dirty, fishy hands covering mine, his nasty breath on my neck, cigarette ash crumbling down my back, he would do his stepfather-ly best to guide my hands to cast properly.

Just get the damn line in the water, please, so I can go sit on a rock for the next five hours, starving and staring into this river/lake/ reservoir/body of water.

There were a couple of joyous occasions when a fish would tug at my line. It was thrilling because for a few moments, I felt like a boy. I did my best to reel the poor sucker in, but secretly hoped it would disengage, saving me from having to deal further with it.

"Keep your line taut!" Ruben would scream in his high-pitched, almost effeminate voice.

"I am! I'm trying!"

"Don't let that bastard get away."

The fish breached the water and flipped triumphantly skyward as my line went slack.

"What did I tell you, you fucking bookworm? You let it get away! You fucking pansy. Re-bait, and get that line back in the water before I kick your sorry ass," Ruben coached.

Bait, cast, wait, repeat.

A little tug that turned out to be a snag on a rock was enough to lose the bait.

Reel it back in.

Bait, cast, wait again.

Another tug. This time, it was a seriously strong tug that nearly ripped the pole out of my hands. The spool was unwinding fast as the fish darted downstream. Just in time, Ruben leaped over and took control of the rod and started reeling. When it emerged from the water, it was a beautiful, enormous Rocky Mountain Rainbow trout, with iridescent scales that reflected the Colorado sun and cast an array of colors across the water. It was a brief moment of shared success, and I felt a tinge of hope for my miserable self.

"Looks like *someone* gets to eat tonight after all," Ruben announced.

Ruben's game plan was always clearly enunciated at the start of each fishing trip to Hell.

"We catch what we eat, and we only eat what we catch. If you don't catch nothing, you don't eat nothing," Ruben would warn with his best "I work as a Ford parts manager" grasp of English grammar.

Once the big trout was subdued, Ruben handed back my line with said fish attached, telling me to unhook it and put it in the trunk of the car. Still flopping in my lap as it fought for the last moments of its fishy life, I squeamishly removed the hook from the trout's mouth, impaling my forefinger on the hook in the process.

Before it gave up the ghost, the fish looked at me as if to say, "Uh huh. See what's it like to have that hook in you? Well, buddy boy, I'm outta here, but you—you little bookworm—ha ha, get it? Worm? You, bookworm, is gonna be wishing someone would put *you* out of your misery. Later, sucker. Trout over, and Trout out."

I opened the Granada's trunk and removed the lid from the fish blood-and-goop-stained Styrofoam cooler, already laden with Ruben's catch. I laid the big trout on top of the others and replaced the foam top, knowing a food fight was ahead.

The temperature began to drop, as the mountain sky began its rapid descent into darkness. I breathed a huge sigh of relief mixed with dread as the last of the fishing gear, coolers, and Mom's lawn chair were packed in the trunk.

Ruben sped the Granada down the dangerous curves of Highway 34, or Fall River Road as it was called by locals. We were a good twenty miles past Estes Park, with no restaurants, gas stations, or public services to be found. At some point, Mom's overactive bladder inevitably required an emergency stop. Ruben was evil; he would slow down, slam on the brakes, then squeal the tires as he resumed top speed.

"Honey, please," Mom pleaded. "I really have to go now. Your driving is making it worse."

"Yeah, me too. Can we please stop somewhere?" I added a show of solidarity.

Ruben continued on in silence for a few minutes until Mom begged again.

"Ruben, honey. Please. I really need to stop, and so does Denny. Please. I'm about to pee my pants."

"Fine," Ruben said curtly, as he veered the car to the side of the road. There was no rest stop in sight, but Mom was used to the drill. She went around to the trunk and grabbed her trusty roll of toilet paper that she kept in a quart-size Baggie. Taking the TP, she hurried behind the roadside bushes to squat.

I was sitting in the back seat on the driver's side, which was the side facing traffic. As Mom scurried to the underbrush, I got out of the car, careful of the cars that were flying past us, the gusts from which rocked the Ford. I was careful to maintain a tight grip on the rear passenger door, but between the wind coming off the mountain and the breeze generated from a fairly steady stream of cars (each filled, no doubt, with happy families concluding their photo-album-perfect weekends), the car door closed hard. Slammed, actually. Definitely too hard for Ruben's liking.

Before I knew what was happening, Ruben leapt from the front seat and grabbed me by my right arm, nearly dislocating my shoulder.

"What the fuck did you just do to my car?"

"I just closed the door, that's all."

"You *slammed* the fucking door, didn't you, you little son of a bitch."

"No! I didn't slam it!"

"You talking back to me, you little faggot bookworm?" He hit me square in the mouth, his "Ford Parts Manager of the Year" insignia ring on his right hand slicing my upper lip open.

Mom heard the scuffle and hurried back from the bushes, zipping her Gloria Vanderbilts as she stumbled over the rocks.

"Ruben! What happened?" she yelled.

"Your little sissy of a son slammed the car door, so I reminded him who was boss."

Mom grabbed a linty Kleenex from her purse and began to dab the blood from my mouth, as she moved me to a nearby boulder.

"Let me look at your lip," she said. "I can't believe he did this to you."

Then to Ruben she said boldly, "You ever do something like this again to my son, and I will leave you."

"How about I leave *you*?" Ruben said, as he started the car and peeled out, spraying gravel at us.

"Oh shit," I said.

"Don't swear," Mom scolded.

"How are we going to get home now?"

"He'll be back. I know he will. He wouldn't just leave us here."

Soon, it was dark, with the only light coming from the occasional passing car. Traffic, such that it was, had thinned out, and the flurry of station wagons and Jeeps had greatly subsided.

"What do we do if he doesn't come back?" I asked.

"I don't know," Mom said, now visibly shaken from fear and

shivering in the cold air.

"We'll hitch-hike, like in the movies."

Before we could get our thumbs warmed up, Ruben came speeding back up the mountain road, pulled a fast U-turn, then skid to an abrupt stop in front of us, spraying us with more gravel. The passenger window was open.

"Well, are you getting in, or do you want to sit here all night?" he yelled.

No arguments or hesitation from us as we jumped in the car. No one said a word the rest of the way home.

Upon arriving home, I went straight for my bedroom. Ruben unloaded the car, then tossed a fish in a frying pan atop the harvest-gold GE stove. Knowing I hated fish, Mom started to make a peanut butter sandwich for me.

"And what do you think you're doing with that?"

"It's for Denny. He hasn't had anything to eat in hours," Mom said.

"He'll eat fish with us, or he doesn't eat at all."

"Ruben, please."

He started to raise his hand to Mom. "You're gonna look awfully pretty at work tomorrow with a bruised mouth."

I heard the typical commotion and came down the hallway to take my role in the scene that had played out after many fishing excursions. "I'm not hungry. Can I just go to bed?"

"As long as you don't eat, I don't give a crap *what* you do," Ruben sneered.

"He needs to eat," Mom continued.

"He'll survive."

Mom and Ruben ate the big trout, and then Ruben settled into the once-nice, gold-velvet chair, now ruined from cigarette smoke and encrusted with the thick layers of boogers he had wiped on its sides. He sucked on a Merit, staring into space, one hand on the cigarette and the other in full picking mode, excavating the left nostril. Mom hid the sandwich she had made for me in her nightgown and padded silently down the hallway to my room, tapping softly on the door.

"Denny, here. Don't let Ruben see," she said as she passed the sandwich to me wrapped in a towel.

Ruben didn't discover her misstep that night. Other nights, however, she wouldn't be so lucky.

13

Bilbo's Last Dance
NORTH LONGMONT: 1977–1978

I loved animals and always had at least one pet. But either I was a crappy caretaker, or I had horrible pet karma because the critters didn't last long. There had already been the first dog Puffy, the jar of grasshoppers, and the turtle that got stepped on during one of Kempferland's operating days.

There was the white mouse I dragged home from school that proceeded to bite me, requiring an emergency tetanus shot. It also ran incessantly in its exercise wheel. The noise pissed off Ruben, so away the mouse went.

There was the dog Ruben allowed me to select from the Humane Society, a cute black-and-white little mutt that I named Beauregard. But after it peed in the house, Ruben "accidentally" backed over it with his truck. Even so, I was blamed for killing the dog because, according to Ruben, I was the idiot who let it pee inside.

Then, there were the goldfish. They required no attention and little maintenance, other than cleaning their tank once the chains of fish poop outnumbered the fronds of the fake underwater plant.

But even the goldfish didn't like me.

One by one, they would jump out of the tank, making for several traumatic mornings when I discovered yet another fish had committed suicide during the night. I would scream for Mom. Ruben usually arrived on the crime scene first.

"What's wrong, little fairy-boy pansy? Too afraid to touch a fish? Then why the hell do you have them? Pick it up and flush it. Or do I have to make you eat it?" Ruben sneered.

Then came the gerbil phase.

I got a new buddy for my birthday, an overweight gerbil I named Bilbo after the main character in *The Hobbit*. During the summer of 1978, I started a savings plan, drawing a huge red thermometer on poster board with my $85 goal. I was obsessed with buying one of the multi-plex cages called a Habitrail.

Constructed of translucent orange and yellow plastic, a rodent pet owner would start with the base unit and, from there, build an entire kingdom of turrets, tunnels, twists, turns, towers, and t-connectors to neighboring units. I updated my goal chart every day after mowing lawns, then went to K-Mart to study the entire Habitrail product line, making written notes of the pieces and parts I would need to build a dream house for Bilbo. After all, my poor critter was living a miserable life in a boring, undecorated, rectangular wire cage. But with a Habitrail? I imagined the hours of elated fun he and I would have as I watch him scurry through his wonderland of play zones and hiding places.

During those trips to K-Mart, I had also been checking out the disco records in the music department. It was, after all, on the way to pets. I already had one Donna Summer album—her double LP set *Once Upon a Time*—from joining the RCA Music Service. You know, any six albums for a penny? I had fallen in love with Donna's voice and wanted all of her records. Plus, on July 2, 1978, the iconic disco song "Last Dance" was released, and I bought it the minute it came through the door at Record Bar.

The day came when I had the eighty-five bucks I needed to build Bilbo his private Disneyland of gerbil cages. Hands shaking, sweat pouring, I raced on my bike to K-Mart, made a quick stop at the disco records, then went back to gerbil gear. Maybe it was just me growing up, or maybe it was the cute guy looking at KISS albums, but in one life-defining moment, I scurried back to records and grabbed all the missing LPs I needed to complete my Donna Summer record collection and hightailed it to the check-out line.

What was I doing? Did I work this hard all summer just to tank at the finish line? And what would Bilbo think? Do gerbils even think? Would he even care if he got a new cage? After all, a cage is still a cage.

My mind was spinning with thoughts, questions, reasonings, and justifications.

Perhaps it was just a mere transportation problem. Instead of having to schlep home a cumbersome load of Habitrail boxes balanced on my handle bars, I had, in one paper K-Mart bag, all of Ms. Summer's recorded works through 1988 tucked tightly under my arm.

Once home, I cranked the 16:49 album cut (the entire A-side of her debut album) of what was already Donna's signature song, "Love to Love You, Baby." I was warbling, moaning, and vocally writhing along with the Queen of Disco when I heard Mom's familiar knock on my bedroom door.

"Turn that down! You're making my migraine worse. Where's

the Rabbit-Trail or Make-a-Trail or gerbil cage thing or whatever it's called?" Mom asked.

I simply shrugged an innocent shrug, as I nodded to the Donna Summer records splayed across my NFL bedspread. "I guess, I, well, uh, changed my mind."

Good thing, since there was a tragic day late in August when I had given poor Bilbo a taste of freedom by letting him run around the back porch in his clear plastic exercise ball. It was one of those sweltering, hot summer days when I loved being outside creating something in the backyard. As long as I was creating something, I was happy both indoors and outdoors.

But whatever the activity, on that day, I totally forgot about Bilbo. When I remembered his whereabouts, I ran to the porch only to discover that a plastic exercise ball also makes an excellent Dutch oven for a pet rodent.

Bilbo was dead.

Thanks to my stupidity, my absent mindedness, I let my rodent buddy and only friend succumb to the dangerous heat inside that poorly ventilated rolling death chamber.

I cried for a week.

But at least I had Donna Summer to console me. "MacArthur Park is melting in the dark, all the sweet green icing, flow-ow-ow-ing dowwwwwwn. Someone left the cake out in the rain…"

Rather, someone left the gerbil out in the sun.

14

It Gets Worse
NORTH LONGMONT: 1976-1977

On Friday nights, Mom and Ruben went to dinner at a Mexican restaurant on the corner of 3rd and Main called La Cocina. Occasionally, I was included if Ruben had had a good week at Ford. More often than not, a babysitter was arranged, and mercifully, I was left at home. As bad as it was as a kid when a group of grown-ups would linger at a restaurant table over pot after pot of coffee, it was even worse when Mom and Ruben would park themselves at a table in La Cocina and knock back margaritas. Mom was never much of a drinker, but her default setting was to please her husband, so in this case, that meant drinking whatever Ruben ordered.

One night, after they returned home and the babysitter was dismissed, Ruben made more drinks for himself and Mom. Although we will never know what he may have slipped into her drink—or why he did it—Ruben laced Mom's after-dinner margaritas with some potentially toxic drug. As the arguing and yelling intensified, I snuck down the hall to check on Mom.

I had never seen Mom in such a state. She was staggering, slurring her speech, and soon laying in just her bra and jeans on the cool cement step to the patio. Her moans became unintelligible until she seemed to fall asleep. She must have caught me out of the corner of her eye and, upon seeing me, urged me to go back to my bedroom, ensuring me everything was OK. I did as I was told but kept a vigilant ear pressed against my bedroom door.

Mom came back inside and told Ruben she needed to throw up. Ruben blocked her path. Voices were raised, a punch was thrown, and Mom was knocked to her knees. She struggled to open the basement door that was the first doorway on the left in the hallway. In an effort to flee from this drunken Jack-Nicholson-in-*The Shining* lookalike, Mom started down the basement stairs when Ruben ordered her to stop. He jumped down the stairs and slugged her hard in the face, sending her tumbling down the remaining six or seven steps. She landed in a crumpled heap.

"What did you do to my Mom?" I yelled at Ruben.

"Get back in your room, you little pipsqueak titmouse, or so help me you'll be next."

Pipsqueak titmouse?

Had Ruben been reading one of my Dickens novels?

I stole a look down the basement steps and was horrified. I dodged a blow from Ruben and scurried back into my room, barring the door with my wooden desk chair. I tried to quietly pry the window screen off, so I could go find help.

Then I heard Mom's voice in the hallway. Her speech was slurred. "Denny, everything's all right. Please go to bed. I love you."

I assumed Ruben was sitting in a chain-smoking, nose-picking trance in the orange booger chair.

Mom spent the rest of the weekend sleeping off whatever

Ruben had put in her drink. On Monday morning, with the skill of a Hollywood makeup artist, she expertly masked her bruises with Cover Girl and went to work.

Then, things got worse.

By this point, Ruben had effectively bullied any shred, any remaining shard of wobbly self-esteem out of me. Dennis had laid the rock-solid foundation of abandonment and self-worth issues. Ruben added the flimsy structure that helped cement a lifetime of self-hatred.

The bathroom in the 19th Avenue house was similar to those in Aurora and on Ashcroft Drive. Sink and toilet on the left, glass shower doors straight ahead, and towel bars on the right. This bathroom was decorated with ugly wallpaper, even by 1970s standards, that featured raised-relief purple roses and pink gladiolas splattered against a background of shiny green and silver leaves. A textural swirl tied the whole hideous design together.

I don't know how I provoked Ruben's wrath that day. Fact is, it didn't take much on any given day. He hated that I preferred to be indoors, sometimes reading a Nancy Drew book or furiously banging out typewritten pages of some story I was writing. He hated when I worked on my various crafts, everything from crochet to candle making. Ruben was disgusted by all of it and would call me Gertrude, Nancy, Matilda, fairy boy, or his favorite go-to, faggot.

Somehow, I made him angry that Saturday night, and he nearly broke my left arm as he pulled me into the bathroom. He slugged me across the mouth, then grabbed my head and slammed it into the bathroom wall until it had all but broken through the drywall, save for the nasty wallpaper. There was a head-shaped indentation in the wall.

I collapsed on the floor and blacked out.

* * *

As if my crafts and writing weren't enough for Ruben to despise me, my singing really pissed him off.

I discovered musicals in the way most kids of the late '70s discovered musicals; *Grease* was on the big screen. In my case, *Grease* was being shown on *both* screens of the north Longmont Twin Cinemas. I literally wore out the A-side of record one of the two-album set. If you grew up with the movie and had the album, you know what I'm talking about. A-Side: "Grease," "Summer Nights," "Hopelessly Devoted to You," "You're the One That I Want," and "Sandy." Five great belt tunes in a row without having to turn the record over. Pure belt-along awesomeness.

Then, I watched *The Sound of Music* on television. I usually attribute my becoming a singer—particularly a high tenor—from singing along with Julie Andrews. I could sing in Julie's range and match her note for note on nearly every song. Well, except that last B-flat of "Do-Re-Mi."

Far more than just singing, *The Sound of Music* stirred something deep inside me. The central theme of the main character, Maria von Trapp, is her trying desperately to discern and do the will of God. In my sixth-grade brain, I figured that doing God's will meant doing something I had absolutely no desire to do. If I, like Maria, tried to take the Austrian high road and obey God, would it mean I had to become a monk? Shave my head? Never speak again? Live inside formidable walls hand-copying Bibles? Looking back, there could have been worse vocations.

Years later, still struggling with the idea of doing God's will, I figured I would have to become a pastor or a Christian singer. But I suppose, had one of those vocations been God's will for my life, then it would have happened.

There was always a part of me that desperately wanted to do God's will, if I could only find out what it was. Answers were maddeningly elusive. So, like Maria spinning around on her Austrian mountain, I frittered away my adult years, spinning in every possible direction, on every possible hillside, and often, simply spinning completely out of control.

Interlude #1

Still Spinning
HOLLYWOOD: 2008

I still couldn't stand or walk, only crawl in my own slimy waste. The spinning was relentless.

Again, I prayed. "Dear God, Jesus, Universe, guardian angels, my higher self, my future self—please, anyone, someone—dear God please, please, please make this room stop spinning."

I knew I needed medical help, but I couldn't figure out how to work the motel phone to call 911. What a blessing it was that I never made that call. After being taken to a hospital and placed on a medical hold, my next stop would have been to prison for drug possession, hiring an escort, and who knows what else.

I don't know how many hours into the overdose I was—it might have only been minutes; time was always strange when I was high. Would I ever be able to walk again? Each time I attempted to stand, I fell, crashing face first into a piece of the motel room's disgusting furniture. Each time, I ended up back on my knees. And each fall to my knees intensified the panic and the slurred, barely intelligible requests to God.

Not once did it occur to me to ask for forgiveness rather than just begging for help as if it was owed to me.

15

Dr. Fruitcake
NORTH LONGMONT: 1978–1980

Junior high was a frightening, intimidating new world. The shred of confidence I had developed in sixth grade being in the "senior class" of elementary school quickly morphed into the awkward seventh-grade year of starting over.

Longs Peak Junior High was fast-paced and confusing, with the day carved into seven periods with five-minute allotments for using the restroom and getting to your next class. The first few days were a rough adjustment period for all seventh graders, but my peers adapted quickly. Not me. I struggled to navigate a huge rectangular maze of individual classrooms. The older guys were bigger and rougher, as they swaggered down the halls with pretty, cheerleader-skirted girls hanging off their broad shoulders. And there I was, an awkward kid in corduroy bell bottoms and tan Hush Puppies, braces still on my buck teeth and a face full of newly sprouted zits.

Eighth grade was even worse. Friendless and hopelessly depressed, I shuffled down the hallways with my head hung so low my chin nearly scraped the ground. Unless we were assigned seats, I would sit as far back as possible in each class, trying to blend in with the woodwork and praying I wouldn't be noticed. I hid behind my hand, firmly positioned against my forehead like a visor, shielding me from the world. I refused to look up or around, and often, I was silently crying, just wishing that the suffocating depression would finish its job and do me in, once and for all.

I had one teacher—my English teacher, Mr. Taggett—who believed in me and thought I had a talent for creative writing after reading the novelette I'd been writing since fifth grade. It was a stupid juvenile adventure story about a young boy who longed to be a botanist, then discovered a rare plant that brought him fame. With Taggett's assistance, he put a copy of my manuscript in front of his friends at the Denver Book Critics' Circle, who, in turn, offered positive feedback. The final comment: "A promising young writer. We hope to see more of his work." The compliment made a lasting impression. If an eighth-grade loser like me could bang out an 80-page novella on his Mom's old Smith-Corona and be praised for his work, well, that was something.

But it wasn't enough.

It was during this time that a mantra emerged and was chanted at me by everyone I encountered: "Believe in yourself. Have confidence in yourself. Just believe." Each well-intentioned person offered a slightly different variation on the theme, all trying their best to pull me out of my spectacular plunge into negative quicksand.

I tried to believe in myself.

Was there just nothing about me in which I could believe? I wondered.

The reflection in the medicine-chest mirror offered a clue: an ugly, zit-faced, metal-mouthed loser who had no friends, no prospects of friends, and little reason to live. Nothing worthwhile at all.

It was the late 1970s, the crescendo of the "Me" decade during which Americans looked inward while vigilantly looking out only for themselves, as the self-help book that was once given to me espoused.

One of the philosophies in Robert Ringer's book, *Looking Out for Number One*, that became permanently embedded in my brain was his "One to a Box" theory. I still imagine the cartoon drawing I made of some poor schlub sitting alone in a funeral store display casket, while the salesman shrugged at his confusion for the single-serving container.

"We come into this world alone and go out alone," the book proclaimed, building its case for learning to count on the only person in the world one could count on: one's self. Well, that's just fabulous. *If that's the secret to life*, I thought, *I'm pretty much screwed.* Because what stared back at me in the mirror was nothing I could count on.

I've spent more than fifty years flailing about, trying to believe in myself. I think the mantra was flawed and misguided from the get-go. What I wish someone had told me was: "Believe in God. Believe in Jesus. Look up to your Father in Heaven, not down at your feet." Perhaps if someone had said those words to me (and it's quite possible someone did), the next four decades might have taken a different course.

But what Father in Heaven could be proud of this walking disaster? My own father certainly wasn't. Ruben definitely wasn't.

I envied the kids who appeared to have it all together (and remembered where they put it), the ones who seemingly had it all figured out. Kids like Scott Douglas, who came from stable, unbroken homes, attended Sunday school with their siblings, and acted like they didn't have a care in the world. I, on the other hand, ever the Charlie Brown of my own not-so-funny comic strip at thirteen years of age, was carrying the weight of the world on my back. And it showed. I was put down and ridiculed by those kids for always being depressed, which just made me more depressed. But no one knew what I was enduring at home.

My head hitting had expanded from the gymnasium to my classrooms and even the hallways. It had become my method of self-punishment, and I didn't care who saw me hurt myself. I was the only kid at Long's Peak who was regularly sent to the counselor's office—at least twice per week. I mean, no other kid dragged himself between classes with head down and eyes fixed on the floor while silently chanting, "I hate my life. I hate myself. I want to die."

And after repeated threats to kill myself, the school counselor made an urgent recommendation that it was crucial for me to see a professional therapist. Mom dragged me out of school and sent me to a psychiatrist, whose office was conveniently across from the junior high. Drab brown and coldly clinical, the place was decorated in "Early Depression." The waiting room was comprised of a handful of gray metal folding chairs, some old dog-eared copies of *Highlights* magazine for kids, and a dead ficus tree. Seriously, if one wasn't already depressed when he walked in, he certainly would be by the time he left.

My first session began with both Mom and I sitting on opposite ends of a hideous, flowered sofa in the psych's office, the walls of which sported an assortment of degrees and tacky—and probably inappropriate—Kama-Sutra artwork. Mom did the talking, as I sat there holding my head down as far as it would go without my neck snapping in two. With my face hidden behind shaking hands and silent tears rolling down my pimpled face, I had nothing to say. As I sat there, an immobile, invisible figure, the doc gave Mom advice on dealing with this gloomy, suicidal mess of a kid she had on her hands. I mean, what thirteen-year-old kid willingly reads Sylvia Plath poetry?

Before one session, I had a moment of boldness and insisted I be allowed to talk to the psychiatrist alone. After all, wasn't I the one who was supposed to get help?

"Well, Dennis. You know why you're here, don't you?" He, like other adults, used the full, formal version of my first name that I loathed.

I shrugged.

"Come now, Dennis, you need to open up to me. Otherwise, we're just going to sit here for the next hour, and I will have to tell your mother how *very* uncooperative you were."

"Nobody likes me," I managed to squeak out.

"And why don't they like Dennis?" he said, referring to me in the third person, as if I wasn't there.

I shrugged again, studying a stain on my left shoe. "I dunno."

"Oh, surely there must be a reason. Is it because you're not like the other boys? Or is it maybe that you *like* the other boys, you know, in a certain way?" the psychiatrist pried.

He had called me on the carpet and, in five minutes of so-called therapy, had uncovered my deepest, darkest secret.

Yes, Dr. Fruitcake, I like other boys. Happy now?

I shifted my weight in my chair and alternated hands holding my head and hiding my eyes.

"Hands down, Dennis. Come on, Dennis, you can tell me. Your secret is *safe* with me," the doctor said with a disturbing wink.

"Yeah, I guess, a little." I felt like he was ripping my chest open and could see straight into my black little heart.

"Yeah, you guess a little—what, Dennis?"

This jerk wanted me to verbally confess my horrible secret.

"I like other boys, OK?"

"And what is it that Dennis likes about the other boys, hmm?"

"They're better looking than me. They play sports, and everyone likes them."

"Ah, now we're getting to know the *real* Dennis, aren't we?" His emphatic use of third-person singular put me even more on the defensive. "Do you wish you could be with the other boys? Touch the other boys?"

"I don't know what you mean."

"Oh, sure you do, Dennis. I think you know what I mean. Your mother says you *bother* other boys by calling them on the telephone and by writing notes to them."

"I don't mean to bother them." *Crap. He got through, broke me down.* "I, ah, just want someone to be my friend," I admitted.

"I can be your friend, Dennis." Fruitcake offered.

"It's not the same. You *have* to like me. Mom's paying you."

"Just what is it you don't like about Dennis?" He was back in third person.

Fine. Talk at me like I don't exist. I wish I didn't exist. I wish your office would catch on fire and trap you, your stupid degrees, and your disgusting sex paintings inside.

"I don't like anything about me," I answered.

"There must be *something* to like about Dennis, now isn't there, hmm?"

"Nothing I can think of."

"Well, you're just not trying very hard, now, are you?" the psychiatrist continued, as he picked and flicked out pieces of brown gunk from under his finger nails.

That was it. I could take no more. "I'm just a worthless piece of crap, just like everyone says I am. Just like Ruben says. Just like everyone says and thinks. A total worthless piece of total shit."

Then, grabbing me roughly by the arm, he pulled me off of the sofa, flung open the door from his office into the dingy hallway, and practically dragged me down the corridor. He opened the door to a one-at-a-time, "one-holer" bathroom, the private kind teachers got to use at school. He locked the door and pushed me down onto my knees.

Dr. Fruitcake dropped his pants and saggy underwear and plopped his hairy butt on the toilet seat. "Well, Dennis, if you're a piece of shit as you proclaim, then this is where you belong, in the toilet with your fellow turds. No greater happiness is known than that which is found when in the midst of your own kind, becoming the person—or shall I say in this case—the object you were born to become."

He farted and expelled what sounded like big, nasty turds into the commode. A sickening stench permeated the small room. I thought I would throw up right there on his filthy feet with their twisted yellow toenails poking out of his grimy hippie sandals. Fruitcake didn't wipe. He just stood up and stepped back to survey his disgusting masterpiece.

"So, Dennis is a piece of shit. Very well then," he cooed as he locked my head under his stinky left armpit and pushed my head down into the toilet, just above the unspeakable mess in the bowl. "Well, let's show Dennis where a piece of shit belongs," he announced as my face nearly made contact with the putrid brown glop.

I managed to scream, "Noooooo!"

"What was that?" Fruitcake cupped his ear toward the commode. "I thought I heard a piece of poop crying out from inside the toilet. Is it possible, just possible, after all, that excrement is capable of somewhat intelligible speech? Simply fascinating."

"Noooooo! I'm not a piece of a shit, OK? Please, please, please let me go, please."

"Well, Dennis," he said as he reluctantly released his vise grip on my neck. "I'm very, *very* disappointed because I thought we had made real progress today. I thought we found your true place in world. The place where you could be happy. I'm rarely wrong, but, oh well."

Progress? What was this maniac thinking? How on earth would forcing my head into a wretched toilet full of his crap fix anything? I wanted to disappear, to just die and get it over with. Maybe I should have let him have his filthy way and allowed me to drown in the toilet. *A fitting way to go for me, the stupid loser,* I decided. *I missed a good opportunity.*

Dr. Fruitcake pulled me back into his office, tossed me a Kleenex to wipe my tear- and sweat-stained face. "Compose yourself, Dennis. And wipe that brown splotch off your forehead. Wouldn't want it walking around like that, now would we? Time is up for today," he said, rising from his desk and adjusting his hastily zipped, rust-colored corduroys. "I assume we will be seeing it—and by 'it' I mean Dennis—again next week? Hmm?"

I made no attempt to answer.

"Dennis, how I *do* look forward to our next session. I'll see to it your mother schedules you for an extra-long session. We'll need the time," Fruitcake said with another wink.

There were at least three more visits to Dr. Fruitcake's little mind-shrinking lab, and at least once, a similar scene ensued. But it was 1979, and in those days, kids had few rights, certainly not in the way children enjoy the extreme rights and protections today. Bottom line was I could never tell Mom what the psychiatrist did to me, lest she think that I had provoked the scene.

A rare stroke of luck came my way when my orthodontist appointments required rescheduling in the Fruitcake timeslot. "Thank you, God. Thank you, Jesus. Thank you, whoever's up there," I whispered under my breath. I guess someone was looking out for me.

And I no longer had to look out for number two.

16

One Corndoggie to Go, Please

Dan Armstrong was the be-all and end-all in an otherwise invisible eighth grader's life. He was cool. He was edgy. He was rough around every edge and carried himself with the prowess of a wildcat that had seen and done everything.

Around sixth grade, I discovered that I could sing pretty well but had no outlet for it. Although I would belt out show tunes and disco standards from the safety of my bedroom, I was deathly afraid to sing in front of anyone. Fortunately, Mixed Chorus at Long's Peak Junior High was an open elective class, meaning no audition was needed. All one had to do was sign up and show up.

Because my voice was in its post-puberty transition (I would later be a high tenor), I was placed in the baritone section and assigned a seat next to Dan. And oh, how I wanted to be near him, to be with him, to smell him—to *be* him. I wanted to be anyone but me, and Dan was as far from "me" as I could get.

Dan occupied my every thought and embodied all of my hopes for a best friend. Much to my surprise, he seemed genuinely interested in being my friend. Maybe the loner in me spoke to something in him.

In his worldly way, Dan broke all the rules. He wore high-top black Converse Chuck Taylors and a fleece-lined, navy-blue windbreaker with a golf-course logo on it. It smelled like cigarettes—and him. One time, he left his jacket in the choir room, and I took it home—for safekeeping, of course—and slept in it before returning it to Dan the next day.

Dan was in ninth grade, and the teachers didn't seem to mind that he could often be found outside the side doors near the woodshop classroom smoking his unfiltered Marlboros. The smoking, the cool shoes, and the worn-out windbreaker were all part of his mystique, as was his course language and frank talk about sex.

I probably learned more from Dan's impromptu sex-ed teachings on the east side of campus than I did from the required sex education module taught to us eighth graders in the middle of the school year.

Like the *Scared Straight* films of the 1950s that warned teens of the dangers of drunk driving, the films shown to us boys gathered on the wrestling mats in the small gym were equally, if not more, disturbing. It was a merciful blessing that we were given a bye week from learning how to grapple during PE, even if it was to watch a ridiculous animated sperm in a tux swimming stupidly toward a lady egg in a prom dress sporting a blonde bouffant hairdo.

Then, there were the highly detailed illustrations of the female genitalia splayed across the retractable projection screen. We were told to pay strict attention, as (a) we would be tested, and (b) this was what we would be chasing if we weren't already. Accompanying the artwork was the film's narration by a monotone male voice.

"The vulva is comprised of both external and internal parts.

On the outside, we have the labia, the clitoris, the opening to the vagina, and the opening of the urethra, or pee hole," explained the male narrator to a wrestling mat full of giggles. "And above the vulva is the *mons veneris*, a fleshy lump that will be covered with pubic hair, like this."

A disembodied hand added black scribbles to represent pubes, evoking more giggles and the occasional "ew." I was imagining Maria von Trapp making up a rhyming ditty to help us learn the sacred parts. "*Oh, the clit, the lovely clit.*"

"Next, going inside the vulva, we have the vagina, the uterus, the cervix, the fallopian tubes, the ovaries, the hymen, and the G spot."

It was enough to make me want wrestling to resume. Almost.

* * *

In his true rebel manner, Dan read smut novels and made no attempt to hide their provocative covers. One day before class, Dan was engrossed in a paperback titled *Seventh Avenue* by Norman Bogner. The cover promised "a spellbinding tale of love, lust, and greed inside the seedy world of Manhattan's fashion industry."

Dan had dog-eared one of the pages on which he circled a bit of explicit dialogue between the bad boy main character and one of the females with whom he had just had a sexual tryst. Dan noticed my interest and read the passage aloud to me, right into my ear in his raspy, smoker's voice then gave my right knee a playful nudge.

"He fed it slowly into her mouth," Dan read aloud. "...and she felt it oozing."

"Felt what oozing?" I asked stupidly, with a grossed-out look on my face.

"Think about it, dude," Dan replied.

Lightbulb.

I was all at once enthralled and embarrassed. I'd never heard such things and was amazed that a book was allowed to contain this tantalizing scene.

Dan continued dramatically. "'Spit it out!' said the dude. 'That what whores do?' said the chick. 'Spit it out!' the guy said again.'"

That weekend, when I went with Mom to Horizon Park Mall, Mom went to Fashion Bar while I made my usual beeline for Waldenbooks. This time, I was desperately searching for my own copy of *Seventh Avenue*. It turned out that the book had to be ordered, and there was a puzzled, disapproving look on the prehistoric clerk's face when she saw this overly eager kid asking how fast she could get it in stock. A week or two later, I had my copy and quickly found Dan's favorite passages. Just carrying the book somehow made me feel closer to Dan. It felt like I had purchased admission into his exciting and dangerous world.

* * *

Shortly after winter break, the spring musical was announced, and we, in loser chorus, were informed that being part of loser chorus obligated us to be in the show as a final class assignment. Ever since *Grease* came out on the big screen two years prior, it seemed the entire world was obsessed with the 1950s. Although the stage version of *Grease* was available for schools, the royalties must have been far less expensive for a highly forgettable musical knock-off called *Rock 'n' Roll*.

I didn't have the confidence to audition for a speaking role, so I happily chewed the scenery as one of a handful of nondescript chorus boys. Dan, being the ninth-grade superstar and little-g god that he was, got the leading role. His character, Corndoggie, was a black-leather-jacket-wearing, slicked-back-haired rebel without the slightest clue. The female lead character, Betsy Lou, was a goody-two-shoes chick from the right side of the tracks and was played by a goody-goody chick who was over the moon for Dan.

And so was a certain nondescript chorus boy.

Someone dropped out of the show during the rehearsal period, and I was promoted to a speaking role, Bub, one of Corndoggie's cohorts. I had one line that I promptly forgot on opening night: "Way to go."

Way to go, Kempfer. You had one shot to impress Dan, and you blew it.

Forgetting my lines and lyrics would become a regular problem for me in subsequent shows throughout my performing career. I still have vivid nightmares in which I'm on stage in front of a large, unforgiving audience, grasping for my next line and coming up empty handed, or mouthed, as the case may be.

The end of the production's two-show run in Long's Peak's "auditeria" (a hybrid cafeteria and auditorium), fell on the weekend of my fourteenth birthday. After a great deal of pleading with Mom and Ruben, I was granted permission to have a small birthday get-together in the basement of the new house on 24th. Great emphasis was placed on "small," as they didn't want the house to be overrun with hoodlum kids.

In what would become one of my character traits, I now had a project, a goal, a *raison d'être*, and as such, I set out to give 110 percent to its completion, consumed with creating a themed masterpiece.

The unfinished basement was a blank canvas for a themed party straight out of *Grease* (or from the low-budget knockoff we were doing). I moved Mom's old turquoise record player into the event space and placed stacks of records around it, carefully selecting the soundtrack for the event. I decorated a rickety card table to hold Mom's custom-made cake that featured the Decca Records label of a certain Judy Garland tune, which had nothing to do with the '50s.

I handed out my invitations at school and probably bugged Dan eighty-seven times for his RSVP. The night of my birthday party came, and disaster struck. One poor sucker showed up around the start of the party then blew the joint after he shoveled a piece of my gay-as-a-goose, "Over-the-Rainbow"-themed cake in his pie hole.

One hour into the event, and there was no sign of Corndoggie Dan. I kept asking Mom if he had called. Nothing.

Then, in true drama-queen fashion, I cranked up Leslie Gore and blasted "It's My Party" *ad nauseum* until I drove away the other three kids that had bothered to show up. I should have paid attention to them, been grateful for their attendance, and nurtured those friendships. But no, I was pouting in a corner over some guy who I wanted desperately to be my best friend, the older brother I didn't have, and the father I never had. And those were a lot of shoes to fill.

Sometimes, even the saddest tales have happy, if not bitter-sweet, endings. Around 8:30 that night, after my three guests were long gone, Dan showed up, probably stoned. Wiping my pitifully tear-stained face, I showed him the basement décor, he grabbed a hunk of cake, wished me "a good one" and bolted. I cried for nothing over some dude who ultimately didn't give a crap about me, all the while alienating potential friends.

Oh, how the patterns start young and become engrained.

17

The Night the Lights Went Out at Malo
ESTES PARK, COLORADO: 1981

Big changes happened while I was in ninth grade. Mom left Ruben and married a nice man who lived in Broomfield, a suburban city about forty minutes south of Longmont. We moved, and I started high school with a priceless new opportunity to reinvent myself. Via a self-promo kit, I used my ninth grade performing experience in my school's ultra-elite, eight-member vocal group and my turn as the Tin Man in *The Wiz* to launch myself into Broomfield High's show choir. It worked, and I was cast as the only sophomore in the all-upperclassmen choir.

Each year, the new cast of the Broomfield Eagle Express show choir would go to the mountains for a weekend retreat to learn a concert's worth of music. Although we did learn the new music, we also learned a lot about our cast mates' personalities, backgrounds, and body parts.

The retreat was held at the infamous Camp Saint Malo, a YMCA venue outside Estes Park. A Catholic-run camp, its thin wooden walls had no doubt witnessed many conversions from childhood innocence to teenage wanderlust. It had also been the location of my first trip away from home during sixth grade when two classes of the eldest members of Northridge Elementary took to the woods surrounding Saint Malo for "Eco-Week," a nearly week-long venture to study nature, shower together, and compare the growth patterns of newly sprouted hair from pubescent groins. With plenty of adult chaperones on that trip, the most shameful thing that happened during my Eco-Week adventure was losing power one night. That was 1978—the era of big, feathered, *Saturday Night Fever* hair on both genders. Sadly, it was determined by Malo staffers that it was the *boys'* hair dryers that blew the fuse. Thanks, Travolta.

My first show choir retreat had only one chaperone, the choir director herself, who had to manage the primal urges of fifteen seniors, two juniors, and one particularly horny sophomore. Rumor was that every year at least one choir member lost his or her virginity on the retreat. I'd like to be able to say it was me. I'd *like* to say that, but it wouldn't be true.

Shortly after we returned from the retreat, it was Homecoming 1981. A school tradition was Spirit Week, a weeklong celebration that today would seem stupid, at best. It was during this week, steeped in tradition, that we were allowed and encouraged to dress according to a different theme for each of five days. Although BHS was a public school and we didn't wear uniforms, it was still the early 1980s, and there was a fairly strict dress code. Spirit Week for us was the high-school equivalent of casual Fridays in the workplace.

Two of the senior singers took an interest in me, albeit for different reasons. Phil, a wonderfully talented singer and songwriter, had his own band and invited me to sing with them for one of the Homecoming events. He was a great role model and mentor.

Jack, however, took an interest in me that would prove to be more than platonic. Although he ignored me during the retreat—perhaps because he was under the ever-watchful eye of Tammy, his then-girlfriend and later wife—Jack almost instantly befriended me once we had settled into the school routine. Since we both sang tenor, that gave him the opportunity to sit next to me in show and concert choir.

At first, I didn't think much of the occasions when Jack's leg would push against mine with ever-increasing pressure. I have to admit, the warmth and the physical connection with another guy was not at all unpleasant, so when the warm leg pressed into mine, I responded with an enthusiastic nudge. Soon, we were sharing a music binder, each of us holding one side of the large black vinyl folder. Jack's right hand started to find my left and playfully brushed against it, securely hidden behind the safety of the folder. Eventually, those innocent little finger brushes became hand-holding under the choir chairs.

Jack lived less than two blocks from me and usually walked me home. Other times, when he drove his brown Pontiac Cutlass to school, he would collect Tammy and me, take her home first, then linger in a slow ride home, holding hands with me.

One day during Spirit Week, between "Wear Your Clothes Inside-Out Day" and "Wear Your School Colors Day," Jack asked if he could borrow a pair of my sweatpants for the next day's equally lame "Wear Your Sweats to School Day." I had several pairs and thought nothing of loaning him one.

About two weeks after Sweats Day, I asked Jack if he still had my gray gym pants. He said he hadn't forgotten, then whispered, "I wear them at night to feel closer to you."

I blushed with understanding having slept a night with Corndoggie Dan's jacket. "That's cool," I answered. "Well, if you like them that much, I guess you can keep them a while longer."

Jack returned the sweats the next day with a handwritten note tucked inside confessing his attraction to me. I was flattered and instinctively knew it could only lead to trouble. But trouble was fun and exhilarating.

In October, show choir had a group outing to see *West Side Story* at Boulder's Dinner Theater, and Jack arranged to have me at his table, at his side. Conveniently, Tammy was ill and couldn't attend. During Maria's second-act ballad, "I Have a Love," a moist-eyed Jack pushed in closer to me, squeezed my hand under the tablecloth and whispered, "I love you, Denn" in my left ear. I echoed his sentiment, feeling elated and like I had found the one—already.

Well, that happened fast!

In my naïve tenth-grade head, I foolishly believed that we could make a successful go of it, just the two of us against the world. But make a go of *what*, per se? I couldn't even answer my own question. Best friends? Sure. Roommates? Eventually, I hoped. But how did the hand holding and other physical embodiments of this relationship fit in? They didn't, at least not from anything I'd ever seen. As is standard operating procedure for me, I charged in head first without a plan, just hoping everything would work out for the best. That and a lot of finger-crossing, star-wishing, and fervent "I'll never ask for anything ever again" prayers.

The next week at school, Jack arranged for me to become his locker roommate in senior hall, which made the perfect repository for exchanges of sickly-sweet love notes, all of which I carried home tucked deep in the pockets of my navy-blue puffer jacket. I squirreled them away in my top dresser drawer, behind my underwear and near the two remaining Percocets I'd managed to hide after the previous year's wisdom teeth extraction. *Because no parent would ever look there.*

Then one night, Jack's parents and brother were away from home, and I was invited over to watch *South Pacific* on cable TV. It was also the night that things progressed from quasi-innocent hand-holding into more dangerously exciting territory. Around the time that the sailors on the beach were singing how "there's nothing like a dame," the guys on the couch had their shorts off, embarking on their own enchanted evening.

After that fateful night, Jack and I became inseparable. And folks began to notice. *His* folks, to be precise. Especially his father. Jack's dad was a hardcore Southern Baptist preacher and was starting to question the nature of his son's keen interest in his younger playmate.

Convergence came quickly. Around this time, Mom found one of Jack's notes in my jacket. The note was immediately passed to Jim (Mom's new husband) for inspection, who promptly marched up Miramonte Boulevard to present the note to Jack's strict, right-wing father. As you might imagine, this had the success of sailing a lead balloon.

Jim returned home and scolded me. He didn't get into the minutia of what Jack and I did physically that was detailed in the note, rather stating that "for a variety of reasons" the relationship could not and would not continue. I was to make friends with kids my own age, and Jack's father had forbidden him to ever see me again in an unsupervised situation. And of course, I was grounded for two weeks.

I've always said that Jack was the first to break my heart. Perhaps that's not entirely accurate. It was more so the relationship's sad outcome that broke my heart. The rebel in me wanted to go against everyone's word and just run away with Jack, and I think Jack wanted the same. I thought I loved him, and maybe I did on some naïve level. I'm not sure if it was love on Jack's side. He certainly spoke as if it was. I found Jack's proclaimed affection suspect when he made no attempt to continue our relationship, despite his father's decree. I don't know what Jack wanted out of our little romance, and it's quite possible, he didn't know either.

But to me, a wide- and starry-eyed young teen, Jack was Dennis, Mike Leak, Sonny, Scott Douglas, Matthew Laborteaux, and Corndoggie Dan all in one package. Rather, I was trying to cast all of those hurts, crushes, and broken friendships onto Jack for him to redeem and heal me. He was the first to unwittingly bear this burden. That's a tall order for any one person.

So, as fast as we became friends, we were forbidden from speaking to each other, and I retreated to my bedroom, sulking and crying in an uncanny flashback to Mike Leak.

* * *

Time proved to be the great healer, and between show choir, newspaper staff, a job at McDonald's, and the 1974 Dodge Dart that appeared in front of the house just prior to my 16th birthday, I had pretty much squelched every last bit of shyness. And for at least this time in my life, I wasn't hitting my head nor hating myself as much.

The Dodge Dart was a cool looking car, red with a *Starsky and*

Hutch sport stripe that made it look pretty bad ass. Not shabby for a choir boy when my cohorts were driving hand-me-down ugly station wagons. But there was a catch.

When Jim gave me the Dodge Dart for my birthday, it came with a two-page driving contract, and I was, most likely, the only driving-age kid in Broomfield (possibly even in the state of Colorado) who had an ironclad legal contract that had been expertly prepared by my well-meaning stepfather. The document was presented to me on the eve of going with Jim to obtain my learner's permit. I was flummoxed but sat dutifully at the avocado-green kitchen table, trying to pay attention to most of the contract's legalese. There was a lengthy list of infractions that would warrant Jim to invoke the "Taking the Keys Away" clause.

Yeah, yeah, I was thinking. *You'll never enforce this.* The key enforcement mechanism involved Jim taking odometer readings prior to and upon conclusion of my use of the Dart. One of the top violations, second only to breaking curfew, was driving outside my approved driving radius, which was equivalent to one round trip to the AMC movie theater complex at Westminster Mall, about five miles one way.

The driving contract was reviewed at length, I was quizzed on its content and stipulations, and Mom notarized the thing. I even had to write an essay to convey my understanding.

Once I finally earned approval for solo trips for recreation, I snuck in as many prohibited journeys as possible, concocting flimsy excuses for the extra miles logged. I was thankful for the car, but the contract made me want to buy my own, stipulation-free vehicle.

It was also a chick magnet, and the last thing I wanted was a chick.

18

All-State Romance

FORT COLLINS, COLORADO: 1983

Shortly after winter break, Ms. Leighton, the choir director, encouraged me to audition for the 1983 Colorado All-State Choir. The competition would be brutal, but based on my scores at the regional vocal competitions, she was convinced I could get cast. Not nearly as difficult as some of the Saturday vocal competitions I'd been doing, I gave a stellar audition and, along with a senior girl from my school, was picked to be part of the 300-voice choir. I had been spoiled with an unprecedented number of solos in both BHS choirs and had decided that being a "solo artist" was more my thing. But All-State Choir carried a distinction with it that would look good in a yearbook. Plus, the 1983 event was being held at Colorado State University (CSU) in Fort Collins—about ninety minutes north of home—which meant two glorious nights away from parental supervision.

On the first day of rehearsal, we worked in smaller break-out groups in the morning. In the afternoon, we were sorted by vocal part and arranged in long curves of chairs in an enormous rehearsal hall. About thirty chairs from me, in the bass section, sat the most gorgeous brown eyes I'd ever seen. Better still, each time I stole a

145

glance down the row, the brown eyes were staring back. Eventually, smiles were exchanged. Then a wink. And on the next break, I met the brown eyes that were attached to Scott from Fort Morgan.

Of course, his name was Scott.

After rehearsal, we couldn't wait to talk to each other.

"So, Denn, do you have a girlfriend?" Scott asked.

"Well, not really. I mean, I have friends who are girls, but you know..." *Did he know?* "Do you?"

"Hell no. There's a girl I take to dances, but that's because I live in a small town. You know how it is, right?" he said with a wink.

"Oh, yeah. Totally," I said, unable to make eye contact.

We walked behind the rehearsal hall and with a loading dock as cover, Scott pulled me to him and kissed me.

Was it too soon to tell him I loved him?

Reeling and gasping for breath, I began a barrage of questions. "You said you work at McDonald's. Me too! I work drive-through. What about you?"

"I usually work grill." At my store, grill guys were usually straight and gorgeous.

"Hot. Do you have to wear those ugly green uniforms?"

"No, my store wears the ugly rust-colored ones."

"Lucky."

"And the stupid paper hats?"

"Yeah, but I usually wear the Manager-on-Duty hat because I'm training to be a shift supervisor," Scott explained.

"I got to wear one of those hats once. I still have it."

"So, have you ever had a boyfriend?" Scott asked, shifting the conversation to more interesting ground.

"Um, yeah. Last year. It didn't last long. His dad is a preacher, and well, you know, that didn't go over so well."

"Do you want to be my boyfriend?" Scott asked.

"Oh my God, yes! Anything! I'd do anything to be with you." *Shut up, you pathetic idiot*, I told myself. "I feel like I've known you my whole life. Maybe even in another life, if there's such a thing," I gushed. "But how does this work? You live so far away."

"I'll be graduating in a few months, then I'm moving to Denver. It will work out. You'll see." Although he lived in a small town on the northern Colorado plains, he somehow seemed worldly. And I could never resist "worldly."

At last, the stars had aligned, and I had met my soulmate. It was a match made in All-State-Choir heaven, or so I thought, and we instantly fell hopelessly, madly, and recklessly in love with each other. We spent our spare moments of the remaining two days of All-State sharing our life stories, pledging our love to each other, and sneaking into each other's hotel room.

On the final night, hundreds of parents jammed the CSU parking lots to come hear the 1983 Colorado All-State Choir perform. Once it was over, our respective parents would whisk us all back to from whence we came. Unless, like Scott, one had unlimited driving privileges and got to drive himself home.

I could barely make it through the concert without choking up. From Broomfield, Fort Morgan was three hours away by car, and per my driving contract, that was a strictly prohibited destination. There would barely be time for a decent goodbye after the concert before we were swept our separate ways. We had traded phone numbers and addresses and vowed to call each other and write to each other every day until I graduated and could go flying off into his embrace.

What a dumb schmuck I was.

Tears burned my cheeks as I cried silently all the way home to Broomfield. I prayed the phone would ring the next day. In those Paleolithic days of 1983 before cell phones, email, and texting, all we had were landlines and the Postal Service. It was a horrible wait, but the next day, the chocolate-brown rotary phone on the kitchen wall *did* ring, and it was Scott. We talked for more than an hour before both mothers started squawking in the background about long-distance rates.

Faithful to his word, within a couple of days, the first of many daily letters started to arrive. I, of course, upheld my end of the deal, and being an overachiever, wrote Scott *two* letters per day. I mean, I had to make sure he knew how much I wanted him, right?

About six weeks after All-State, the Broomfield choirs were scheduled to give their final concert of the school year. Since I hadn't been allowed to drive to Fort Morgan for Scott's end-of-year concert, he planned to come to mine. Oh, and we were so clever. He had attended All-State with a girl named Brenda; I had attended with a girl named Susan. We fabricated a story that Brenda would be coming with him, and the four of us would be going out on a double date after the concert. It seemed like an infallible, plausible, innocent-as-a-malt-shop ruse.

But Mom must have suspected something. Perhaps all those daily letters? After the concert, Mom watched me like a hawk as

I rushed to meet Scott. There were no girls with us, as we darted out the side door, hopped in his 1979 medium-pine, metallic green Mercury Capri convertible, and drove off into the night. We went to Broomfield's "Inspiration Point," where we parked and managed to thoroughly steam all the windows. I lost track of time but had the nagging sense that it was probably "around my curfew" and reluctantly told Scott I had to get back to my car, still parked in a now empty school parking lot.

I rushed home and walked casually into the house with a huge, shit-eating grin on my face and an even larger hickey on my neck.

Oops.

"You're late," Mom barked, blocking my path as I tried to cross the living room.

"Oh, yeah. I'm sorry. We all lost track of time."

"Uh huh. And who exactly is 'we all'?"

"You know, me and Susan and Scott and Brenda," I replied as nonchalantly as I could manage.

"And what is that on your neck?" Mom retorted.

I glanced in the living room mirror to see a trio of big, ugly, purple hickeys on my neck. I beamed inside when I saw them, so proud of my tacky little trophies. "Oh, oops, I guess, hmm, I don't know. Maybe my tie was too tight?"

"Those are hickeys!" Mom yelled. "Where did you get them?"

"Um, well, Brenda and I kind of made out."

"Brenda, huh? Well, I didn't see any *Brenda* with you tonight. You got those from Scott, didn't you?"

Oh, crap. Should I perpetuate the lie? Should I be honest?

I decided to go with bold, cocky honesty.

"Yes, I got them from Scott. We love each other."

Oh boy.

"I don't want to hear any of this nonsense. You're grounded. Forever! No phone, no car, no nothing. Go to your room, and don't come out until I tell you to. And you won't be talking to Scott ever again," Mom growled.

Mom and I didn't speak for at least a month. I resented her for trying to keep me from Scott. Although I was grounded and phone use was forbidden, I managed to sneak a call to Scott and let him know what had happened. He seemed aloof, distant.

"Hey buddy," Scott said as he greeted me on the phone.

"Buddy? Never mind. You'll never believe what happened," I said, as I started to blurt out every tragic detail.

"Yeah, hey, sorry your Mom acted that way. But hey, you'll never believe what happened to me! I'm going to Dallas to train as a flight attendant for six weeks, then I'll be getting my own apartment in Denver! So pretty soon, we'll have a place where we can be together."

I was ecstatic. I was ready to quit school and have his babies. Except of course for the fact that I was indefinitely grounded. "I'm grounded, like, forever," I said.

"Ah, you won't be grounded forever. Look, I'll call you after I get settled in Denver, and you can come down and hang out."

Scott's tone was different and concerning. "Yeah, well, sure. Call me, I guess," I said in defeat.

Mom eventually softened, and we started speaking again. Now in my senior year, I was no longer grounded, and Scott finally did call; it was just six months later than expected. It was a Saturday when he invited me to his new apartment in Denver's Capitol Hill area. Scott had a wonderfully dumpy one-bedroom apartment all to himself in a five-story building at the corner of 14th Avenue and Emerson. His unit was at the far-right end of a hallway on the top floor. He came down and showed me where to park, then we hurried into the rickety, chrome-plated building that was littered with graffiti.

We wasted no time getting reacquainted, although, I firmly stated that hickeys were off limits. He agreed. Other things, however, were not off limits (but probably should have been). I thought all had been restored, and like the stupid kid in the grade-school book waiting by the rainy window, I assured myself that good things truly come to those who wait.

But, wait.

Scott did go through flight attendant training, but for some reason, there was a delay in getting hired. Meantime, he was working at the McDonald's on 6th and Broadway as a shift leader, making the tidy sum of $4.50 per hour. My brain was going ninety miles per hour planning our life together.

I could quit school, move in with Scott, and work at the same McDonald's. It would be perfect.

Not so fast. It seemed Scott and I were no longer sharing the same dream.

"Well, now that I'm in Denver, I just want to enjoy my freedom. I mean, for the first time in my life, I'm on my own and out of that small town. I've had a lot of catching up to do," Scott explained.

"Oh, I see." *I didn't see.* "Um, what kind of catching up?"

"You know, messing around, having fun, meeting a lot of different guys."

I mentally repacked my suitcase.

"I don't want to be tied down," Scott continued.

"Well, I'm kind of a one-guy guy," I said. "I don't think I could be one of your, I don't know what to call it—your harem or your stable of guys."

"You never know; you might like it. You need to loosen up. I'm on a quest."

"A quest?" A warbled underscore from *Man of La Mancha* started to play in my confused head. "What do you mean by quest?"

Scott giggled, suddenly shy. "Oh, you wouldn't understand."

"Try me."

"I'm on a quest to sleep with as many guys as possible and see who has the biggest dick."

I couldn't believe what I was hearing. I gathered my things and started toward the door, red-faced and hurt. I was going to slink away without a word. Then I turned around.

"You know what, Scott? You want to find the biggest dick? Look in your fucking mirror. *You* are the biggest dick. You, Scott, you. So good luck with your fucking quest. I hope you find what you're looking for."

It was the first real sting of what felt like romantic reality. Apparently, the real world wasn't quite the Hallmark card I imagined it to be. Everything felt wrong. Wrong, dark, and sour. I drove home with a face full of tears, reeling from everything that had just happened.

About a year later, I became friends with an African-American club DJ who knew Scott intimately. He confirmed that Scott was indeed on a quest, and that he had been declared the winner. Still, Scott wasn't satisfied, and as such, the friend feared for him. This was 1985, and the AIDS epidemic had just begun to reach smaller metropolitan cities like Denver. Male flight attendants were to blame, people said.

Scott died from AIDS on August 15, 1993 at the age of 28.

19

I Need to See You in My Office
BROOMFIELD AND DENVER: 1984

By the fall of my senior year, I found myself without friends. I had been so busy hanging with the Classes of 1982 and 1983 that I snubbed my own classmates. It was a bad move that lacked forethought. I was back to being a loner. And although it wasn't my style to accept the friendship of a guy three years my junior, I did so rather hesitantly and perhaps with only a modicum of caution.

Mike was only a ninth grader but had clearly been around his own particular block many, many times. While I thought I had been exposed to all manners of sexual escapades, my experiences were suddenly tame compared to Mike's. He shared stories about being sexually abused by an uncle at ten years old, but unlike most guys who are traumatized by such an unfortunate violation, it simply piqued his interest, as he pursued a portfolio of older guys to repeat the scenario. He said guys offered him money, and once in a while, he'd accept it for ice cream and records and stuff. And so, he pursued me until I gave in to his boyish charm. While I didn't find him all that attractive, the idea of having a new gay friend was appealing.

Mike was following in my footsteps as the youngest student-singer cast in show choir, effectively topping my once-impressive achievement. I needed to top him, I suppose. I just didn't imagine it would be in my office during school hours.

Let me back up a step. During my junior year, Broomfield High went through a massive renovation, combining the former middle school with the existing senior high, creating a four-year institution. During that renovation, the journalism lab added a new layout room for the newspaper, a dark room for the photographers, and an unassigned, tiny office tucked behind the lab. As a second-year Editor-in-Chief of the *Eagle* yearbook, Mrs. Babb, the journalism advisor, offered me the space from which to work. I quickly relinquished my locker in senior hall and went to pick out office furnishings from a storehouse of retired desks, rickety chairs, and battered filing cabinets. Soon, I was set up with my own office, complete with a Mr. Coffee.

Early into our blossoming friendship-courtship, Mike wanted to see my new digs while a third-period journalism class was in session just one wall away. Mike knew what he wanted and wasted no time. He barred the door with my desk chair, and as fast as you could say "Denise's ho-ho," Mike had his pants down and was bent over my desk, with his flat, wide, pale moon of a butt wiggling at me for attention.

"Whoa. What the hell are you doing?" I asked.

"What do you think? Do me," Mike said quite casually.

He's played this scene before, I thought.

"We can't do that here. Not at school," I said.

"Why not? No one knows we're back here. Don't worry, I'm pretty quiet…"

"*Pretty* quiet?"

Perhaps partly out of curiosity and partly just to get him out, we did the deed. The whole scene was crude and disgusting. No romance or pleasantries. And Mike was not, in fact, quiet. Soon there was a jiggling of the door knob and a knock on my door followed by the awkward and hasty buttoning of two pairs of 501 jeans.

Mrs. Babb never asked, never said a word. But she knew. And she knew that I knew she knew. A raised eyebrow and a look that conveyed "tsk tsk" was all I got from her. I made sure it never happened again. At least not there.

Ultimately, Mike proved to be a little too young and ironically, far too experienced for me. Decades later, thanks to social media, I learned that Mike had also succumbed to AIDS. I wasn't surprised, and at the time I found out, I took a holier-than-thou, serves-him-right attitude.

* * *

Mercifully, at some point early in my senior year, Jim gave up on taking the odometer readings and loosened the contract-sanctioned travel perimeters. That, and a new girlfriend named Becky at Arvada West High School (about thirty minutes south) afforded me some hard-fought freedoms for my senior year.

With the driving sanctions relaxed, I started to grow more adventurous and, like Alice down the fabled rabbit hole, increasingly curious about what was beyond the sleepy borders of Broomfield.

Mike had personally introduced me to a gay cruising area that was conveniently in the same general vicinity (if one considers a ten-mile detour as "general") as Becky's area.

Built in 1906, Inspiration Point Park on Sheridan Boulevard was created as a picnic spot where visitors could view the fast-growing city of Denver and the Front Range of the Rockies. With time and cultural changes, the park deteriorated into a gay cruising destination. Give us gay boys a thing of beauty, and we'll quickly turn it into a haven for cheap sex.

All too soon, the red-and-white Dart and the blonde-haired boy behind the wheel became a regular fixture on the circular loop around the inner-city respite of natural wildlife. Truth be told, the real "wildlife" was occurring in the backseats and bushes between boys and men of varying ages and experience. Too often, a late-night drive—with the temptation for just one more time around—through the park became the reason I pushed the limits of my midnight curfew.

Keep in mind that in 1983, it was all word-of-mouth among gay guys where to meet others for fun. This was a year before the personal computer became a household thing and more than ten years from the introduction of anything that resembled the Internet. There were the 1-976 phone lines for "meeting local guys" with per-minute charges that were just shy of extortion, but if a guy was still living with his parents as I was, those were calls he did not want appearing on the family phone bill.

As I continued to grow increasingly adventurous, through the gay grapevine, I learned about a larger playing field: Capitol Hill's Cheesman Park. In my youthful naiveté and utter stupidity, I had no clue that the park was much more dangerous than I realized at the time. It was only years later that I learned of the police sting operations and guys being arrested for pants-down in the public restrooms. One time, I was wandering the playground area and stopped to casually perch on a swing while keeping my eye on a construction worker making his rounds through the nearby underbrush. I was approached by a cop and nearly wet my pants from fear. But being young, blonde, and stupid, I was able to concoct a flimsy excuse for being in the park after dark—"my niece had to use the restroom"—and got off with a smirk and a warning.

Rumor had it that Cheesman was built atop an old cemetery, which added a creepy sense of the impending doom that AIDS was starting to bring to our collective doorsteps in 1984. There we were, hoping to get laid, lying on top of those long-since dead.

The park became first on my list of hangouts. On the hot summer days in 1984, I would drag a VW-sized boombox to the center of the open expanse of grass where I slathered myself in baby oil and splayed myself across a *Psycho* movie poster beach towel, as I desperately tried to get tan lines. The area in which I frequently laid was exactly dead center of the buried cemetery.

When I moved back to Colorado in 2016, a Facebook friend wanted to meet at Cheesman because he didn't have a car and the park was in walking distance from his apartment.

"You can pick me up near the swings," he suggested.

"Um, hell no," I protested. "The cops bust guys for cruising the park."

"Seriously? No one cruises parks anymore. We have the Internet, remember?"

"Oh, yeah. True. The last time I cruised Cheesman, I was blasting Wham! and Whitney Houston, laying out in a tiny Speedo."

"Eww. A Speedo?"

"Yep. Pubes hanging out the sides and everything. I was a real class act."

But back to 1984.

Becky had no clue about my extracurricular activities, and I doubt she could even imagine such things. Her family owned a video rental store at 64th and Wadsworth and travelled frequently. On one such occasion, she was having a school friend, a lifeguard named Joe, housesit. Lifeguard was the only word I needed to hear and, in my growing ability to lie, appeared at Becky's door the first night she was gone.

Joe answered the door in just his red Speedo, still wet from a swim in the backyard pool.

"Um, hi, hello, I'm Denn, you know, Becky's boyfriend?" I announced, trying to keep my eyes above his bulge.

"Yeah, cool. I know who you are. What's up?"

"Well, I was here last night, and I left my driving glasses somewhere."

Nice ploy, Kempfer. And how did you get here today without your driving glasses?

"Oh, no problem. Come in. We'll find them."

And so the Hardy Boys set off on a mock search of Nancy Drew's house. I put on my best act, knowing all the while that the glasses were stuffed far back beneath my front seat in the Dart.

After an hour of exhaustive searching, Joe asked if I was hungry. "Let's walk away from this for now. I'll drive. We'll grab some pizza and movies from the video store and come back and hang out. I'm sure we'll find what you're looking for."

Joe's words hung in the air like a cartoon-dialogue bubble as he pulled on his thick-ribbed corduroy Ocean Pacific shorts that were all the rage. I had a pair of my own that cost me two weeks' McDonald's pay only to have them confiscated by Jim the first time I attempted to wear them in public.

I was stopped abruptly in my driveway by a stern voice emanating from the garage. Jim asked, "Just where do you think you're going with your genitals hanging out?"

My sassy response resulted in a two-week grounding and full revocation of car privileges. Yes, the shorts were short, but it was 1984.

And Joe's OP shorts left little to the imagination, perhaps just as the designer had intended. We hurried back with food and a stack of VHS tapes and camped out on the living room floor. As we ate and watched some boring *Terminator* movie, Joe's leg occasionally brushed against mine. I hesitantly brushed back. Before long, there were two male bodies tangled up among the pizza boxes and video cases.

During the two weeks that Becky's family was away, I was a frequent visitor to their house, finally admitting I had never lost my glasses. Joe said he figured as much and was glad for the way things worked out.

Then, like a scene from a bad teen movie, Becky and company returned a night early. We were indulging in Becky's bed when we heard voices downstairs. We jumped into our clothes and ran red-faced down to meet our fate. Being a good Mormon family, no one suspected foul play, but the question was raised as to my presence.

"We were working on a surprise for you, sweetie," I lied through my teeth.

"Oh, what is it?" Becky exclaimed.

I hesitated. Joe jumped in. "It's not ready yet. Anyway, I gotta get to my shift at the pool."

Smooth move, Joe. Leave me holding the proverbial bag.

"Oh, never mind the surprise. I'm just so glad to see you," I lied again. "Want to go get ice cream and drop by the pool?"

"The pool? Why? You just saw Joe."

"Oh yeah, that's right."

I was a horrible liar.

My relationship with Becky fizzled, but the sparks between Joe and I remained. With my ever-increasing gay-boy knowledge, I told Joe about a gay bar for guys between 18 and 21. The Grove was widely known as a "chicken bar," referring to the slang of the period in which an under-aged gay boy was un-affectionately called "chicken." At that time, Colorado still had what was known as "3.2" beer, meaning it had 3.2 percent alcohol, roughly half the alcohol content of full-strength, grown-up beer. Joe and I reached our eighteenth birthdays within weeks of each other in early 1984 and hit the bar to celebrate.

The Grove (also known as the Grave and the G-Spot) was a run-down, former straight dive bar that had attempted to dress itself up for the style-savvy gay crowd but had only managed to change itself into a *gay* dive bar. Like lipstick on a pig, there was only so much that could be done with smoke and mirror balls to hide the filthy, torn carpeting and stale aroma of beer, sweat, and piss. The best night to go, if one wanted to meet guys over the legal age, was on Drown Night—also known as Chicken Hawk Night. (A chicken hawk was an older man who liked young, almost mostly legal guys.) Every Tuesday, for a mere pittance of four bucks at the door, one could get a big, bold rubber-stamp imprint of a chicken on his right hand for a night of limitless beer and, well, chicken.

But the Grove wasn't Joe's scene, and he left early in disgust. Had I been wise, I would have followed suit, but I wasn't wise; I was never wise. I wasn't even sure if we had gone to the club "together" as boyfriends. (Apparently, we had.) I wasn't there to drink, as I had no taste or tolerance for beer. I certainly wasn't there to dance. Only on rare occasions have I been seen on a non-country music dance floor, as I've never been adept at freestyle gyration. But if there was a guy dancing whom I was smitten with, well, I'd get my butt on the floor and flail about looking like a imbecile.

As such, it was truly a momentous occasion when I was on the Grove's dance floor and among the first to hear what would become a top-twenty record by a then-unknown singer with a religious name. "Lucky Star" became a sort of personal anthem, as I wandered blindly into the darkness of being gay.

20

Unlikely Rent Boy
DENVER: 1985

As much as I enjoyed Madonna's music, I blame Cyndi Lauper for this whole mess. No, that's an unfair statement; I don't know the woman. But I do know that her twelve-inch extended-mix single of "She Bop" was in frequent rotation on my senior-year bedroom turntable. In addition to teaching me how to conjugate the verb "bop," she also unwittingly introduced me to gay porn with the mysterious reference to seeing her dream boy every night in *Blueboy* magazine.

Without the present-day convenience of typing queries into Google, in early 1984, all one could do was subtly ask around. Or ask the old biddy clerk at the mall's Waldenbooks. "Um, do you, ah, well, carry *Blueboy*?"

"I'm sorry, dear. I didn't hear you very well."

"Yes, ah, *Blueboy*," I repeated sheepishly.

"I can barely hear you, dear. Are you asking who wrote about Bluebeard, the pirate?"

I'm pretty sure I'm asking about a different kind of pirate.

"Um, no. Do you have something called *Blueboy* magazine?"

She led me to the magazine wall where she muttered to herself,

"*Redbook*, no that's not it. Book reviews, no. Sunsets, no. Sports cars. Oh!" she exclaimed in sudden realization. "You mean the *Kelley Blue Book*. It has pricing for used cars."

I was pretty sure that wasn't it. But maybe. "OK, I'll take that."

Later, I proudly showed my best lesbian friend my accomplishment.

"Really? Come on. I'm a dyke, and even I know what *Blueboy* is."

"So, it's not about whether a car has a stick or not?"

"The models in the magazine you want *all* have sticks."

* * *

In the autumn of 1984, I was attending Metropolitan State College in downtown Denver but was still living with my parents. As such, I was still bound by the "under-my-roof" rules, which included the same strict midnight curfew I had in high school. Jim made it perfectly clear that if I wanted to attend college on his dime, I had to do so while living at home and under his household statutes.

I started planning my escape.

I had graduated from McDonald's and was working as a waiter at Pizza Hut, pulling in surprisingly good tips on Friday and Saturday nights. Kim, my lesbian friend, was also a server and had helped me land the job. Together, we plotted to get our own apartment right in the heart of the predominantly gay Capitol Hill area. I spent as much time as I could manage in the area, soaking up the local culture and dreaming of the day when I would be free—out on my own. I even started to collect kitchen utensils and cleaning supplies for my yet-to-be-found first apartment.

Despite Jim's confining parameters, I managed to cultivate a fairly active social and sexual life. And given my affinity for guys named Scott, it shouldn't have come as much of a surprise when Scott #3 appeared on the scene.

I met Scott #3 at one of my regular stomping grounds, and through him, I was introduced to the gay social circle in which he ran. One of the most memorable characters was the effeminate-yet-charming banker named Kirby. Although I didn't find him attractive, I was in love with his second-floor apartment in a hacked-up Victorian mansion on Clarkson Street. It was nothing like I'd ever seen having grown up with stark white walls and boring architecture. I told myself I'd have an apartment just like Kirby's one day.

New Year's Eve 1984. Scott and I were about one month into dating, although dating might be a generous interpretation of whatever we had going. Our dates were usually the result of my incessant pestering with way too many phone calls. Most of the calls were answered by his annoyed mother who would eventually and emphatically state that, "No, Scott is *still* not home. And maybe you should wait for him to call you." A great little nugget of advice, and one I would ignore for years to come.

Scott was a player and was sleeping with a whole slew of guys, but I was too lucky-star-eyed and too naïve to acknowledge such a possibility. Then, the miracle happened, and I was selected to be Scott's date for my first grown-up New Year's Eve. I begged permission from Mom (who, in turn, begged permission from Jim) to stay overnight at Kirby's place, where the "quiet get-together" was to take place. Another miracle: permission granted.

It was a busy Friday or Saturday night at Pizza Hut, and I

hurried as fast as I could to close out my tables, do my side work, and rush over to Scott's house. Being New Year's Eve, the restaurant was so busy that I didn't get my usual break or dinner. I did a quick change out of my greasy pizza boy attire in Scott's living room and off we sped to Denver in his bad-boy Nissan 280Z. First stop was the liquor store where Scott used his fake ID to buy a trunk full of booze. Soon, we were parked behind Kirby's mansion on Clarkson, sneaking a pre-party kiss and grope.

We didn't remain long at Kirby's. Turned out the actual party was a few blocks away in a run-down apartment complex, just off the notoriously seedy Colfax Avenue. When we entered the third-floor apartment, there were guys (and a few girls) everywhere in various states of intoxication. The pungent and overwhelming stink of pot smoke formed a dense cloud in the living room.

My gut told me, "Hey, Denn! Yeah, you, pizza boy wearing all the Madonna bracelets. This might not be a place you should be."

I told my gut to keep quiet.

I wanted to impress Scott and to hold his attention among the stiff competition. I was painfully shy and sat tentatively within earshot of Scott as I nursed a beer.

"C'mon. It's New Year's Eve! You need a real drink," Scott said, as he threw a friendly arm around my neck.

A rum and Coke was poured for me that was thankfully more Coca-Cola than rum. The sweet concoction went down easily.

"Good job," Scott cooed approvingly as he planted a cigarette-and-liquor-tinged kiss on my lips.

Another drink was mixed for me. "You can add more rum this

time," I giggled.

"That's my boy."

The second drink went down as fast as the first, although not without a grimace as my throat burned from the alcohol. It didn't take me long to loosen up, unbutton my shirt, and even dance a bit. Scott was proud of me in a way that no father had ever been. "That's what I'm talking about. You actually might be more fun than I thought. Have another."

The drinks continued to flow, like a bad reenactment of the *I Love Lucy* "Vitameatavegamin" scene in which Lucy gets plastered. Soon, I was drinking rum straight from the bottle, all in an effort to prove something to Scott and to win his heart. Once I ran Captain Morgan onto dry ground, I grabbed a bottle of pink champagne, and said, "Why not?" Soon, I was shirtless and singing show tunes. (As I would later learn, when one thinks he's the life of the party, he is usually dead wrong.)

The sweet champagne proved to be a disastrous chaser to the straight rum. I'm still not sure where champagne fits in the "beer before liquor" rule, but before long, I was bent over the toilet, as Scott said, "worshipping the porcelain goddess." My whole body was shaking and convulsing as I vomited, gagged, and poured sweat. Scott was kind enough to initially hold my hand while I "worshipped." After what felt like five hours in the john, I emerged to find that most of the party-goers were either gone or passed out on the floor.

"C'mon, Denn. Let's get you out of here," Scott said tenderly, putting his arm around me and helping me drag myself back to Kirby's place as a light snow began to fall. Kirby, ever the perfect hostess (as he referred to himself), had prepared sleeping palettes on the floor of the half bedroom at the back of the apartment. The room was a precarious add-on, a second-floor sort of shanty that always looked as if it would fall off the mansion at any moment. But at that moment, to be wrapped in warm blankets with Scott next to me, I didn't care if the whole house fell off the planet. I was blissfully content.

Around 11 a.m., Kirby had scrambled eggs and Pillsbury cinnamon rolls waiting for us. We gobbled down the late breakfast, and I called Mom to explain that we had overslept. Fortunately, she and Jim were dealing with my colicky and troublesome baby half-brother and let the tardiness slide.

Later that night, feeling the party let-down, I called Scott from my bedroom phone only to get a cold shoulder. "Yeah, it was fun, wasn't it? Well, I'm beat. I'll catch up with you later."

He never did.

Quick to overcome the latest crush, I needed activity to distract my broken heart. To meet the right guy, I surmised, I needed to live in the heart of where the boys were. I thought it was a sign from the "gods" when one of the basement apartments in Kirby's building became available. With Kirby's recommendation, my steady employment, and a hard-earned $100 deposit, I signed a six-month lease. My budget was based on Kim and I sharing the damp, one-bedroom basement dump, and nervously, I went home to share the news. It didn't go over well, and I was once again reminded that if I proceeded with my plan, the college funding would indeed be cut off. I scoffed.

Jim can't be serious. Mom will convince him otherwise.

Shortly after breaking the news, Kim backed out on me,

leaving me holding the one-bedroom bag. Still, I was determined and had already started packing my bedroom full of possessions. I knew there was a budget deficit to be addressed, but as would be the case throughout my life, I threw caution to the wind and just hoped for the best.

Sometimes, my timing leaves a great deal to be desired. OK, most of the time. This was one of those incidents of poor timing and poor judgment.

February 11, 1985. Mom was in the hospital. Having a hysterectomy. On her birthday. And I moved out that same day. I broke her heart but raced off to my freedom.

At first, having my own place was a surreal dream—a cozy, fuzzy, fluffy little dream in which I had no clue about life or finances.

Kirby gifted me an enormously long sofa (he called it a Davenport, an East Coast brand name for a sofa) that I was all too eager to get into my apartment. Between the two of us and a third friend, we managed to get the nearly nine-foot-long monstrosity down to the first landing of the basement stairwell. But alas, the behemoth of a couch wouldn't make the turn. No problem, I figured; we'd just push the thing back up and park it in the alley. Except the thing wouldn't budge and was stuck blocking all access to the basement, which included two other apartments.

One borrowed chain saw, two butch neighbor guys, and a lot of dusty old Davenport fabric and stuffing later, I had a sectional. A wobbly, messy, two-piece sectional.

So, I still needed furniture.

Having recently established a scant amount of credit, I was

approved for a Montgomery Ward credit card with a generous $250 credit limit. I maxed out the card in one shopping trip for the following items: a bargain-basement, scratchy Herculon fabric loveseat for $99 not including delivery; a Wards brand canister vacuum for $69; and six gallons of paint in six different colors, plus painting supplies for around $70. The rest went to sales tax.

The Wards delivery guys barely got the loveseat down the narrow stairway, resulting in a torn corner, but they were ultimately successful. It was a hideous piece of furniture, but it was all mine.

Long before HGTV showed the world how to decorate, I took it upon myself, without landlord permission, to paint the apartment—each room a different color. The bedroom was pale blue. The bathroom was pale green. The living room was dusty rose. And the kitchen, poor thing, was smothered with high-gloss, baby pink paint. Not just the walls, but the cupboards and even the refrigerator door. If I had a deposit coming back to me, I'm sure I lost it in that mess of paint.

Budget reality struck as March and the next rent check approached. I wasn't close to having the full rent amount and decided to drop out of school to take on more hours at Pizza Hut. And as warned, all financial help ceased. *Fine*, I thought. *I can do this.*

For a young guy with virtually no real-world, marketable work experience, jobs didn't come knocking on the basement door of apartment number five at 1145 Clarkson Street. I resorted to taking a third-shift position as a clerk at a 7-Eleven. If there's one defining quality about my life it's when I do things, I do them big—however wrong, bad, or stupid. The convenience store job fell under the "stupid" category.

I was assigned to a 7-Eleven on a rough corner in a sketchy section of East Colfax. I was whitewashed and squeaky clean, fresh out of the sheltered suburb of Broomfield and looked alien to the late-night denizen of downtown Denver. I received thirty minutes of training, and on my first night, the exiting mid-shift clerk left the store in my hands as he handed me an enormous metal chain with the door key attached to it.

"If anyone gives you any trouble, just start swinging this," was his sage advice.

Perfect.

I survived only two weeks seeing all sorts of pimps, prostitutes, homeless dudes, and drug dealers. One night, I came in for my shift to find that there had been a shooting nearby and a stray bullet shattered one of the front windows. I proceeded to immediately hand in my name tag. And the chain.

There must be an easier way to make money.

The answer came in the form of a tiny classified ad in the Denver gay newspaper, *Out Front.* Something about needing young, good-looking guys for a modeling job. *Hey! Now that's more like it.* I called the number listed in the ad and was given directions on how to dress and where to report.

Wearing my yellow Polo shirt, a pair of tight 501s, and my Sperry top-siders (sockless, of course, and as instructed), I rang the bell at a formidable gated entrance to an expensive-looking home in a posh neighborhood of Denver. An older gentleman welcomed me into his home and offered me a drink. I probably asked for a Pepsi. That probably wasn't what he wanted me to drink.

"What are these pictures for? *GQ Magazine*?" I asked, laughing nervously, trying to picture myself on the cover.

"No, no, they're just for my own use. Now, why don't you just act naturally, and I'll start snapping some pictures."

"Um, sure, OK," I replied, not knowing how to act naturally. I just acted nervously. I struck an awkward pose on the living room's Victorian settee, one of my arms draped casually over one of its rolled and button-tufted arms.

"Maybe you'd be more comfortable if you slipped your shirt off," the man suggested.

"No, actually I wouldn't. I don't like my body."

"Well, I like your body, and since I'm paying, you can go ahead and slip off your shirt. And your shoes. I want to see your feet."

Feet. Eww. Gross.

I had a thing about feet. Hated them, didn't want to see anyone else's and didn't want anyone looking at or touching mine. Something didn't feel right about this situation. But it was worth $100, and I desperately needed the rent money.

I wasn't loosening up to the man's liking, so he said we would be going "downstairs" where it was more comfortable. So, he led me to the basement where he had a black leather sofa and a TV playing a gay porn flick. I thought about bolting for the door, then I thought again about the hundred bucks.

"Take off all of your clothes and get on the sofa," he ordered, clearly losing patience with the stupid kid who had no clue what he'd gotten himself into. "Now. On the sofa."

I complied nervously. The man seemed even more revolting

to me after he undressed; he was easily old enough to be my father.

I shouldn't be here, shouldn't be doing this.

I winced through having the man on top of me, gritting my teeth through the ordeal, thinking only about the money. I felt dirty, disgusting, pitiful. He threw a $100 bill at me as I dressed, while he continued to lie on the sofa watching the porn and stroking himself.

"Um, thanks," I said. The man didn't respond. I found my way out.

I went home and showered for forty-five minutes in an attempt to wash away the filth of my degradation. I didn't care about the money; I just wanted to be clean and to curl up in bed and cry. I felt like such a loser. First 7-Eleven, then prostitution.

Two weeks later, when the next batch of bills were due, I saw a slightly different version of the man's ad in the new edition of *Out Front*. I went back, as awkward and nervous as the first time, but allowed the man to do what he wanted and collected my hundred bucks. He told me, in no uncertain terms, to *never* call him again, thus ending my short-lived career as a rent boy.

Living on my own wasn't turning out to be the dream life I imagined. The real world was harsh and uncaring, just as Jim had warned. But I had no desire to "eat crow" and move back home and be back under iron-fisted rule. I was working as many hours as I could manage but barely made ends meet. And every Tuesday night, I dutifully and faithfully hauled my cookies out to the Grove with the hope of meeting the right guy to fix my mess. Someone who would complete me, rescue me.

21

The One That Got Away—Part One
BOULDER: 1985

I was in my customary spot, holding down a corner of the bar at the Grove, nursing a watered-down Coors Light from a chipped, red, hard plastic cup. It was a Tuesday Drown Night, and I usually would drink my full four dollars' worth while being completely ignored before slinking off to my multi-colored basement apartment. However, on this particular night, I ran into a friend, who pulled me out on the dance floor. It was April 23, 1985, and that same relatively new recording artist, Madonna, was now a bona fide star and had a hit song blasting from the blown speakers around the small patch of dance floor, something about enjoying material things.

I made a fool of myself trying to dance and only managed to work up a huge sweat. After the seven-minute extended mix ended, I made my way through the packed bar toward the front door with the goal of getting some fresh air. I didn't expect to run into the guy who would change my life.

Mitchell was nearly two years older than me, worldly and experienced. He was a charmer with a crooked grin and a beguiling gap between two of his front teeth. He moved like an elegant wild-cat on the prowl, dashingly handsome with his tennis tan and pink

Polo shirt.

"Easy there, Tiger," Mitchell said as I fell into his hairy arms. Interestingly, he called me by the name of the animal I was mental comparing him to. (I should note that Mitchell only used the full version of his name, never just Mitch, and made this point clear with his introduction.)

"Oh, I'm so, so sorry! I'm such a klutz," I said.

"You're a cute klutz. Do you have a name?"

"Yes, um, it's I don't know. I mean, Denn. I was just running out for some air."

"Ah, you're not getting away that easily," Mitchell said with all the charm of a rattlesnake.

We talked and had another beer, then Mitchell pulled me close and kissed me hard. His mouth tasted like beer and a real man's cocktail, which he probably had prior to coming for chicken. "Let's get out of here, Tiger."

At that point, I would have followed him anywhere. Turned out, I only needed to follow him to Boulder. He was the strong male figure I had always hoped for, and that night, he swept in just as my newfound independent life was hitting the rails.

We figured out the logistics of having two cars parked in the vicinity of the bar, and he decided I would return my Dodge Dart to my apartment. He followed me, then swooped me away in his dark blue Eddie Bauer edition Ford Bronco II. I was over-the-moon happy and never wanted the night or the feelings to end.

Mitchell lived in Boulder near Colorado University, about a twenty-five-minute drive from downtown Denver, at least in those days. I wondered for a moment about getting back home and hoped he wouldn't leave me stranded. But after that brief moment of worry, I no longer cared. We got to his third-floor, college-modern apartment and as soon as the door closed, we flung our clothes in every direction as he pulled me into his bedroom.

The experience with Mitchell that first night forged the foundation for my adult sexual desires. On that particular night, the intimacy was magical and tantalizing with an undertone of danger as he introduced me to blindfolds and light bondage using the business ties he wore to his bank job.

I was completely relaxed, in the moment, and inexplicably comfortable with Mitchell, allowing him to take the lead. He was the loving father, masculine older brother, and caring best friend I always wanted all in one. Of all the guys I've forced into those myriad roles, Mitchell was best equipped to juggle them. And as fast as he swept into my life, I bulldozed into his with nineteen years of baggage.

Mitchell lived in Boulder near the University of Colorado, about a twenty-five-minute drive from downtown Denver, at least in those days. But when we got to my apartment, we were both having trouble saying goodbye. I threw clothes and toiletries into a gym bag and followed him back to Boulder.

The glow of the first night had worn off, as first-night glows tend to do, but I was ecstatic to be with Mitchell, hoping for a repeat romantic night. That hope died as he informed me that on Wednesday nights, he played basketball with his buddies at the local YMCA but requested I stay put until he returned.

The whole time, I was nervous and excited to be alone in his place, surrounded by his things. For a while, I sat quietly on the sofa, studying my hands and constantly checking my plastic Swatch, wondering how long he would be gone. This was long before the days of smart phones, so there was little to do to pass the time. His cat ignored me, and I couldn't find anything to watch on the three TV channels.

Eventually, curiosity got this particular cat, and I started poking around. First stop: his underwear drawer. I don't know what it is with underwear drawers, but they have always held a fascination for me and top the list of popular hiding places. I should know. That's where I stashed those leftover Percocets in ninth grade. Naturally, I wanted to dig for buried treasure and see what secrets his underwear drawer would yield.

I found a letter from an ex-boyfriend, a couple of animal-print thongs, a well-worn jockstrap, and photos of an attractive girl around our age with a lovey-dovey inscription on the back of each, "*Te amo, mi amor*, Mitchell." Neither the girl nor Mitchell were Spanish, so I figured it was a college thing. Later, the cards and love letters I would receive from Mitchell always had a lengthy section written in Spanish detailing the depth and breadth of his love for me. I couldn't read a word of it.

My search took me to his bedroom closet to look for more clues about his life. The closet proved to be less interesting, holding only his work and casual clothes and an assortment of sports equipment, including skis, roller blades, a baseball glove, a tennis racket, a kayak paddle, and a pair of Speedo swim goggles.

He's into sports. Really into sports. Well, crap.

Sports had never been my thing.

It appeared Mitchell lived a busy life between his two jobs, one at the bank and the other as a weekend waiter at Village Inn, a Colorado chain of pancake restaurants. The sports gear, the photos of numerous friends, the two jobs, I wondered how I could fit in.

I paced and chewed my nails as I waited for Mitchell. Again, the little voice reminded me of the stupid childhood poem about waiting. I tried to tell the voice where it could go stuff it. Mitchell got home around ten that night from basketball and immediately took me into his sweaty arms. I was in heaven all over again as he pulled us into the bedroom.

Thursday morning came, and I needed to go home and deal with my own life and feeble finances. Mitchell didn't want me to leave, and he decided in that instant that he needed me to be closer to him, not wanted but required. He asked me to move in with him shortly after telling me he loved me. A million questions flooded my mind: What does this mean? Are we committed to each other? What about the girl in the underwear drawer? He wasn't one for explanations, just exhortations of how he wanted things. Mitchell wanted me and wouldn't accept no for an answer. Like I would have declined the offer.

So as quickly as my few belongings had been stuffed down the narrow basement stairwell, they were shoved back up the stairs and into the back of the Bronco II. I was two months into my independent life and was already hauling my stuff to its second address on Glenwood Drive, apartment number 302.

As I settled in, there were numerous discussions about what part of the closet I would use (the back half), locations for the pieces of my ramshackle furniture (crammed in the patio storage unit), and how the kitchen would be set up (as he already had it with his oh-so-Eighties, red-and-black dishes, red utensils, and red Rubbermaid sink mats).

Then, there was the towel fight. I have no idea why I pushed so hard when it came to the towels. They weren't even my signature color, turquoise. They were ugly mauve with the scratchy, sculpted filigree on one end. But maybe it was because Mom had bought me that new set of towels for my first place, and I wanted to keep using them. They were familiar. And with so much of me being packed into patio storage, I felt I needed to retain something that said, "I live here, too."

This didn't bode well with Mitchell, and we had our first fight, the first rift in our newly-formed and fragile relationship. I ultimately won the Battle of the Towels but would later lose the war.

* * *

On his nightstand, Mitchell had a book called *Tales of the City* by Armistead Maupin, the first installment in a series of books about a group of straight, gay, and transgender characters living in 1970s San Francisco. Up to that point, my only exposure to gay literature had been the steamy, naughty Gordon Merrick gay "romance" novels covertly written in the 1940s. I asked Mitchell about the book, and he insisted I start reading the whole series; there were six books at that time. He was on the third book, *Further Tales of the City*.

Mitchell grabbed the first volume. "Tiger, read this section with me," Mitchell said. "It really sums up what I'm looking for."

One of the main characters, a gay man named Michael Tolliver— nicknamed "Mouse" by his lesbian roommate—was lamenting the state of his romantic life. Fresh from a broken heart, Michael had a conversation about marriage with the book's main character, a straight woman named Mary Ann Singleton. They agreed that, most of the time, they believed in marriage, and Mouse shared how he "got married four times yesterday on the 41-Union bus."

Mouse continued to explain that his idea of marriage wasn't a flamboyant drag wedding in Golden Gate Park, rather more like being good friends—someone with whom he could buy a Christmas tree.

For the better part of three decades, Mouse's idea of marriage became mine as I searched in vain for the guy I could buy *my* Christmas tree with. But in that moment, reading aloud with Mitchell, I was in heaven—he and I were literally on the same page. The "little-g" gods had smiled upon me, and I knew I had been saved from years of frequenting gay bars looking for my soul mate. *Equivocado, mi amigo.* (Wrong, my friend.)

* * *

Saturday night, April 27, 1985. I was settled in, and it was our first date night together. I was hoping for a romantic dinner in a secluded booth at some charming little bistro on Boulder's Pearl Street Mall followed by secretive hand-holding at the movie theater. Mitchell, of course, had other ideas.

"We've been invited for dinner in your old neck of the woods," Mitchell announced. "My friends Tim and Tom are cooking and want us to come over."

Tim and Tom. That was just too precious for words.

"Oh. I kind of thought our first Saturday night together could be, well, never mind."

"What, Tiger? What do you want?"

"Well, I wanted to be alone with you."

"Ah, Tiger, we have the rest of our lives for that," he said, squeezing the back of my neck and tousling my hair as a father might have done.

"Yeah, I guess you're right. What time must we be there?"

"Soon. I told them we were on our way."

We did a quick change of clothes and soon were *en route* in the Bronco II to south Pearl Street in Denver's Capitol Hill area.

Tim and Tom were a surprisingly masculine gay couple, who had seemingly been together for quite some time, if one were to judge by the walls covered with photos of the pair on camping trips, hiking, and lounging poolside on numerous vacations. They were a bit older than Mitchell and me, perhaps by ten years.

"I want you to see a real, successful gay couple who have made it work," Mitchell explained, as we pulled up to the stucco-coated apartment building and were buzzed into the subterranean parking area. "They've been together ten whole years, Tiger."

Tim was a great cook, and we had an excellent steak dinner in their tastefully decorated living room. Drinks were flowing, and I loosened up much to Mitchell's approval.

"Let's all go to the hot tub," Tom suggested, stripping off his purple Izod Lacoste shirt and exposing a perfectly tanned washboard. Tim and Mitchell were quick to shed their clothes. I hesitated, as usual, despising and embarrassed by my body, only to be tackled by Tom and Mitchell as they pulled off my clothes and tossed me a Speedo.

After a thorough soaking and shriveling in the hot tub,

we returned to the apartment where we remained in our towels and trunks.

"Let's go to the bedroom and cool off," Tom said.

Soon, four naked male bodies were lined up on the double bed. A gay porn VHS was playing. When Tom and Mitchell started kissing, I was in shock and didn't know what to think. I thought *we* were a couple—he and I—me and Mitchell. But I didn't dare say anything and just laid there, wishing my new lover and I could just leave and be alone. Tim, who was the less masculine of the couple, started to caress my leg. As soon as I put a tentative hand on his, he smothered me with a wet, sloppy, and unpleasant kiss.

Before long, I was entwined with Tim while Mitchell and Tom took things to third base. (I have to admit I never "got" the whole first, second, third base thing, and to this day don't know what activity goes with which base. But clearly, they were close to a home run.)

Against my will, I soon became the center of attention as the three guys focused their sexual energy on me. After two sweaty hours and every possible configuration among the four of us, it was over, and Mitchell announced it was time to head out. Seems that as an old "married" couple, Tim and Tom were approaching their bedtime.

As we were gathering our things, Tim pointed out the window to a condo across the street. "Did you know that Ann B. Davis has a place right across the street from us?"

"You mean *the* Ann B. Davis? Alice? From *The Brady Bunch*?" I asked.

"That's the one. She's a grand old dyke from way back," said Tim.

"Wait, Alice is a lesbian? I would've never guessed."

"Oh yeah. A carpet-munching marvel, a big ole lesby. We have her over for dinner when she's in town," said Tom.

I'll bet she doesn't do the four-way thing with you guys, though.

"Oh, cool. I'd love to meet her." I never did. I'm not even sure if Tim was telling the truth. Gay guys were notorious for fabricating gossip and fashioning urban legends.

Mitchell and I headed back to Boulder, as a million new questions triggered a headache. Was this "dinner party" an anomaly? Or was this the norm? I thought we were going to be committed and monogamous, just like a straight couple who was married. I couldn't figure out how we got from reading about buying Christmas trees with a partner to having group sex. I was about to ask the question, but Mitchell spoke first, as usual.

"Well, how was your first orgy? Technically four-way. An orgy involves a lot more guys."

"Orgy." The word stuck in my mouth. "Oh, well, I don't know. Hard to say, I guess," I stammered. "Do you, um, hang out like that often with Tim and Tom?"

"Yeah. Occasionally. We like to kick back and let our hair down, you know?"

"Oh, yeah, sure. It was…fun, I guess."

"Well, it sure looked like you were enjoying yourself, Tiger. Tom is hot, huh? Bet you liked his hairy chest."

I giggled stupidly in response.

Idiot. Now he thinks you're on board with this swinger scene.

Mitchell squeezed my left knee in approval. "There's a lot of fun things we can do together. I'll show you. Trust me."

"Trust me," said the boa constrictor as it coiled around its victim, I thought.

* * *

One evening after work, Mitchell announced, "We should go look at new cars. Have you seen that cool new Fiero?"

Again, a million questions. "No. Not sure."

"Let's go drive one. We'll take your car, so you can see and feel the difference."

So, our next fateful trip was to Pollard Friendly Motors in Boulder where Mitchell did all the talking, and before I could say "Why do they call it an orgy, anyway?" we were behind the wheel— rather, he was behind the wheel—of a bright red 1985 Pontiac Fiero. Those were the days when the salesman didn't have to do insurance-mandated ride-alongs. Besides, in the two-seater car, there was no room for him. Further, Mitchell knew the guy from working at the bank.

I'm not sure if I was more enamored with my cute boyfriend behind the wheel or the factory-installed stereo, complete with an auto-reverse cassette player, but I was not thinking clearly. The new car smell mixed with Mitchell's Polo cologne was intoxicating. Plus, the sporty Fiero reminded me of the DeLorean that was the central character in a soon-to-be-iconic summer blockbuster.

Mitchell drove the stick shift like a pro. I came to my senses for a moment. "Wait, this isn't an automatic. I can't drive a stick."

"Eh, don't worry, Tiger. I'll teach you to drive it. The main thing is, do you like it? And you *do* know how to handle a stick quite well; I've seen you in action."

"Well, yeah, it's great, I guess."

He pulled the car over to the side of the road on a residential street and told me to get behind the wheel. Mitchell patiently talked me through the mechanics of the clutch and the different gears laid out in the standard "H" pattern. I tried to shift the Fiero from neutral to first gear, while slowly releasing the clutch with my left foot and applying pressure to the gas pedal with my right. The car sputtered and stalled. So, we tried again. And again. Through each failure, Mitchell was infinitely patient, unlike Dennis or Ruben. It did something to cement the idea that the right male partner could be everything I never had and always wanted.

Keeping a close eye on the time—Mitchell wore a man's hefty metal watch, not a silly plastic fad like I had on my wrist—he had us trade places again as he raced the Fiero back to the dealer. Once we were back, he had me sit behind the wheel and run my hands over the leather-wrapped steering wheel, while he cranked the stereo. Billy Ocean was on the radio, singing the praises of some Caribbean woman with royal features. I was head-over-heels in love—with the car, with Mitchell, with my new life with Mitchell. It was all so nearly perfect. Maybe a little too much.

"You were meant to drive this car, Tiger. It suits you. You look better in it than that old beater you have now."

With a stealthy, knowing nod to the salesman, a service attendant pulled away in my Dart, and soon, we were inside one of the requisite glass-walled sales rooms. A matrix of numbers was presented to me on a sheet of paper. This much down, this much for your old car, this much every month for the rest of your life. It was my first experience buying a new car, and I would eventually learn through a tangle of too many bad car deals, there's a certain theatricality about the process, all designed to incite the buyer's emotions while purposefully confusing them at the same time.

I looked at Mitchell, helplessly. He squeezed my leg and said, "You can afford it. Remember, you've got me now."

I met his Cheshire-cat grin with a sheepish one of my own. "OK, where do I sign?" I stopped short for a moment. "But wait, you're going to teach me to drive this car, right?" Another knee squeeze. "OK, where do I sign?"

Yeah, so that phrase, "Where do I sign?" quickly made its way into my vernacular.

What I would soon discover was I could not, in any way, afford the car payments or the higher car insurance premiums. I would also learn that I broke Jim's heart trading in the Dodge Dart, as he had spent two cold weeks rebuilding its engine during winter break of my senior year after I "innocently" blew a rod "carefully" driving back from the "mall."

Mitchell drove the new car home, as I fretted over the decision I'd just made. I was busily crunching numbers in my head, and they were crunching right back, giving me a migraine.

"Honey, I can't afford this car."

"Sure, you can, Tiger. You just need a better job. That's the next step."

"Oh, OK, cool."

I dropped out of college and have only my meager income from waiting tables at Pizza Hut. I'm sure a great new job will just land in my lap.

Mitchell made some calls, and within two days, I had an interview with a stern, uptight woman named Betty at United Bank of Boulder. There was an open position being some kind of runner/liaison/delivery boy between the local branches of other banks.

I got the job and started the following Monday, feeling on top of the world as I drove the Fiero (stalling at nearly every intersection) to the bank. But it was only five hours per day, and the hourly rate was barely above minimum. I wasn't sure how it would solve my car payment dilemma, but I got to do a lot of driving around in the new Fiero, delivering checks from one bank to another, feeling like hot shit in my shiny red sports car. This was well before electronic banking, and when a check was written by one bank's customer to a person or business who banked with a competing chain, the check in question had to make its way back to the guarantee bank. That way was me. And soon, the driving practice made me an accomplished stick-shift driver.

The best part was I got to drop in on Mitchell every mid-morning at his bank. I'd go to his teller window, and we'd sneak a brief hand-holding across the counter. He'd give me his trademark wink and some instruction of what he'd like for dinner or where he wanted to go out. I counted the hours until I'd see him again.

22

The One That Got Away—Part Two
BOULDER: 1985

First new car, first non-restaurant job, first orgy. I was racking up new experiences quickly. Exactly one week after the dinner party at Tim and Tom's, Mitchell announced plans for the evening.

"It's been a really long week, hasn't it, Tiger? You know what would feel great?"

You giving me a backrub?

"Soaking in a hot tub," Mitchell said.

Even better.

"You said it," I said. "But where do we do that?"

I had heard of a place in Denver called Time-Out Tubs where anyone with 40 bucks and an ID could rent a private room with a hot tub for an hour. Similar to a tanning salon with a bunch of rooms behind flimsy, hollow-core doors, it was popular with straight couples wanting to have hot-tub sex. The business' name had always seemed odd, almost an adult version of the infamous time-out corner in kindergarten.

Now, Denny, you've been a very bad boy. Go soak in the time-out tub.

Anyway, I figured that was where we were heading. As usual, I was wrong.

Mitchell was driving the Fiero, as it had become *his* new favorite toy. He pulled down some seedy side streets around lower Broadway, eventually finding a spot to parallel park the Pontiac.

"We're here." Mitchell grinned with a strange glimmer in his eye.

"Where's 'here'? Never mind, let me get my Speedo out of the back." The Fiero had a sliver of a trunk under the front hood in addition to the suitcase-sized cargo hold in the rear. This was because the Fiero's engine was considered to be a mid-mount, which really meant the motor was right behind the driver's back. I always feared that if I were to be rear-ended in traffic, I'd end up with a Fiero engine up my butt.

"You won't need trunks, Tiger. This is the Ballpark."

Oh crap. I should've known when I saw all that sports stuff in his closet. He wants a sports guy, and that's definitely not me.

"The ballpark?" I asked, as I tried to quell the mental panic. "Um, I'm *really* bad at baseball. I mean horribly bad. I don't think this is a good idea."

"I've seen you handle a bat. You'll be fine," he said with his usual devilish wink.

It turned out that a different type of ball was played at this park, and that the Ballpark was a clothing-optional, all-male "resort." OK, resort was stretching it. It was a bathhouse—the last of its kind in the new era of AIDS.

We checked in via a double-pane glass window with a little

slide-through slot for proffering cash and driver's licenses. In return, two locker keys on plastic coil bracelets and two thread-bare white towels were shoved through the slot, as the effeminate guy at the window wished us a "good time," blowing a little kiss at Mitchell with a wink that said, "How you been?" And because membership was required, even for a single visit, I was issued a membership card. Plastic and the size of a credit card, the front featured a stylized logo of a bat and two strategically placed baseballs.

With the administrative process complete, the counter queen pushed a button, which sounded a loud buzzer and triggered the clunk of a heavy door being automatically unlocked.

And so, we entered the Ballpark.

We stripped and stashed our clothes in two separate lockers and draped the white towels around our waists. The stretchy key chains could be worn around one's wrist or ankle while playing "ball." I was having trouble keeping my towel in place, and Mitchell showed me how to wet one corner prior to tucking to make it more secure. Like everything I'd seen so far from him, Mitchell was a pro.

Mitchell took me on the "grand circle tour" of the place, and I was amazed by how much they had crammed into a seemingly small building. Actually, the Ballpark was distributed over four floors, and each floor had its own main attraction. On the second floor was an elaborate tropical paradise-themed pool, complete with a two-story-tall waterfall, as well as a private cove for relaxing or doing whatever. Across from the pool was a set of double doors leading to the steam room maze.

Both the second and third floors had dozens of private spaces that looked like tiny motel rooms, each with a vinyl-covered thin mattress, a huge mirror, and a TV mounted high above the bed play-ing three channels of porn. The third floor also featured group play rooms, with leather slings hanging from the ceiling.

The basement served as a sort of catacombs to this queer fun house and was an adventure in its own right. Tucked behind the porn video room and just beyond the glory-hole maze (mazes were plenti-ful at this place) was an actual semi-truck cab. The whole thing, tires and all. If one's fantasy was to get it on with a trucker in his semi-cab, well, the Ballpark had it covered.

There was so much to take in, so much to see. I hadn't felt this visually overwhelmed since visiting Disneyland as a kid. This was the *adult* Disneyland of gay Denver, with a dark side and seedy underbelly, keeping many secrets within its black-painted walls and purple glow lights.

Back at the pool entrance, Mitchell re-tucked his white towel around his waist. His impressive bulge looked enormous under the wet terrycloth. "I'm gonna cruise around on my own for a while. Meet me back here in an hour or two."

An hour or two? What on earth was I was going to do with myself for that long?

I sensed it wasn't appropriate to ask Mitchell if I could go with him, so I quietly acquiesced, as I studied my bare feet, hoping I wasn't picking up athlete's foot from the slimy floor tiles.

"Oh, OK, well, have a good time or whatever," I said, visi-bly dejected.

"I will. You do the same, Tiger," he said with a wink and a nod toward the steam room.

I tried to enjoy myself, but truth was I just wanted to be with my boyfriend. The pool was warm and soothing, but because I still couldn't swim, I perched inside, clinging to one of the sides near a decorative rock wall. I was petrified to drop my towel and go naked into the pool, but it seemed to be the only way. And everyone else was naked, too. Afraid I would lose my towel, I took it into the pool and stashed it in a fake palm tree behind me. It eventually fell into the water, but at least it still provided a covering for my nakedness.

Taking a cue from others, I stood under the waterfall, letting the water pound on my back. It did feel amazing, and I've never felt anything quite like it since. If there is one good memory about the Ballpark, it was the warm waterfall massage. I ventured back into the secluded cove, only to find an orgy already in progress. I quickly waded back through the waterfall to safer territory, as I had no desire to be pulled into a group scene with a bunch of fat old men.

I was chilled after getting out of the warm pool and decided to check out the steam. I saw a row of towels hanging outside the glass doors, so I figured no towels were allowed. I hung up my towel, trying to take a mental snapshot of which towel was mine and precisely which peg I had left it on.

The steam was so thick, it was nearly impossible to see, let alone breathe. The air was heavy, burning my lungs with something that tasted like Vicks VapoRub. As I stumbled through the tile walls and bench seats, it became evident that it was also a maze with plenty of wrong turns and dead ends, probably a prophetic harbinger of my future as a gay man.

The steam room was like one of those haunted house attractions where costumed actors jump out, grab an unsuspecting person, and manage to scare his pants off. Except I had no pants to scare off. And the hands that grabbed me were slick with sweat and sticky lubricant (or worse) and touched me in places I didn't want to be touched. I worked my way out of the steam maze and searched for my towel. Only two towels remained on the rack and neither was mine. I had two choices: walk naked to the front desk on the first floor to request a replacement or grab someone else's. Shyness made me choose the latter option, but the towel I picked was gross, with a variety of untold substances on it. I held it in front of me like a fig leaf as I darted down the steps to the check-in counter to plead my situation.

"Well, well, what have we here? Chicken's first time at the bathhouse, and you lost your towel? My, my, what a problem," said the queen with the most disgustingly effeminate gestures I'd ever seen. "Well, you'll have to give me that filthy towel you're holding up before I can swap it for a fresh one."

I complied, painfully aware of my naked body standing in full view of the check-in lobby where a line of fully clothed, soon-to-be patrons waited to be processed. I felt a dozen pairs of eyes studying my body, as I desperately wanted to be anywhere but there. I was only nineteen but had already developed love handles and was ashamed of myself.

Leaning on his elbows in mock intimacy, he asked, "So what happened, honey? Did your boyfriend run off and leave you alone?"

"It's not like that."

"Oh, uh huh. Tell mama all about it."

"No, really, we're in love."

"Funny place to take a date, wouldn't you think, little chicken?"

"Please, can you just hurry up with the towel? I feel really naked."

"That's 'cause you are, Blanche, you are," he said, referencing a movie I had yet to know.

The queen took his sickeningly sweet time rummaging around a few shelves behind the check-in counter, changing a VHS porn tape, taking a hit of poppers, then flitting out of the room. He tossed an equally wet towel at my face. "This is all I have. It's wet, but clean. Sort of, I guess. Who knows?"

"Whatever," I said, as I snatched the towel and draped it around my waist.

"Careful with the attitude, little bitch. I can eighty-six you from this place like *that*," he warned with a catty finger snap.

Fine, go ahead. Ban me from this horrific gay theme park. See if I care. I will never be back.

I returned to the designated rendezvous spot to meet Mitchell, but there was no sign of him. So, I set out wrapped in the dirty, wet towel to search four floors for him. I passed rooms with open doors with guys brazenly performing sexual acts (for all the world to see) or guys lying on the wafer-thin mattresses touching themselves (for all the world to see) but never making eye contact with any of the passersby—at least not this passerby. I even had a door slam in my face when I was trying to get a glance for the sole purpose of finding my supposed boyfriend.

On the third floor, there was an old guy hoisted up in a leather sling with a group of men gathered around his bare butt. It seemed they were playing a game of "hide the hand." I wanted to vomit.

One final pass through the basement video lounge and a peek into the semi-cab, and I was done. I dressed, grabbed my car keys, and raced back to Boulder. The sun was coming up, and I felt exposed, filthy, and disgusting.

Back at our apartment, I waited for Mitchell, fearing the worst. As expected, he was upset I had left him at the bathhouse, but as I explained, it was well past our meeting time, and I had no way of knowing if he was even still there.

"Guess it wasn't your scene. I thought you'd enjoy it. I'm sorry, Tiger, I really am. We'll never do that again."

Mitchell never explained what he had done (or who) or how he had made his way back home. As I had already learned, Mitchell was always in charge, always took the lead, and was never to be questioned. I was just relieved to have him back home. But the minor rift that began with the bathroom towels split further open that morning. Something had changed between us. I could sense it, feel it, and it scared me.

* * *

During our remaining time together, Mitchell took me to his family's estate in Aspen, where I met his parents and his sister. He had two motorized dirt bikes and insisted we go riding on the nearby dirt hills. I made an overdramatic and unnecessary fuss over how I couldn't do it and ruined what might have been a fun experience.

Mitchell helped me get a Saturday morning job with him at Village Inn waiting tables so we could spend more time together. He was adept at juggling breakfast orders for twenty tables; I freaked and ran into the kitchen to hit my head on the tile wall when I had only two tables and dropped a pot of coffee.

More romantic cards were exchanged over candlelit, home-made meals. There were no further orgies or trips to the Ballpark. I breathed a heavy sigh of relief and felt we had weathered the storm.

That is, until one rainy night, I came home from an evening shift at Pizza Hut and heard giggling coming from our bedroom. I stood in the entryway, dripping wet and reeking of pizza grease, as I held my breath trying to hear if it was my small, black-and-white TV that we had on Mitchell's tall dresser—or if he had a guest. It was distinctly two voices: one was his, and one was—a girl's?

As I stood there stewing and steaming, I could no longer hold back. I tried to make a casual oops-I-didn't-hear-you-in-there entrance to the bedroom and found that Mitchell was in bed with the girl from the underwear drawer. So, there *was* something there, as I had worried.

"Wait, Tiger, I can explain," Mitchell said, as he pulled on work-out pants. Underwear Drawer Girl pulled up the blue plaid blanket to cover her ample breasts.

"What's there to explain? I thought we were going to be monog-amous, committed. Or that if we played, we played together—or something—I don't know what, but that we were going to be monog-amous, some 'buy a fucking tree together' crap."

"I've been meaning to talk to you about this," Mitchell said, as he nodded to Underwear Drawer Girl to start dressing. "But not while she's here. Please, just go outside, and give me a little time. Go take a drive and come back in, like thirty minutes. And we'll talk."

I didn't want to leave. I wanted to yell, scream, throw, and break things and then, storm out in a rage. I ran to the Fiero and slammed the door so hard I nearly shattered its driver's side window. Between the rain pounding, the windshield, and the tears filling my eyes, I could barely see. And I didn't care. It was the first of many times I would be behind the wheel of a car thinking serious thoughts about driving it off a cliff.

I thought of my worthless, ridiculous, already-messed-up adult life and wasn't finding many reasons to not kill myself. Then, I thought of Mom and how much I loved Mitchell and the chance it could still work. I had to find out.

I sat in the parking lot of our apartment building for nearly an hour, waiting until Underwear Drawer Girl gave Mitchell what appeared to be a sloppy kiss goodnight before disappearing into the rain. Then, I ran up the outside concrete steps.

"Tiger, please. Don't be upset."

"I don't know what to think. The four-way, the bathhouse, and now this *chick*?"

"I told you I was bi-sexual and still into women."

"Um, no, you never said that, Mitch."

"Mitchell. Not Mitch."

"Whatever."

"I'm quite sure I mentioned being bi. In any case, sex doesn't mean anything. And from time to time, I will be having sex with other people. Her included."

"Well that's not the way I want things to be," I protested. "I thought we were going to be the couple who buys the goddamn Christmas tree together. I don't want to share you."

"Well, that's the only way you get to have me."

"Then it's over." I lost my temper and started throwing my clothes into a gym bag and pulling my boxes of belongings out of the patio storage room.

"Don't do this. Not tonight. Not this way," Mitchell pleaded.

"Fine. I'll be back tomorrow with a truck."

I'm not sure who I coerced into helping me move out the next day, but I managed to wrangle help and a pick-up truck. Probably Kim and a couple of her lesbian pals. Mitchell watched silently, sitting in his spot on his cherished, overstuffed leather sofa.

As the last load went down the two flights of stairs, I stayed behind, searching frantically for a missing box.

"Where's the box with my yearbooks?" I asked.

Mitchell walked in his cat-like manner to the living room closet and produced a box. I went to grab hold of it, and he placed his foot on top of it. "Not until you pay me your half of this month's rent."

"I don't have the money right now," I pleaded.

"Then I'll keep these until you do."

"You better give them to me. You're probably going to throw them out or ruin them."

"You should know me better than that, Denn." It was odd to hear him call me something other than Tiger or honey or baby. "They'll be here, safe in my closet until you can settle your account with me."

Settle my account with him? Who did he think he was? The Bank of Mitchell A. Hole?

"Fine."

I borrowed the money, returned later that day, paid my rent, got my box, and made a silent retreat from what had promised to be such an epic romance. And maybe it could have been epic. I was trying to force-fit us into the perfect picture of what I thought our relationship should be. The clues had been there, painfully obvious, that he valued togetherness, but that sex was recreational and not exclusive to the two of us. And if I could have accepted that, well, who knows.

* * *

Time, sometimes, has an uncanny way of healing broken relationships as it folds back on itself. Five years later, after I had moved to Phoenix, I was back in Colorado visiting my family. Taking a much-needed break from my whiny, then seven-year-old brother, I escaped to downtown Denver. The Grove was gone and so was David's, another popular gay watering hole near the Clarkson apartment. Having gotten into country music living in Phoenix, I decided to check out Charlie's, the Denver location of a three-location gay-bar franchise. (There was a Charlie's in Phoenix, as well as one in Chicago.)

I got my beer and perched myself in a corner overlooking the dance floor. A familiar voice and a gentle touch on the small of my back startled me.

"Hey, Tiger."

Mitchell and I exchanged warm smiles and hellos and shared a solid embrace. Small talk ensued, as we caught each other up on the last five years. We didn't hate each other and were both happy for this impromptu reunion.

And just as though I had fallen through some crack in the space-time continuum, into some oddly pleasurable time warp, I took my rental car and followed Mitchell back to his place in Boulder. Not the same place, but some condo he was sharing with another guy and some girl. The night of April 23, 1985 repeated itself in the bedroom. After Mitchell had fallen asleep, I laid awake recalling the headline feature on *Oprah* that day: "Sex with Your Ex: Should You Do It?" I chuckled softly with a resounding, satisfied "yes" on my lips as I watched Mitchell sleeping.

The next morning, he had to work a breakfast shift at the crunchy-granola Boulder restaurant where he was a full-time server and trainer. He invited me to tag along. It was a short shift, and he quickly got it covered so he could spend the day with me. As we sat and ate a breakfast of granola mixed with plain yogurt, we continued to catch up before embarking on a day around Boulder. He was driving an old beater car, a late-1970s Subaru. As Mitchell drove, he explained the joys of having a paid-off car and no debt. Seems he had worked hard, paid everything off, and was back in school to earn his teaching credentials. He wanted to teach history at the high school level.

We returned to his condo and met his female roommate, who I was relieved wasn't Underwear Drawer Girl. She snapped some candid shots of the two of us on the couch. It had been a wonderful yet stingingly bittersweet visit.

Throughout my life, this more mature version of Mitchell has come to mind. I've admired his financial prowess and desire for simplicity and have attempted to emulate him. Thus, in many ways,

Mitchell remains a silent inspiration.

We lost touch during the pre-internet years, as was so easy to do. Over the years, Mitchell was the one person for whom I searched online most frequently. To see what he was up to, how he was, to learn if he had ever achieved his dream of simplicity. There was never a trace, not a single clue.

Then, in 2013 while writing the first draft of this chapter, I found his mother's obituary from 2004. It stated she had been "preceded in death by her husband and son Mitchell," and I started an exhaustive search to find out the cause of his early death. Probably something athletic or adventurous, I figured. Skiing accident? Racecar crash?

I eventually learned that Mitchell succumbed to AIDS on November 26, 1997. I hope he's resting in peace. I will forever regret my decision to walk away from him, and I've missed him every day for more than thirty-four years.

And what of the Ballpark? With the early years of the AIDS epidemic already in full swing, bathhouses had become a health hazard for gay men who didn't know how, or simply didn't want, to play safe. Back then, there was a "Whatever—it will never happen to me" mentality. On June 16, 1986, the club played its final inning and soon after was demolished. The corner lot on which it stood at south Broadway and Bayaud remains a vacant lot, carefully guarding the secrets of the gay water park buried several feet under dirt, its plumbing long since filled with cement by the club's owners, ensuring no one could ever revive the place. And the basement attraction—the semi-truck cab? It's rumored that the filthy thing is buried under four stories of rubble. Good riddance.

23

The Night Was Alive
DENVER: 1985–1986

I had been out on my own for only six months and was already at my third address, this one, an apartment near 72nd in north Denver on Hooker Street. Yes, Hooker. And aptly named. This second-floor sliver of a one-bedroom was time-trapped in the '70s with its hideous green shag carpeting, avocado appliances, and a smell of something like dead cat mixed with Lysol. It wasn't at all me, and I vowed to move as quickly as possible.

I wasn't allowed to paint, so I lined. I meticulously lined each kitchen cupboard shelf with thirty bucks' worth of woodgrain-pattern Con-Tact paper. I lined with a purpose and a vengeance, as if I was trying to bury my mistakes under sticky adhesive. Then, I unpacked everything and threw out the boxes. For someone bent on not staying put, you couldn't tell it from these activities.

I'll admit it took the better part of thirty-some moves to learn the value of leaving non-essential stuff packed, always ready to be loaded on the next moving truck. I must have inherited from Mom the gene that makes you feel the need to move every time a problem arises.

At least the Hooker apartment was close to work at Pizza Hut.

That would save gas, I reasoned.

The job at United Bank of Boulder had already ended badly. Reading aloud the computer screen over a co-worker's shoulder proved disastrous. I incorrectly assumed my colleague had the customer (with an unfortunate last name) on hold while she researched something on the account.

"Massengill? That's the customer's last name? Massengill?" I said loudly.

"Um, Denn..." the co-worker tried to shush me.

"Massengill?! What? Did her husband invent feminine hygiene? Massengill! Oh my God! That's hilarious!"

"Denn, she's at the counter."

Upon this realization, I ducked behind a half-wall partition, but it was too late. Mrs. Massengill had heard me and was not amused. I thought I was hysterically funny but really just came across as a douchebag. I was promptly fired.

And after the split with Mitchell, maintaining the Saturday waiter job at "his" Village Inn wasn't in anyone's best interest. So, I was down to one job and one nasty-ass apartment. Plus, I couldn't afford the Fiero—never could—so Jim helped me get into a more affordable ride: a 1981 faded red Buick Century with a stained white velour interior and AC that didn't work. The ugly car went perfectly with the hideous apartment and my broken heart; it was all a recipe for depression.

* * *

I was fighting hard to build a social life outside of Pizza Hut, but more importantly, I was in the hunt to catch some new guy who might call me Tiger. I had stayed in touch with a guy I dated prior to Mitchell, and even though he was far from the "take home to Mom" type, he was single, good-looking, and still interested in me. He was worldly—or what today we might call edgy, sketchy, or just downright nasty. I think his name was Kyle. I think. We'll just go with that.

Kyle was about a year older and talked, drove, and lived fast. He picked me up for our first post-Mitchell date in his souped-up, white 1980 TransAm with the stock Phoenix bird, the "Screamin' Chicken," decal on the hood. The interior reeked of a variety of types of smoke. The backseat was littered with smelly Nikes, stinky Reeboks, and aromatic Adidas; there was some kind of a shoe thing going on back there amidst the fast food remnants.

I had a typical date night planned: dinner at my favorite downtown restaurant, Racine's, then Michael J. Fox at the AMC Tivoli—my seventh time to see *Back to the Future*. When we pulled into the parking lot of a motel of questionable repute on East Colfax Avenue, it registered as a bit odd, but Kyle quickly explained that he was staying there temporarily due to a bad breakup and wanted to change his shirt—which wasn't a bad idea as he reeked of body odor. He threw on another shirt, ostensibly cleaner than the other, then fished around under the bed for a metal box.

Ah, he hides his valuables. Very prudent of him.

Kyle proceeded to dump from a large Baggie a small mountain of white powder onto the motel room table. Then, in another pile, he shook out the contents of what appeared to be ordinary flour or possibly baking soda. He pulled out a few dozen of the tiniest—and as I thought at the time—cutest little Ziploc-style bags I'd ever seen, each just scarcely large enough to hold a quarter.

"Hey, just bear with me here. I have to get this cut," Kyle said, as if I had a clue what he was talking about.

"Oh, will it take long?"

"Cool it, baby. Give me a few. I gotta get this done."

Once we missed our dinner window and were now only twenty minutes from Marty McFly skateboarding onto the big screen, I wondered what was so urgent about making three dozen tiny bags of flour.

"Can I help you? I'm good at crafts."

I'm good at crafts? Really? Was I that stupid?

I must have appeared to be the most ignorant goody-goody that ever lived. Not that Kyle even knew I was there. As he pulled a kitchen scale from his backpack, I asked, "Oh, does each one have to weigh a certain amount?"

"Quality control," Kyle said, as he divided the first white powder into neat little piles then added an almost-equal amount of the second type of powder. He used a credit card to mix the two and what appeared to be a Slurpee straw to shovel the results into each bag.

Looking at my turquoise Swatch, I realized we had missed the 7:30 movie, and I hoped Kyle would be done in time for a later showing. I sat squeamishly on the filthy bedspread and picked some pizza sauce off the band of my Swatch. Meantime, Kyle was making several straight lines on the table with just the first mysterious powder, using the credit card to make them nice and neat. Then, he rolled up a dollar bill and snorted up three lines in succession.

Oh no, this must be the cocaine I've heard about in that Eric Clapton song.

"This is good, good, good fucking shit. Want some?" Kyle asked, as he was shaking his head, sniffing and snorting and pushing stray coke in his nostrils.

"Oh, no. I've never tried the hard stuff," I said proudly. "Just the occasional beer, that's all, thanks. Do you think we can make the 9:50 showing?"

"Of what? That Marty McSpuds crap?" Clearly, Kyle was already going eighty-eight miles per hour.

"It's actually McFly. Spuds McKenz—"

"Whatever. Cool. Cool. Cool. Sure you don't want a line, baby?"

I shook my head.

"Suit yourself. Fuck, this is good shit. Good, good fucking shit."

He snuffed up the remaining four lines of cocaine, wiped his nose, threw a bath towel over his little production set up, and announced he was ready to go.

Kyle drove like a maniac. I thought maybe it was to impress me, but more likely it was the effect of the drugs. I didn't feel comfortable and was car sick, so I asked to be taken home to Hooker Street. He complied, then peeled out, leaving a trail of rubber down the street with the unfortunate name.

I didn't realize it then, but had the cops busted him that night in his motel room, I would have been arrested as an accomplice and would have had a felony on my non-existent police record. I probably would have done some amount of time and community service, and my future would have been officially screwed.

I saw Kyle again on September 25, 1985, the week of a typical early and heavy Colorado snowfall. We rented tuxes to attend a

Dynasty season kick-off party at someone's apartment in Boulder. Booze, cigarettes, joints, and cocaine littered the coffee table. Things were nice and romantic until Kyle did three lines of blow.

Ultimately, Kyle and I had an argument that night, and I slammed my fist with car keys in hand on the roof of my car, sending my keys deep into a snow drift, never to be found. My angry outburst required a ride back to Hooker to beg the landlady to let me in to retrieve my extra car key. It also cost me a $50 door unlocking fee and a sketchy boyfriend.

The strange thing about that night was that exactly one week earlier I had a dream in which every detail of the *Dynasty* party played out vividly, including losing the car keys in the snow. It was my first premonition dream, but it wouldn't be my last.

* * *

Hooker Street was decidedly straight and seedy, and I felt isolated from the gay community, such that it was in 1985, which was more of a bar scene than a community. In any case, it seemed imperative to move back to Capitol Hill.

At a bar, I ran into Kirby, who was vacating his enormous second-floor apartment in the Clarkson Street mansion. I jumped at the chance to take over his lease. I loved the house and what remained of its turn-of-the-century charm. Now, my entrance would be through the huge front door and up an elegant wooden staircase, rather than through the broken-down basement door around back. I loved that apartment with its original hardwood floors, floor-to-ceiling windows, its funky bathroom with a Victorian-style tankless toilet, and an *I Love Lucy* back door to the kitchen from the rickety fire escape. All that in addition to the precarious half-room literally hanging off the bedroom where Scott #3 and I had slept off the drunken merriment of New Year's 1985.

I needed help moving, but Kim was no longer available as my go-to dyke, having recently moved to some lesbian commune in New Mexico, a place that sounded hot and smelly.

Being back where the action was, I started to find my footing. New Year's Eve was just days away; however, after the previous year's vomit-fest, I opted for something lower key. So, with no boyfriend prospects in sight, I went alone to a late-night showing at the Tivoli to see the recently released film version of *A Chorus Line*. The movie awakened something so deep in my soul that I made a midnight vow to myself that in 1986 that I would go back to performing.

In January, I auditioned for a production of *Grease* at Metro State. Auditions were open to current and former students, so I had my uncoordinated foot in. After miserably failing the dance audition, I ran out disgusted with myself and proceeded to pound my head on the cement block wall across from the audition space, in full view of the other actors.

I received a call from the director asking me to play a dual role of Eugene (the nerd) and Teen Angel (the dream singer), neither role required any dancing. As would always be the case, it was my singing voice that won me the roles. There was one caveat: Never hit your head in front of the cast again or be fired from the show.

Once in rehearsals for *Grease*, I vigorously auditioned for any possible acting gig I could find, petrified to be without a show when mine ended. I was driven by the same need for attention—for approval, for validation—that thrust me onstage in the first place.

During that audition season, I struck out due to a combination of low self-confidence, lack of audition experience, and my abysmal dance inabilities. The worst audition was for Lancelot in *Camelot* at Boulder's Dinner Theatre (BDT). In my limited experience, BDT was the epitome of professional theater, highly regarded and critically acclaimed, and so, of course, there was a level of prestige for anyone lucky, blessed, and talented enough to work there. I was too young and too green for the role of Lancelot and went in with the tune "If Ever I Would Leave You" in a key two keys too low for my high tenor voice. I sang a shaky thirty-two bars and received a terse "I don't think so, but thanks," accompanied by a group chuckle from the house. So, that dream was shattered. I had imagined working at BDT as a launching pad to greater things.

After *Grease* closed in early March, I was miserably depressed and went out alone to a large gay dance club called Tracks (the original location, for anyone who's keeping score) in downtown Denver. To this day, I wouldn't be able to tell you where the place is, other than it being near railroad tracks and across a street from another gay bar called the Foxhole where Mitchell played volleyball on Sundays. Tracks had a second level above the dance floor, and it was there that I parked myself to drown my audition sorrows in full-strength Coors Light. It was still 1986, so I was still one year away from being twenty-one and legal, but Kyle had taught me how to make a fake ID, and on that particular night, the ID worked and wasn't confiscated.

Then I saw *him*. He exuded charm and confidence, was extremely attractive, and looked like the quintessential boy next door. My confidence boosted with barley and hops, I found a moment when he wasn't in his large group of friends and dared to say hello.

"Um, hi. I'm Denn," I stammered, not a clue what I would say next and without any concept of my end game.

"Hey! Nice to meet you! I'm Martin Moran. Marty," he replied in the most cheerful voice I'd ever heard. My heart began to melt.

"You look like you're having a lot of fun," I said, as I scraped at the label of my Coors bottle.

"Oh, I am! I'm meeting up with a bunch of old friends I haven't seen in a few years. I live in New York." Marty was exuberant with more confidence than I would ever hope to have.

My heart ceased to melt and beat at the same time.

Damn it. Of course, he doesn't live here.

"Oh, well, I'm sorry to have bothered you," I mumbled, as I stared down at my Adidas Stan Smiths. If I wasn't beating my head in frustration and self-punishment, I was hanging it in defeat.

"Why are you sorry? Hey, don't look away. I still want to talk to you," Marty said.

"Don't mind me, I'm just having a bad week. A bad life, really. I bombed at three different auditions."

"You're an actor? So am I!" Marty bubbled.

"Oh, do you perform in New York somewhere?"

"Yes, actually. I'm about to take over the role of Huck Finn in *Big River* on Broadway," Marty said.

Perfect. Just great. He's beautiful, and he's about to be a Broadway star. Time for loser me to walk away.

"Well, congrats. I guess I'll let you go," I said, dejected as I fished my car keys out of my tight 501s and turned for the stairs. I had yet to learn how to be happy for another's success.

Marty gently grabbed my arm. "Denn, don't leave. Let's talk. Hey, let's go outside where we can hear ourselves think."

Heart-melting sequence resumed.

We went out to my embarrassingly ugly Buick and leaned against its dented driver's door. It was a crisp evening, and although we both had light jackets on, at one point, Marty slipped a conciliatory arm around me. Marty told me how he grew up in Denver, went to New York City about five years prior, and worked a plethora of odd jobs just to squeak by: selling typewriter ribbons by phone, sewing balloons for the Macy's Thanksgiving Day Parade, and, of course, waiting tables. He had been on the national tour of *Doonesbury: A Musical Comedy* and had enjoyed some Off-Broadway roles. It was all hard-earned, and Marty was humble and spoke with amazing gratitude for every opportunity. I adored him.

Marty explained how he lived in a renovated warehouse loft in New York's SoHo district with several friends who comprised an eclectic and artistic family. One of those people was Marty's lover, Henry.

My heart sunk again.

Well, of course he has a lover, you idiot, I told myself. *What gorgeous, successful, been-on-a-national-tour, gonna-be-a-Broadway star wouldn't?*

I wanted to cry, get in my car, and drive off a cliff somewhere. I knew I would never have what Marty had. I suddenly felt like I wasn't even good enough to speak with him.

We continued to talk, as I unsuccessfully tried to suppress tears.

"I want to do what you do," I blubbered. "But I'm not

good enough."

"You can't tell yourself that. It was damn hard for me these last several years. But I got through it by staying focused and doing something—anything—every single day that was for my career. Whether it was making a phone call, going to an audition, taking a class, studying scripts—you name it. But always doing one thing every day connected to my goal to keep me focused."

"I kind of already do that myself. Some days, I'm not good at it and just want to give up, feeling stupid and worthless."

"You can't think that way, Denn. You have to fight those bad feelings and keep telling yourself you can make it, whether that means working here or going to New York."

"I'd love to go to New York, but I don't have the money or experience or anything. I'm not ready. I'm probably not good enough," I said.

"You won't know if you're good enough unless you go and try. And it's not always about being good enough; sometimes, it's just right place, right time. If you can get yourself to New York, I'll introduce you to some good people."

"Gee, I don't know. I guess I'll think about it."

Marty gently said that he needed to get back inside to his friends. I felt so alone. With barely a word, I started to get in my Buick. Marty stopped me and gave me the longest, warmest hug I'd ever known. More than thirty years later, I can still feel the warmth of that embrace. It wasn't romantic. It wasn't sexual. But it was magical.

I watched Marty walk back into Tracks, feeling at once warm inside and more dejected than ever. How would I ever get to New

York? I couldn't even get cast at a lousy dinner theater. I slunk into my car and pounded my head on the steering wheel until my eyes crossed.

* * *

Shortly after meeting Marty, I was cast as Prince Charming in the Rogers and Hammerstein musical version of *Cinderella*. It was a nice leading role at the art deco Aurora Fox Theatre. Although it wasn't a professional production, it was heavily publicized. I wanted to tell Marty—although I feared he wouldn't remember me—but in that pre-digital, pre-social media era, it required a bit more effort to get in touch with someone if you didn't already have their phone number or address. Being ever-resourceful, I sent a letter to Marty in care of the Eugene O'Neill Theatre in NYC where *Big River* was playing, not expecting it would reach him. I certainly didn't expect a response.

I was delighted to receive a lovely, two-page letter from Marty dated April 7, 1986.

♦ ♦ ♦

It's a curious thing. Sometimes strangers can meet and have an exchange more potent than one between old friends. I was afraid I had simply spoken mere platitudes and clichés, but I'm glad that you felt OK about what I said. I believe you said the truest thing when you said "we all have bad weeks."

This is a grueling, frightening, and joyful line of work. Hang in. You sound very wise and positive about "doing something each day." That's how I survived my first two years as a pauper/waiter in N.Y.C.

◆ ◆ ◆

The letter concluded with a reiteration of the offer to connect if I made it to the city and his offer to help if he could. His salutation was those same three words that have been blasted at me by every well-meaning soul I've ever encountered: "Believe in yourself." I still haven't figured out how to do that.

The night I met Marty has had a profound effect on me, as over the last three decades, I've pursued everything from being a theater performer, country singer, country recording artist, theater performer again, theater owner and producer, Disney production manager, and now, memoir writer. Always, there was Marty's sweet voice and kind words of encouragement, always front in my mind.

I caught up with Marty again in 1998 when he was performing on Broadway in *Titanic*. He got me great house seats, and we had a brief chat outside the Lunt-Fontanne after the show until his partner Henry came out to meet him for their long subway ride back to some area far, far north of Times Square. As I watched the two of them leave and saw such sweetness and warmth between them, I hated myself even more. I was still single, struggling, and just as broken as ever.

24

Annie Get Your Snake

I was halfway through the run of *Cinderella*. It happened one Sunday matinee when I went backstage for a costume change and a touch-up of my heavily applied makeup. I was playing Prince Charming, but someone should have told me I was wearing more eyeliner than ole Cindy herself. As I was making my way to the dressing room, the stage manager handed me a note; Dennis and Sharon were in the audience, and he wanted to see me.

I was dumbstruck.

He's pretended I don't exist since I was eight, and now, sixteen years later, he shows up out of the blue and wants to see me?

I wondered how many jars of pennies he had to empty to purchase two tickets.

Mom never missed a chance to tell the jars-of-pennies story. One time, as a kid, we went with Grandma to the Vilas Park Zoo in Wisconsin. Dennis brought with him one of his enormous glass jars of pennies and proceeded to dump the contents all over the ticket cashier's counter and slowly counted out admission for three adults and one child. Mom was embarrassed, and Grandma was pissed. So, the fact that he and Sharon were attending a production at fourteen bucks per matinee seat was fairly impressive.

I wasn't sure what to do and spent the second act fretting whether I should meet Dennis or stage an escape through a side door. I didn't need to make that decision because after the curtain call, lo and behold, there was Dennis, standing backstage. Being a non-pro, non-union production with lax rules, he probably waltzed right in.

He approached me cautiously with teary brown eyes. He looked old and haggard. "Oh, Denny, you were so wonderful, so talented. I had no idea you could sing like that. What an amazing, amazing voice!" Dennis gushed.

"Um, well, thanks," I said, never quite knowing what to call him. Dad was far from appropriate after all the time that had passed. "How did you know..."

"I saw the notice for your show in the *Denver Post*. I couldn't believe my eyes. But you always *were* special."

A million angry thoughts buzzed in my brain like a nest of pissed-off wasps.

Yeah. I was so special I didn't get mouse ears. I was so special you made me ride a horse until my inner thighs were severely bruised. I was so special you threw me in the Pacific and left me to drown.

"So, where's Sharon?" I asked with no interest in the answer.

"She stayed out front. I wanted this moment to be all about us."

I didn't realize we were having a moment.

"I've got plans with the cast," I lied. I had no intention of spending another moment with the man who had crushed Mom's soul and had set me up for a difficult and exhausting life of self-hatred.

"Oh, I understand. I know you must be very busy," Dennis said, still fighting tears. "Here's my number. Will you call me some time?"

I responded with a sort of half nod.

After a week or so, probably out of curiosity more than anything else, I called Dennis. Sharon answered in her high-pitched, squeaky voice. Arrangements were made for me to come by their house in Lakewood the following Saturday. That day, perhaps out of years of guilt, Dennis offered to help me in some way—financially, if it were possible. I made a list of my credit card balances, and after a cursory review, he offered to pay the $200 balance on my JC Penney card, the smallest of my credit card debts. Such a bargain. No child support or alimony to Mom for fourteen years, and he gets off easy with a mere two-hundred clams.

The house was a veritable dump. Sharon served warm, watered-down lemon Kool-Aid in sticky Tupperware tumblers that were pulled from a dilapidated yellow cupboard. We sat at a stained dinette in a nasty kitchen, the walls of which were covered in 1960s-era wallpaper and caked with cooking grease. When I had to use the bathroom, I laughed at the cracked, pink padded toilet seat that probably came from Goodwill. After choking down warm lemon water and stale dollar store cookies, we said our goodbyes, and I sort of promised to stay in touch.

* * *

As theater opportunities continued to elude me, I had to travel further from Denver for rejections. I found a tiny dinner theater in Berthoud, forty-six miles from my Capitol Hill apartment, that

served as a sort of minor league launching point to larger dinner the-
aters (but still—dinner theater). Although I had completely bombed
the Highlands sword dance audition for *Brigadoon*, I was invited
back to audition for *Annie Get Your Gun*. Again, I could sing but not
much else.

In May 1986, I was cast in my first professional—as in, it paid
something—show at Ye Olde Wayside Inn Dinner Theatre (WIDT)
for a three-month summer run.

A longtime fixture in northern Colorado, customers would
drive sometimes hundreds of miles to the Wayside just to eat the
exceptionally tasty fried chicken at the circa-1930s restaurant. Then,
in 1983, a former opera singer named Sally opened the small dinner theater in the adjoining banquet room, complete with three tiers
of seating for maybe ninety guests and a stage the size of a post-
age stamp.

My first role was Foster Wilson, an old curmudgeon who runs
a hotel and is on stage for Annie's first big number, "Doin' What
Comes Natur'lly." As Wilson, I had a couple of marginally comic
scenes early in the first act before I scrubbed off the age makeup and
sang and moved scenery for the remainder of the show. I did get
to play a Native American every night, tripping on my floor-length
shawl or cloak or whatever it was while walking in a circle. I told you
my dancing was *that* good.

For my main role of Wilson, I was assigned a tacky checkered
suit. When we did the costume preview for the director and the production team, one member let out an audible gasp when she saw
me. The previous summer, a guy named Darrell wore the same suit
in a different show. No biggie. Costumes get recycled all the time.

Except that Darrell was one of Colorado's earliest AIDS victims and had recently passed. And I gathered that, in that suit, he and I looked a lot like brothers. Once I learned that, it was a bit creepy to wear his costume, but I'd read enough about the disease to know that I wasn't going to contract HIV from a suit.

What was strange was how Darrell (who I had never met) appeared in at least three of my dreams during the run of the show. Maybe I just had him on the brain, maybe the suit held some essence of his spirit, or maybe it was something else. In each dream, Darrell and I were in some clouds. He would approach me, and tell me that he loved me and wished we could have been together, but it wasn't meant to be. That certainly appealed to the gay-romance novel reader in me. Well, and we were both naked. So, yeah. Weird.

But then, each time, just before he would disappear back into the clouds, he would issue an ominous warning: "Denn, you need to be careful. I don't want to see you ending up with AIDS like me." With that, he was gone, and the dream was over.

My second production at the Wayside was a rarely performed and highly forgettable musical by Kander and Ebb called *A Family Affair* (it's about a Jewish wedding not the television show that had the butler named Mr. French). I was promoted to waiter, which meant my show days were longer and I took home much-needed tips.

We worked in male-female pairs for the service portion of each show. Typically, the guy would handle the food (since the trays were heavy), and the female would handle the cocktails (since they were prettier and could sell more booze). Occasionally, roles were reversed if the female was too young to legally serve booze, albeit frothy, fruity booze in a souvenir show-logo glass.

My partner for the fall show was a staunchly religious girl named Loretta, who relentlessly badgered me to come to her church. It seemed her church always had a service going on, so the "I'm busy that night" excuse didn't fly. But there was that word again: *church*. It made me cringe and recoil. Good heavens; the word still curdles in my mouth.

I gave Loretta the twenty-second summation of my church experience.

"Oh, silly, it's nothing like that, Denn. We're all about worshipping Jesus."

There was that other word. That name, Jesus. At that point in my life, He was merely a concept I couldn't grasp, and I only used His name as a shoddy cuss word. "J–C! I spilled the soup on table B4!" or "J–C, my tire blew out on the freeway," or "J–C, no one's ever going to love me." I'd heard plenty about Jesus freaks, and I was quite sure I didn't want to be one of them, thank you very much.

"Um, when were you thinking about us going?" I asked tentatively.

"We could catch the Wednesday night service," Loretta offered as if we were making plans to catch a movie. Or a bus. Or to get run over by a bus.

"Well, you know I'm moving to Greeley this weekend. Maybe we wait until after I'm moved?" Anything to put off what I imagined to be the equivalent of a colonoscopy. It seemed to keep her at bay for a time.

So, yes, Greeley, a mere sixty-three miles from Capitol Hill. Most of the regulars in the cast at the Wayside lived in Greeley

because most of the regulars in the cast were in the musical theater program at the University of Northern Colorado (UNC). No
one lived in Denver. The per-show pittance I was paid—$15 for the
"second chorus boy from the left" role, $20 for a featured role, or $25
for a lead (I never got one)—barely covered the driving expenses. So,
moving north seemed to make sense.

I found a second-floor studio near the UNC campus. I wanted
to be close, as I imagined myself enrolling and getting into the musical theater program, although I had no clue how I would pay for
tuition after being turned down for a student loan. Like so many
apartments, houses, and parts of houses (as well as jobs and relationships) I thought I could make it work.

I let Loretta have her way the first Sunday night I lived in
Greeley. She said we needed to carpool to the matinee, so we could
make the 7 p.m. service. She also said a guy named Toby, who occasionally worked at the theater, would be meeting us there.

Instantly, my mind started to play Twenty Questions. *Who was
Toby? Was he gay? Was he cute? Might he be interested in me if we met?
Could he be the one?* It was my standard line of mental questioning.

Loretta explained that Toby was struggling with some "personal issues" and the church was doing "a world of good for him."
Toby had "fallen into the devil's snare of thinking he was gay," she
said, but the church was turning him around, cleansing him, healing
him in a program called "Pray Away the Gay." Yikes. I was sure she
was going to sign me up, but I quickly remembered that I had yet to
come out to anyone at the theater.

We pulled up to a building that looked like it had once
been a revival tent that had a church built around it, room by

patched-together room. Here, a kitchen; there, a nursery. And a giant dunk tank?

They better not make me get in that thing. Number one, I can't swim. And second, when was the last time anyone changed the water?

"Oh, you don't have to be baptized today, silly. Well, only if you accept Jesus as your personal Lord and Savior. And, oh, how I pray that you will," Loretta said with folded hands aimed toward Heaven and great emphasis on the word *baptized*.

"Oh, so not necessary," I said, always one to find the loophole. "I grew up Presbyterian and was baptized as a baby. So, I'm good to go, right?"

Loretta emitted her shrill trill of an annoying laugh. "That doesn't count, you silly goose." She seemed thrilled to deliver the news. Like she wanted to throw the baseball that would dunk me in the tank.

"Um, why not? It was water and done by a minister."

"But, as a baby, you couldn't make a personal decision to accept Jesus."

I learned much later that this is the commonly held belief by most Protestant churches, both the dunking and non-dunking kind. Thankfully, Presbyterians were sprinklers not dunkers. Catholics believed something else entirely that remains a mystery, as does most of their belief system.

At the church service, I was hoping for some familiar ground, however unpleasant. But it was beyond casual. No printed program, no pews. Just some folding chairs and a lot of open space. Upon entering, Loretta was immediately pulled into a prayer huddle that was laying their hands on some old goat with a bad ticker. Others were already singing a repetitive hymn of sorts. Clumps of church-goers sang, rocking back and forth, to and fro, raising their hands in the air. As the praise band cranked up the tempo and the volume, the crowd began jumping up and down as if in a group trance. It was a bizarre scene for an un-churched guy like me. All that was missing were a bunch of lighters held high above the crowd like at a Led Zeppelin concert.

I didn't know what to do. I felt too self-conscious to raise my hands and sway. I stood, with perfect Presbyterian posture, waiting for something familiar. Something—anything—akin to my childhood experience of "stand up, sit down, sing a little ditty" all within the space of an hour tops, of course.

Suddenly, a plump, older woman jumped onto the stage and started rattling off a string of foreign words that sounded like pure gibberish. Loretta whispered that the woman had the gift to speak in tongues. Now, with all due respect, I knew I spoke by using my tongue (singular) like everybody else. But in trying to make sense of this new term, I had a mental picture of the woman's mouth housing some number of tongues like a *Star Trek* alien. *How many tongues did she have? Six? Ten?* It was beyond me.

The jabberwocky continued for maybe fifteen or twenty minutes. After she finished, the plump woman fainted, making an audible "thaw-wump" on the plywood stage. I was concerned for her well-being, but all the church people just let her lie. *Let sleeping tongues lie*, I thought, still wondering how she ate with so many appendages in her mouth.

We'd been there well over an hour, and I still hadn't met Toby.

I feared he was locked away in some nether region of the sprawling church campus in a conversion-therapy session.

After driving from Greeley, performing the senior matinee amidst the aroma of fried chicken and full colostomy bags, and enduring the ridiculously long church service, I was more than ready to call it a day.

"Oh, Denn, don't give up on my church yet," Loretta said, sensing palpable boredom. "The really faithful stay and handle snakes. It's transformative."

"That's a joke, right?" *Wasn't it a snake that tempted Eve and caused this whole mess anyway?* "I'm sorry; I have to go home. I have a lot of unpacking to do."

"Well, definitely next time, you promise?"

Oh yeah. Definitely. There won't be a next time for me visiting this particular freak show.

"Um, yeah, sure. Oh, wow. Look at the time. Can we get going?"

"I'm going to stay, but there are some people leaving early, and they can drop you at your new place."

Drop me at my new place, drop me off a building, drop me…just about anywhere but here.

"Great, thanks."

And thus ended my first young-adult attempt at church.

* * *

Greeley had been yet another mistake. No one from the dinner theater wanted to hang out with me, and the apartment was depressing and unbearably warm. So, I repacked and hauled my junk back to Capitol Hill to an apartment at 14th and Emerson, kitty-corner to the building in which All-State Choir Scott once lived.

The landlady, Claudia, was an odd bird and a self-proclaimed psychic. We hit it off immediately. She told me things from my past she couldn't possibly have known, so that was all I needed to be convinced. She was the one who introduced me to the notion of past lives and, during a hypnosis session called a regression, had me believing I saw a scene from one of my many previous incarnations as a jilted woman who committed suicide.

Claudia also told me a new tenant would be moving in within a few days—a young, handsome, and gay actor named Dexter with whom I had a shared a past life and that we had business to work out in this one. My imagination went crazy envisioning the reincarnated reunion and epic romance that would inevitably spring forth the moment we met. (Seriously, what gay Harlequin Romance novel was I stuck in, anyway?) She also explained that he had accidentally—although she firmly believed there are no accidents—called a tenant in her building when he was apartment hunting. Seems he misdialed, and the tenant gave him Claudia's number. Magical stuff.

A week later than planned, Dexter did move in, we did meet, and we did hit it off—at least sexually.

Dexter had no furniture, and his few belongings were strewn across his living room floor. He was aloof and mysterious, the archetypal bad boy to which I had always been attracted. Romance wasn't Dexter's thing but unsafe sex was. In one of my innumerable stupid decision moments, I allowed him to penetrate me without a condom. Then, he ignored me. As they do.

Word on Capitol Hill was Dexter was a rent boy and had lots

of partners. I was petrified he'd given me HIV. I needed answers and borrowed Claudia's master key to let myself into his apartment to search. For what, I had no idea. Turned out that I didn't need a key; Dexter had already vacated the building and left his door unlocked. Among the Big Gulp cups and Burger King debris were two syringes and a few empty mini-Ziploc bags. I hated that I knew they weren't for crafts, and I doubted Dexter was diabetic. I was too scared to get tested for HIV and decided if I ignored what happened, it would just go away. Just stick a bag over my head as always. After a few months of feeling fine, I figured I had dodged a bullet. But the Darrell dream repeated, and his warning had an increased urgency: don't do that ever again—ever.

* * *

I continued with the Wayside until early summer 1987. I ran lights and dressed the set for *The Star Spangled Girl*. I was the lead tenor in the barbershop quartet in *The Music Man*. I did a major reorganization of the theater's costume storage for a couple hundred bucks. All the while, I was also working the box office full time. Somehow, I was cobbling together enough to barely scrape by. Between that, the bag of groceries Mom gave me each week, and the twenty she'd slip me without Jim seeing, I was living the dinner-theater dream.

That is, until one day at the beginning of my box office shift when Sally, with newborn baby suckling at her left breast, marched in and told me she no longer needed my services. She would be handling the box office herself from that moment on; money was tight, and she was $90,000 in the hole.

Thanks, Sally. Now I was officially deeper in my *own*

financial hole.

I hoped she would change her mind. If not, I'd have to find another day job, maybe waiting tables. Still, I was counting on being cast as Freddy in *My Fair Lady* in the three-month summer run. As a lead, surely I would also get to be a server and be in the pre-show.

I did well enough at the auditions and got a callback. I had just hit my one-year anniversary with the Wayside, so I felt certain that the role of Freddy was mine. When I got the call from Sally, I could barely breathe.

"Hellooooo-oh, Denn! This is SAL-leeeee from Ye Olde Wayside Inn Dinner Theatre," said in her sing-song voice, a frosty formality in her tone. "I am calling to offer you the role of…"

Here it comes. Dear God, I hope I get it. I hope I get it.

"Chorus," Sally said.

I nearly fell on the floor in shock. "Um, I thought you guys wanted me for Freddy, so I'm kind of shocked—surprised, I guess."

"We decided to go with another actor. Oh, and just a reminder that chorus roles pay only $15 per show."

I was totally screwed.

"Sure, I'll take it. Can I ask who the guy is who got the part?"

Her icy coldness nearly frostbit my ear through the phone's receiver. "No, you may not ask, as the offer is still out. But I'm confident—"

"Do you think there's a chance he might—"

"As I was saying, I'm confident he will accept the role, and you can meet him at the read-through."

"Any chance I can wait tables before the show like I've been doing?"

"No, Denn. I have all of that covered with other cast members."

I wanted to scream and tell her what a bitch she was.

So now, I was down to $60 per week before taxes on a four-show week. I searched frantically for a flexible day job. I tried going back to Village Inn, but they said, "No thanks." I tried to parlay one month of marginal experience there at Coco's (another breakfast chain), but they said I could go fry an egg. I couldn't go back to Pizza Hut; they fired me the previous year for missing a shift due to an audition.

The best I could get was a part-time server position at the Dawson Street Grill at the Meadow Hills Country Club golf course south of Denver in Aurora. But there, customers were as scarce as were the tips. Most of them were old farts who only wanted to order Arnold Palmers between nines and slap down a quarter for a tip. There was still no way I could make ends meet. So, after a shift at the grill, I would drive fifty-four miles to the theater. Traffic around Aurora was always snarled, so the drive time was at least two hours. It was costing me more in gas and oil—the ugly Buick drank oil— than I was making per show as, quite literally, the second chorus boy from the left and scenery schlepper.

I got desperate and nearly called the old modeling ad in *Out Front* (miraculously, the ad was still running after two years), then remembered I had been told to never contact the man again.

Then, I met a guy named David at a gay bar called David's. It wasn't his bar, just a funny coincidence. David (the person) was about to move to Phoenix. He had no plans nor job but was more than ready to leave Denver. I made a brief trip to visit him in Phoenix on my "long weekend" week when there wasn't a Sunday matinee and we weren't back on stage until Thursday.

There was something about Phoenix—the soothing warmth, the perpetually sunny skies, and the strangest trees I'd only seen in postcards, well, and from those trailer lots we stayed in when I was a kid visiting California. I ended up with a twenty-four exposure roll of film filled with nothing but palm trees. Palm trees lining a street, palm trees at night, palm trees in a McDonald's parking lot. Photos of little, well-groomed palm trees, and photos of big, shaggy, nasty-ass, grandpa palm trees.

The thought of going back to a show I hated with a cast I detested made leaving Phoenix difficult. As for moving, I figured if David could do it with no plan and no job, then I could too. At least I would know one person there.

I got in touch with the McDonald's regional office in Phoenix. I was able to use my three-plus years of experience to secure an interview for an assistant manager trainee position. I couldn't afford to fly back out for the interview, so given my crappy situation in Denver and no theater roles on the horizon, I just said, "Screw it," and started packing. I held a yard sale alongside the building on 14th, making barely enough to rent the smallest U-Haul trailer available. I didn't know that my car would need a hitch to attach the thing, but Jim was kind enough to step in and help. I think he was grateful I was finally pursuing real, sensible work.

My Fair Lady was a month or so into its long summer run. On the week I returned, each day after the show, I discreetly removed a few of my personal belongings from the dressing room. By the Sunday matinee—and end of the four-show week—I only needed to take my makeup kit and make a dash to my car. I would give no notice. Although I was only a chorus boy, it was in a scaled-down, multi-tasking cast; as such, my absence would be noticed. And that's precisely what I wanted. I wanted my absence to be felt, to hurt.

By Tuesday, I was crossing the Colorado state line into New Mexico with a tiny U-Haul trailer hitched to my red Buick. I was so worried about someone breaking into it that I took twenty-minute naps in the car at rest stops rather than stay in a motel. I called Mom—all was quiet on the dinner-theater front; no one knew I had slipped away in the night.

I continued to rumble along with an overpacked car and an over-the-weight-limit U-Haul trailer that contained my *Sanford and Son* collection of furniture; fifteen milk crates of books, scripts, and sheet music; my nineteen-inch Mitsubishi TV; clothes and costumes; and a bottle of Mrs. Butterworth's that during the trip proceeded to relieve itself all over the Herculon love seat, rendering it not only scratchy, but permanently sticky.

By the time I made it to Albuquerque, the temperature gauge was pushing the red zone, and even with my lack of automotive knowledge, I knew it needed to rest. I slept five hours in a truck stop parking lot. That is, after I had sufficiently cruised the truck stop parking lot.

I reached Flagstaff midday on Thursday. The back tire sounded funny, so I stopped at a full-service station. The problem wasn't the tire. The problem was the extensive record collection in the trunk that proved too heavy for the back end of the Buick, nearly cutting through a brake line. Thank God I had the sense to stop. The next leg of the trip was the long, sharp decline out of Flagstaff that required a constant foot on the brake. Had I not stopped, that U-Haul and my prized Annette Funicello record collection in the trunk would have been littered across the northern Arizona forest.

By the time I got to Phoenix, the curtain (so to speak; there was no curtain) was rising on the Thursday night show.

On Friday morning, Sally called Mom and screamed and cussed at her like a drunken sailor, demanding to know my whereabouts so she could get the $127 I owed her for meals and long-distance calls. Mom wouldn't say.

So much for my burning desire to be an actor or a singer or be on Broadway. In hindsight, that was the perfect moment to make a risky move east to NYC when I was the right age and without a ton of debt. Could have, should have. How was it I had the guts or sheer stupidity to go to Phoenix without any plans and without a job? I had let that stupid little dinner theater shake any bit of confidence I had gained. I was letting everyone down by quitting. But who exactly was "everyone"? Dennis? Marty? Mom?

It took years to answer the question: I let myself down.

Part Two

SHADOWS FORM

Interlude #2

Hail Mary
HOLLYWOOD: 2008

I tried pleading and reasoning with God, firing off more "Hail Mary" prayers.

"OK, I know I haven't been a good Christian. I don't even know if I am one. I mean, I was baptized as a baby, so I guess that counts. Doesn't it? But please, please, please get me out of this mess, and I promise I'll never do it again. I'll even start going to church if You want."

Of course, they were all empty promises, confusion-based lies, all of which had helped deliver me to the floor of the Coral Sands Motel. It wasn't my first time there, not by far. It was just the first time there that I knew I was in serious trouble.

I thought about all my failed attempts for love.

"If I had a partner, I wouldn't be here. I'm only here because I have no one, God. I have no one. I'm so alone. Please, God. Just make this feeling stop. I won't do this much drugs ever again. I'll even try to quit meth. I promise."

This isn't working. There's really no one up there, is there? Maybe I should try praying to Buddha. But do I need a statue? Maybe I should make notes if I'm ever in this shape again. Or maybe I should just quit doing this stuff, but I don't think I can. It's not like I'm an addict or anything. I'm just having a really bad high, right?

Denial is not a river in Egypt.

25

A New Age
PHOENIX: 1988

The room was virtually pitch black. We were seated in folding chairs in a circle around the old woman. I was excited and frightened and grabbed Joe's hand in some attempt at receiving comfort, reassurance that what we were doing here was OK. He quickly pushed my hand away as if it was a big hairy spider.

"Is something supposed to be happening?" I asked.

"Shhhhhh. Just wait."

I squirmed in my hard metal chair, and almost on cue, the woman cleared her throat several times, then coughed like she was trying to dislodge a hairball or a piece of chicken.

"The date is March 12, 1988, and there are several entities wishing to speak," the trance channeler announced. With that, her slight body shook like she had a massive chill from her head to her feet. Then, as quickly as it began, the convulsing stopped.

Now, she was speaking in a deep, manly voice. "I am Chief Ahtunowhiho. I was a great warrior chief of the Cheyenne tribe. I have a message for the woman in the red shirt." The channeler feebly lifted an arm and pointed at a woman who was, indeed, wearing a red blouse.

"Chief I-Want-The-Tuna-Heigh-Ho?" I whispered to Joe. "No way this is for real—I've done theater."

I was hushed again, as the bony finger pointed directly at me admonishing my rude chatter. I could sense disapproving heads shaking in my direction.

The Chief offered ominous news to another member of our group, then the channeler coughed, sputtered, jerked, moaned, contorted, and all but orgasmed (although it is possible she did), as the Chief proclaimed that the next entity was ready to come through. More throat clearing. Apparently, each new entity had to acclimate himself to using the channeler's body and voice, or as a "Ghost Host" explained, the "instrument."

"Top of the mornin' to ye," said an entity with a thick Irish brogue. "I'm Patrick O'Leary. I lived in me beloved country of Ireland in 1758. Please excuse my high pitch; I'm adjusting to the channel's voice box."

What the hell was going on here?

By now, I was a little freaked out and still skeptical.

"There is a lad here who doesn't believe I am who I am. And I sense he does 'the bold thing' [ancient Irish slang for sexual intercourse] with the handsome laddie next to him. Still an' all I have a message for the unbelieving lad. Make no mistake, I am no fekin' eejit, and I see right through you," O'Leary said to me.

"Um…" was all I could squeak out.

"I know ye ere gobsmacked [surprised], and that's good. Keep 'em guessing. You play upon the theatrical stage. Or used to. Ye need to get back to doing that straight away."

"But why?"

"Are ye not playin' with the full shilling? You had wee success, but ye can do more."

Wee? Well, I guess he's correct. A dinner theatre in the tiny northern Colorado town of Berthoud probably counts as wee success. Emphasis on wee.

Again, the channeler gurgled and snorted, and a bizarre interaction between O'Leary and the next entity took place. Seems he didn't want to step away from the mic. But the last entity apparently had more authority.

"Wu nai Yunchang," said a deep, foreboding voice with a marked Chinese dialect.

For his turn at bat, Yunchang spoke mostly in Mandarin. Seems there was a Chinese woman in our group, and he spoke directly to her, imparting what must have been an unpleasant prediction. The Chinese woman began to cry softly. He made a general address— perhaps some ancient Chinese secret—in rough, mangled English to the attendees. Then, he bowed (rather, the channeler bowed) and left the building.

Man, was this ever a freak show and a big bunch of hooey. Not to mention a waste of fifty bucks.

Now, the channeler was exhausted and slumped over in her seat—the only comfortable seat in the room, a broken-down La-Z-Boy. A female assistant/handler helped her stand and ushered her out of the home's living room. Once she was gone, someone flipped on all the lights, and I was momentarily blinded, trying to catch a glimpse of Madam Weirdo, but she was gone. Shortly thereafter, so was Joe. Just another guy on a long list of guys. But, he further opened the door to New Age gobbledygook, and it continued to resonate as I delved into Shirley MacLaine books and 1-900 "dial-a-psychic" phone lines.

* * *

I had charged into the fiery desert furnace of Arizona with a hope I might emerge as some new-and-improved creature, much like the mythical rebirthed Phoenix itself. But old, well-established patterns resurfaced with a vengeance, as old, well-established patterns do.

I tried to fix myself, first by using my middle name, Lewis, instead of Denn. Then, I became a fixture in the self-help aisle of every bookstore in town, as well as the one New Age metaphysical store with sporadic, odd hours. They must have only been open when stars were aligned and chakras were balanced.

I tried healing my past lives, fixing my karma, balancing my chakras, studying Buddhism, buying a bathroom full of oils, incense, candles, and crystals, and prancing through sun-dappled peaceful meadows in fruity guided meditations.

Then, I was introduced to the practice of "willing things to be so." I didn't grasp it in Phoenix, but later in Nashville, in 2006, I bought hard into *The Secret*. Bought the book, the leather-bound journal, the daily desk calendar, the daily pocket calendar, the framed inspirational quotes, the book-on-tape, the video, the bumper sticker, the travel mug, the bedspread, and the t-shirt. Bought it all. And what did I manifest? About $323 in credit card debt. And I still wasn't a lick closer to anything I desired.

It was during this New Age period that I eschewed the notion of Hell and wondered if there truly was an entity known as the Devil or if it was just some age-old, Sunday-school concept to scare children into behaving. During this time of embracing New Age tenets such as karma, fate, and destiny (weren't they a girl group in the '60s?), I pretty much came to my own misguided conclusion that Hell is what we make it, that we get a whole bunch of go-arounds on this planet in multiple lives until we somehow get it right, and if there was a God, He had long since forgotten me.

26

Gone Country

"Lewis, get your ass up here," Jody yelled into the mic. "Get up here and sing, baby. Show us what you got."

I tried to decline but Jody was persistent.

"Do I have to drag your cute Wrangler butt up here myself? Don't think I won't do it. And I've got my helpers, Julie and Vanessa, just waiting to grab your sweet cheeks."

By that point, *all* of my cheeks were red, so I acquiesced.

It wasn't a karaoke night, rather Jody was the lead singer of a country band in a dance club called Marshall's, somewhere southeast of Phoenix in the sprawling suburb of Mesa. Nervous as a long-tailed cat in a room full of motorized rocking chairs, I shyly went on stage, took the mic, and sang two Garth Brooks tunes. It was 1992, and country music was hot.

I received so many positive accolades that I assembled my own band, designed the band's logo, got publicity shots, and recorded a studio demo. As with so many things in my life, it all happened quickly, and it wasn't long before Lewis Kemp & Laramie became the house band at a tiny dive bar called the Branding Iron Saloon on

East Thomas Road (in the adjoining basement to a Ross Dress for Less). Soon, we started landing special event gigs, and as an actor, I was able to get a fair amount of local TV, radio, and print ad work but nothing that went national—meaning nothing paid very well.

Lewis Kemp & Laramie wasn't the best country band in town, but we were far from being the worst. I shortened my last name for stage purposes, but it was still a lousy name for a country singer. (I once received a cease-and-desist letter from Louis Kemp Seafood telling me to stop using their name to sell fish. Um, what?)

Soon, the band was booked nearly seven nights per week. I headlined the Arizona State Fair twice as a local artist, performed solo at special events, and sang on local television, and was even interviewed a few times. My name was getting out.

The most high-profile gig I booked was the opening act for Patty Loveless and Diamond Rio, both chart-topping country acts in 1995, in front of an estimated audience of 250,000 at the City of Phoenix's "Fabulous Fourth of July" event. Backstage, I struck up a conversation with the leader of Diamond Rio. Actually, he pulled me aside.

"So, what are you still doing in Phoenix? You have a killer voice. Nashville is where you need to be," said Marty Roe of Diamond Rio.

"Well, um, gee. Yeah, I've been thinking a lot about that."

"So, what's holding you back? You got the voice, the looks, the hat, the whole package the labels want right now. But you gotta have original stuff, so start writing. And I'd get my ass to Nashville ASAP." And with that, Marty went to tune his guitars.

A dream was hatched, a seed was planted, a cliché was overused.

I went out on the stage to sing "The Star-Bangled Banner" to great hoots, hollers, and thunderous applause. On my next song, when the crowd held their Bic lighters in the air, I felt like destiny had just tapped me on the shoulder and said, "Go east, young man."

27

Easy to be Hard

PHOENIX: 1995

Daryl sat wrapped in a ratty blanket in his eighty-five degree apartment next to mine in central Phoenix. His TV was blaring some game show when I knocked on his open screen door and asked that he turn down the volume. He couldn't easily get out of his chair and told me to come in and adjust the TV if it was an issue. His apartment, aside from being swelteringly hot, had the sick aroma of a person dying.

I found out through friends that Daryl was indeed dying, and the culprit was AIDS. This scared the life out of me, and I never wanted to pass by his open door in fear that I might breathe in the deadly virus. Back then, I was still ignorant about the HIV virus that causes AIDS, and I didn't want to take any chances. I had heeded the first Darrell's advice religiously and always—with the exception of Dexter—played safe.

With a boyfriend, I experienced the massive display of the AIDS Quilt during its 1993 tour stop in Phoenix. When I saw the quilt, it covered the entire floor of a coliseum. I didn't fully understand what I was seeing; I kept asking my boyfriend if all of these people had actually died from AIDS. It was moving and eerie, and it creeped me out. Maybe that was the intended result. There was a silent reverence in the coliseum; no background music, and no one on phones. That alone was moving. There was the occasional baby cry or loud whisper. Or me, who squealed like a stupid schoolgirl when I saw the panel for Michael Bennett, the director and choreographer of *A Chorus Line*.

As I was prepping for a move to Nashville working sixty hours per week by day and taking any performing gigs I could, sleep was essential. Unfortunately, my bedroom wall in the garden-level fourplex was Daryl's living room wall. Over time, the TV volume crept louder and louder. I made two more failed attempts asking—or, rather—demanding that he turn it down. One night, I had it. I had had a late night playing a dive bar in Superstition Springs, complete with a wet and exhausting load-out of the audio gear during a summer downpour. So, when I got home at three in the morning and was greeted by the thundering bass of voices from the next door TV, I flipped. Rather, I went out back and flipped the main power breaker to Daryl's apartment. *Take that, asshole.*

Four hours later, as I was getting ready for my day job, Daryl's apartment was still quiet. Good. Maybe he got the message. Or maybe he had died in his chair. I didn't care.

* * *

With the summer media events and Fourth of July concert behind me, and as a result of the brief chat with Marty from Diamond Rio, I was introduced to a husband-and-wife producing team who developed new country artists and lived both in Phoenix and Nashville. They were interested in working with me and had loose ties with a major record label. When I finally cut bait and moved to

Nashville, it was under the auspices of an artist development deal.

I made an exploratory trip to Nashville where I met with the married couple, Butch and Cathy, sang a couple of tunes in their studio, and scouted potential day jobs. It went well enough that in October 1995, I loaded a much larger U-Haul—a twenty-four-foot truck, in fact—with all of my band gear, a two-bedroom apartment's worth of thrift store furniture, and a couple of cases of leftover Lewis Kemp & Laramie T-shirts and headed stupidly off to another uncharted new life. I didn't have a job lined up, nor a contract with a label, nor a plan whatsoever. I must have smoked twenty packs of cigarettes on the long drive east.

The day I arrived in Nashville, I looked up at the depressingly gray sky, the run-down streets of Madison where I had blindly leased a cheap apartment online, and once again, thought: *What have I done?* I sat there in the cab of my Toyota truck, chain-smoking, replaying everything up to that point.

I thought about my former neighbor. Was he still alive? How was he doing? I asked myself why I had been such an insensitive prick when I had the opportunity to be his friend, to bring him groceries, to watch TV with him, to provide him company, to be a listening ear or a soft shoulder.

I recalled the last conversation I had with Jeff, a guy I had been dating on and off for more than two years.

"So, why are you doing this? You don't have a job or anything," Jeff said.

"Because it's been my dream to be a singer, and this is my shot."

"So just stay here, and be a singer as a hobby. You know you're not going to make it. Don't you know that? You know that, right? I mean, if you were *that* good, they would have given you a record deal and flew you out there."

Jeff sounded just like the negative little voice I'd been listening to my entire life. "Gee, thanks for believing in me. I might make it. I need to find out," I countered.

"But you won't make it. You're not good enough. I mean, sure, you have a nice voice and all, but you're too old, and you don't look like a country singer."

"And you wonder why we've been on-again, off-again. I'm done with you."

"You'll be back. You'll miss this big—"

"Dick? No, I won't. *You* are a big dick, and I won't miss you." Then, under my breath: "Damn it, I sure know how to attract them."

"Well, good luck, I guess." Jeff explained he just didn't want to see me get hurt, to have my hopes shattered. It was a lousy way of showing he cared.

I pummeled my forehead with my fists, calling myself names for running toward the unknown. I felt stupid wearing a cowboy hat and slammed it against the dash, breaking the straw brim of an expensive Stetson. The little condemning voice was there, of course, to add to the silent self-beratement.

But nothing felt right. Maybe Jeff had been right. I had yet again walked away from a job—this time a well-paying job as a marketing director and this time with proper notice—and plopped myself into an unwelcoming environment. Phoenix had been a lot like Colorado, only about forty degrees hotter on any given day. It had the same retail stores, chain restaurants, pace of life. It was an easy adjustment.

But the gloomy, overcast, seventy-five percent humidity steam bath that was Nashville just felt horribly wrong. The Southern way of life was too laid back for me. I still had the country singer dream, just watered down a bit by a strong dose of reality.

The seemingly lovely corner apartment with its own garden-level entrance that I had selected by phone and online photos had been given to another tenant. I was relegated to a three-story building with three long, smelly hallways and apartments stacked so close together I could hear my neighbor fart. Then, there was the stench from Hell that emanated from the cabinet under the kitchen sink. It was obvious some animal had been living (and eating and peeing and pooping) all within the cozy confines of the battered cabinet. The smell permeated every inch of the apartment—my furniture, my clothes, my computer. I was stuck in a three-month lease, but this time, I didn't bother to unpack.

I worked at Kinko's by day, then Butch and Cathy owned my nights. In addition to Cathy telling me how to get my hair cut, what to wear, and what to say to industry folk, at least three nights per week, I was required to perform at songwriter open-mic nights. I had two original songs I wrote while still in Phoenix and another I wrote with a female artist in their artist stable. I detested the open-mic nights with all the hopefuls getting on stage to say something like, "Here's a new tune I wrote after I got off my forklift yesterday." Stories told by genuine, blue-collar boys from behind their well-played guitars.

My guitar, more than ever, was merely a prop. But only chick singers were "allowed" to get on stage with just a microphone; there was a definite double standard. So I strummed what I could, and just like with my band, always made sure I cranked down my volume knob. One time, a well-meaning audio guy yelled across the venue that he wasn't hearing me, that he was getting a signal but nothing else. I was humiliated.

After that incident, I was urged into guitar lessons that proved to be so frustrating I just wanted to smash the damn thing. Thankfully, Butch was on the songwriter circuit as well and became my guitar buddy, doing the actual playing while I faked it up front. He chatted up every audio tech, so they were in on our scam. Still, I was so out of place. I was far better at singing cover tunes at a Phoenix media event with recorded tracks than being in the middle of a cutthroat, competitive process with politics I didn't understand. I was a tiny fish in an enormous pond of better looking fish who could all play their instruments.

When I wasn't out singing, I was expected to be logging time at Butch and Cathy's studio, working on my backup vocal chops, learning to layer my voice across multiple tracks, and recording demos for other writers. I loved the studio part, and my voice recorded well without need for digital pitch correction. I was told mine was a strong, instantly likable voice but that it sounded, at times, too much like a Broadway singer. So, I ratcheted up the cornball accent and felt even more self-conscious and disingenuous with the "Howdy ma'am" and "Shucks, y'all are too nice to me" and "I reckon y'all just came from Shoney's" bullshit patter.

At the urging of my writing partner, Linda, I reluctantly went and stood in a four-hour line to audition for a performance slot at the famous Bluebird Café. I had Butch and his guitar in tow and Linda ready to play keys. I brought my black Washburn guitar but never took it out of the case. I made up some story about a sprained finger.

And so, it was with great shock when I received a call inviting me to set a date to come perform at a new artists' night. Linda desperately wanted to be selected and should have gotten a call; she could write, sing, play, and had album-cover looks. I even tried to give her my spot, but it was against the rules. I chickened out twice then finally committed to a date, did the damn thing, and no one noticed or cared. But, hey, it was the Bluebird. It was a story I could tell my grandkids, I was told. Right. Like I was going to have grandkids.

After the gig, I headed straight to the pawn shop to unload the guitar and put the $75 toward a new acting headshot.

28

This Little Piggy

Lonely, dejected, and depressed describe my usual, comfortable state. But at this point, I was turning thirty in a Nashville gay bar, looking around and seeing guys having a good time, smiling, laughing, embracing. But not me. I was nursing my Bud Light, head hung low, feeling sorry for myself for not having the chops to make the country singer dream come to fruition. It had been a mistake to move to Nashville, a classic case of me blowing smoke up my own ass. Worse yet, I felt like the oldest, ugliest guy in town. Bottom line, I wasn't in the right mindset to meet anyone. And, as usual, I thought being coupled would fix all that was wrong in my life. I was a sitting duck.

The Chute was a tiny Disneyland of a gay bar on 8th Avenue with a front area for billiards, a middle section for dancing to the latest party music, a tiny stage for drag shows further back, and a leather bar in the rear. But to get to the latter section, you had to walk blindly through a dark maze shoddily constructed of Hefty bags and black fabric. In each dark corner of the maze, there were guys paired up, tripled up, getting it up, and getting it on in a group-sex scene. It was disgusting, revolting. Yet, intriguing perhaps? Curiosity must have drawn me into the crude maze that night, and as I walked through, it felt like a million groping hands were grabbing at me. Memory flashed back to the steam maze at the Ballpark. As I emerged, another unwelcome hand took a firm grip on my crotch.

"Bet you've got a big one," said the high-pitched Alabama drawl.

"Excuse me?" I said, pushing away his porky hand as I tried to walk away.

The hand was back and squeezing my crotch. I should have broken his arm.

"I *said* it *feels* like you've got a big one. Aren't ya gonna say 'thank you'? In the South, when you get a compliment, the polite thing to do is say 'thank you.'"

"Sure. Thanks," I said, firmly pushing his hand away as I started to swim upstream through the crowd.

"Oh, c'mon, let me buy you a drink. I'm sorry for being so forward," said the chunky guy who would later be known only as "The Butthole" or BH. ("Butthole" seemed like the less intelligent second-cousin of the superior descriptor "asshole" and, therefore, felt appropriate.)

"Well, I guess. It's my 30th birthday today."

"Well, this *is* a cause for celebration." He glanced at the remaining shreds of my beer bottle label. "Two Bud Lights," he shouted across the bar in an effeminate, lilting voice. "So what do you do, Mister?"

"Well, I work at Kinko's as the manager of a shitty desktop publishing department. I hate it. I moved here because I had a sort of country singer development deal that's kind of already run onto dry ground."

"I work as a motivational speaker, but I do *tons* of theatre and music and know everyone worth knowing in this B market. Nothing like L.A when I lived there and played a major role on a huge show, but sure, yeah, I know tons of people you should meet."

I choked on a swallow of beer. "Really? That would be so amazing!"

"Well, if we hit it off, and I think we already have," he postured, "I might be able to introduce you to some big people." The chubby hand was making wild gestures, as if it was permanently attached to a Fourth of July sparkler.

That was the only carrot I needed to force an interest in this guy who was far from my type. Certainly not the handsome Mitchell with the athletic body and devilish grin. Or any of the Scotts. Or even the drug dealer. This guy, well, he just reminded me of a cartoon pig.

He pushed hard for a relationship, and I acquiesced, I think, because I was desperately lonely and needed some measure of security in a city that ate wannabes for breakfast with a side of grits. The prospect of contacts in a town where I knew only two industry people sweetened the deal, and as much as I hate to admit it, it made him look a little more attractive.

It didn't take long to start seeing the worst of the Butthole. Other than the desk clerk at the Denver bathhouse, he was the most effeminate guy I'd ever met. I saw it in him the night we met, but I chose to look the other way. But he proved to be pathetically needy, horribly co-dependent, and wretchedly gossipy. He had a fat face and pork chop fingers. He wore the same stinky saddle shoes every day, all day. Wore them to work, wore them to go out, wore them around the house. He walked almost on tiptoe, as if a stick were firmly lodged up his butt. I tried to break off the relationship early on but felt I owed him something for the three dead-end Music Row contacts he gave me, guys I assume he had merely slept with. A thank you note and gift card to Luby's Cafeteria, or more appropriately, a fruit basket, would have been enough had I been anything but a stupid, insecure wet blanket.

And so things progressed quickly. Way too fast. Lightning fast. Within only three months, we bought a house in East Nashville. Yes, we bought a house together after only three months. I had a knack for meeting guys who hurried things along. I always pushed hard for a new relationship to solidify into something. And probably because such guys were already on board for the speed round, I'd usually get my way. So, in retrospect, it's hard to play the victim card. But in this case, the "something" I got proved to be a living nightmare.

* * *

With the ashes of my country music career still smoldering, I longed for a way to perform and get the validation I craved. I found a year-long intensive acting course at Actor's Bridge studio studying the Meisner Technique (for those who know, it was kind of like method-acting lite.) The course, I think, was at least two nights per week, with each session having a duration of three hours. This did not sit well with the Butthole.

"What do you mean you're taking an acting class?! *I'm* the actor. You're supposed to be a country singer, but *you* gave it up. This is *not* what I signed on for."

"I didn't realize there were rules about what I can and cannot do."

"Well, you need to drop that class. I forbid it."

"Excuse me? You forbid it? Under what jurisdiction?"

"What does jurisdiction mean?"

Good. I had stumped the Alabama piglet with a ten-cent word.

"Basically, it's about approval. It means someone has been granted authority. What's your issue with me taking an acting class?"

"It means you won't be home at least two nights a week and will probably cheat on me with some guy in your class."

Was I actually hearing this? I should've said, "I already have," just to spike his blood pressure.

"Well, that came from left field. Why would I cheat on you?" I asked.

"Everyone always does."

Hmmm. Might be a reason for that, stinky saddle-shoed queen.

"C'mon, I love you, and we have a house. I just want an outlet to be creative, to perform. This is actually better for you, you know. Had I gotten a record deal I would have been on the road—a lot. Like 300 days a year."

"Well, I still forbid it," he said and stomped upstairs and slammed the door to the upper bedroom.

I was fifteen minutes late getting home from the first night's class and fell all over myself apologizing. It was a nice group of actors, I felt at home, and time got away from us chatting. The BH allowed me this one transgression.

Not long after the course began, Actors Bridge held auditions for a production of Arthur Miller's *All My Sons*. I was cast as George

Deever, and while not a major character, I did have a scene with a long, angry monologue. And I was having no trouble finding the anger well.

After the first rehearsal, which ran notoriously late as most rehearsals do, I drove home at a normal, legal speed.

The BH was in the front doorway. "Where the HELL have you been?" You're ten minutes late. Who was he? What's his name? WHAT'S HIS NAME? Who were you with? WHAT'S HIS NAME?!"

"A red light at West End and Broadway," I said dryly.

He slapped me hard across the mouth, his feminine pinky ring splitting my lip and spilling blood down my chin. I wanted to knock him to the ground, kick him in his ugly face, and shove a saddle shoe up his ass, but he reeked of alcohol, and I already knew he could get violent.

"If you ever speak to me like that again, I'll put you in the ground, you lying, cheating whore. You'll learn. Yooooo-uuuu-ll learn!"

The rhetoric was blown sky-high out of proportion for a grown man who was ten minutes late.

"Look, I'm sorry. Rehearsals don't always end on time. You should know that."

"They always ended on time when I was on TV." He could never let go of that bone, and my research can find no evidence of his being on *any* show, let alone a well-known one.

Scenes like this continued and grew in intensity throughout the rehearsal process. One night, I made the grave error of going to coffee after rehearsal with the leading guy in the play so we could run lines. Michael was as straight as an arrow and worked in the

Christian music industry. That night, when I got home, the BH was just inside the front door and proceeded to knock me down and kick me in the face and chest. Dishes were flung; vases were shattered. But I had nowhere to go and feared leaving my computer—my financial life-blood, as I was working freelance full time—for him to sabotage. (And in 1996, my computer wasn't small, wasn't light, and was comprised of a heavier-than-snot monitor, main CPU, two external Zip drives, one external Syquest drive, external modem, color scanner, plus an impossible tangle of cords and power strips. So, it wasn't simply a grab-and-go laptop.)

Eventually, the Butthole passed out, slumped against a kitchen wall, with an empty bottle of Jack in hand and drool crawling down his jaw. It was a pathetic picture. I pretended to sleep in a different room but was just watching the clock until he left the house. Once he was gone, I loaded my truck with my computer gear, my two fire boxes of valuables, a suitcase full of photos, and, of course, my Annette Funicello records. I figured anything remaining in the house might never be recovered.

I didn't have an end game but drove to the Brandywine apartments in Brentwood from which I had moved when we stupidly and hastily bought the house together. I leased a top-floor one-bedroom on the opposite side of the parking lot and hauled my truckload of possessions up three flights of stairs. Once inside, I locked the door and collapsed on the carpet and slept. I realized that my old apartment complex would be one of the first places he might look for me but prayed he wouldn't. I spent the next morning on a payphone with Mom, going over (and over and over) the situation. Two worriers did not a productive pair make.

"But Mom, I can't go back to the house. I just can't. There's nothing reasonable about him."

"Well, half that house is yours. Why should you have to leave? I worry about you constantly and now more than ever. You could get mugged, and someone will take your computer." Mom tried to be helpful.

So, as a result of insistent begging-by-pager from the BH and nagging, crippling guilt, I backed out of the lease just before the leasing office closed, lost my $500 security deposit, and, tail firmly between legs, moved my stuff back to the house.

I tried to ride it out and gave him several more chances.

He attended my play but only had criticism for me.

He took me on my first trip to New York and spent the week accusing me of cruising other guys.

I took him home to Colorado for Thanksgiving, and it was unbearable. Mom got to see for herself the accusations, the belittling, the nasty comments. I was giving him the tour of Longmont and all the prominent places of my childhood. I owed him this after a grueling three-day weekend at his mother's house in Alabama, where she completely ignored me but still accepted my help running her massive yard sale of crap.

We were getting out of the car to go into an antique store.

"You know that guy? Huh?" he asked.

"What guy?" I was helping Mom out of the car.

"The guy in the yellow jacket. You know him, don't you? Did you do him?"

My jaw dropped at the bile spilling from his nasty mouth in

front of my Mom. "I don't see any guy in any color jacket. And why would I be looking?"

He flicked his hand in dismissal of the subject. "OK, well, you'll learn. Oh, yes, you will learn."

On New Year's Eve 1996, BH insisted we spend it in a bar watching a drag show where I watched him watch other guys. Guy in the yellow jacket. Whatever.

I tried to ride it out a bit further, giving him several more chances than he deserved. Then things got worse, intensified by his drinking. I had to get out for good.

We went to a Chinese buffet on Gallatin Road. I wanted a restaurant full of witnesses if the BH got violent. I flatly told him I wanted out of the house and the relationship. I didn't even care about the couple thousand bucks I'd sunk into a bathroom renovation or the down payment. I had the Quit Claim paperwork with me, which would relinquish my share of ownership of the house. He didn't know how he would make the payments. I told him he'd manage. I suggested he call some of his "industry buddies" for a loan.

The BH started to cry, blubbering all over his Kung Pao chicken and limp chow mein. I held my ground. Reluctantly, he signed the paperwork and told me I had to be out first thing the next day or he would take possession of all of my things and sell them. A friend, a former Marine across the street, was happy to help. I rented an apartment at a different property with the prayer that the BH wouldn't find me.

But find me he did. And he must have done a thorough search of the greater Nashville area because my apartment complex was hard to find. Just ask any pizza delivery driver. Every day for the first few weeks, the Butthole was parked in front of my door or in the adjacent, elevated parking lot overlooking my door. He would sit there for hours and page me. Often, he would come out of hiding and catch me by surprise either in take-me-back tears or with a drunken "I know who you've been sleeping with" rage. He would plaster my front door and my car windshield with nasty notes calling me disparaging names, usually "whore" or "dirty cheater." Truth is, I never cheated on this horrifically screwed-up guy—that was all in his head.

Eventually, I obtained a restraining order, but he still sought me out at work (I had been doing contract design work for his company), so much so that I had to take the issue to human resources. The harassment continued for the next few years, as inevitably, I would run into him in theater circles, at Target, or at the church we occasionally attended together.

The relationship was so troubling and traumatic that I started pursuing relationships with women. Yeah, he spooked me good.

29

Fairy Tales I Told Myself
NASHVILLE: 1997–1999

I stood at the piano trying to sing the most difficult musical theater piece I'd ever encountered, a song called "A Firestorm Consuming Indianapolis." Then, to the man at the keyboard, I said, "Jamey, I can't sing this piece. I mean, I'll eventually get the dissonance and the wild intervals, but virtually nothing in this piece rhymes. I don't even know what the hell I'm singing about." I was rehearsing the title role of an obscure musical called *God Bless You, Mr. Rosewater.*

"The song is Elliot Rosewater's nervous breakdown. He starts with giving a cursory family history then heads into a World War II Dresden flashback and PTSD episode. He sees the war's flames of destruction and overlays it on what he thinks is a prophetic vision," Jamey explained. "Or some shit like that."

"Damn, this is crazy. I'll do what I can, but I'm getting close to my own nervous breakdown."

"I'm gonna beat you to it if ticket sales don't pick up soon."

Little did I know I was less than a year from a serious breakdown.

* * *

Free of the Butthole, I returned to musical theater, successfully stacking role upon role and rarely having a moment without a show. It was then that I began working extensively with Jamey Green, a super-talented musical director I met during a production of *Pump Boys and Dinettes*. I hired Jamey as my private vocal coach and, eventually, music director for my NYC demo project of five Broadway tunes. We even co-wrote and recorded demos of nine songs for our musical adaptation of a classic film.

Once a theater owner in Nashville, Jamey was seeking another opportunity in which he could have total creative freedom. He paired up with a guy named Mike who had money but no idea how to build or run a theater company. Impressed with my marketing background and design skills, Jamey pulled me into his "Euphoria! The Theatre" project to market and help produce the first regional production of Alan Menken's *Rosewater*, which was based on the book by Kurt Vonnegut.

Because of its tricky, elaborate, and hauntingly beautiful musical score, it required a cast of outstanding vocalists, so both Jamey and I pulled in our best theater buddies. One of my contributions to the cast was my friend Lisa who would go on a few years later to play the best Mrs. Lovett in *Sweeney Todd* since Angela Lansbury. She was *that* good. The cast list read like a who's who of Nashville musical theater.

One newcomer was a guy named Keegan who had just burst onto the local theater scene. He was cast in the show and dragged along his boyfriend *du jour* to rehearsals. Almost as quickly as Keegan was cast, he walked out after receiving a better offer. Somehow, he weaseled his boyfriend, Daniel, into taking his role and did so without anyone's knowledge or approval. One night at rehearsal, instead of Keegan, it was Daniel who showed up, script and tap shoes in hand.

Jamey, Mike, and I were all surprised by the switcheroo and peeved that Daniel had a lot of rehearsal conflicts due to his show schedule in *La Cage aux Folles* at the Tennessee Performing Arts Center. Lisa and I went to check out Daniel in the show, who mercifully was playing a male role, the young straight son of one of the musical's leading characters. As we discovered the next year at a theater fundraiser, Daniel in drag made a hideously ugly woman.

As I sat in the audience, I was mesmerized with Daniel; he was the most magnificent creature I'd ever seen. We had only met briefly at a couple of rehearsals, but I sat there with some deep gut feeling that we would get to know each other a lot better. I made a silent vow to, if given the chance, love him all the days of my life.

Daniel was on the outs with Keegan but still living in his house in Donelson, a suburb of Nashville near the airport. I counted the hours and minutes each day until rehearsal when I would see Daniel. And all during rehearsal, my focus was totally on him, this worldly, mysterious, and sexy-as-hell 23-year-old boy, who had an amazing and powerful voice and the most charismatic personality I'd ever known. *Everyone* loved Daniel. He dripped with confidence and walked with a distinct swagger; neither male nor female was exempt from his persuasive magnetism. Daniel always got what he wanted and made it look absolutely effortless. I loved and hated him equally for this quality.

Toward the middle of the run of the show, after a Sunday matinee, Daniel and I stood in the theater parking lot near his beat-up Ford Taurus, its bumper held together with duct tape, and talked until the sun went down.

"So, I broke up with Keegan today," Daniel said.

I tried to maintain a "concerned friend" face rather than the "holy fuck, you're single now?" face I was feeling inside. "I'm so sorry. Are you ok? Is there anything I can do to help?"

"My car won't start. Can you jump me?"

Oh, my dear boy, a million times yes, I thought.

"As it is, the damn thing is being held together with duct tape. Just barely. It's kind of a visual metaphor for my life right now," Daniel continued.

Oh, my dear, sweet boy. You used "visual metaphor" in a sentence. I think I love you.

We attempted to start his car with no success.

"Do you need a ride somewhere?" I asked.

Daniel pulled me gently toward him, taking my hand and delivering a mind-blowing kiss on my mouth. "Well, I kind of need a place to stay tonight, and I thought if it was with you, we could start getting to know each other. I want to be your boyfriend. But I don't even know if you're interested."

I gave an affirmative reply by returning a passionate kiss on his full, beautiful lips.

"I'll take that as a 'yes' then," Daniel said with a devilish grin that I knew only meant trouble.

Daniel came home with me that night and slept in my bed. But we only *slept*, which suited me perfectly. In fact, we only slept—literally slept—together for the first month. Neither of us was in a hurry to allow the relationship to become too intimate too soon. He was raised by strict, church-going parents, and at the time we got together, he was dealing with some confusion over what was biblically correct relationship-wise. I was just biblically stupid, mostly unchurched, and didn't understand his internal grappling with being gay vs being Christian.

And then, in what is truly bad form in any relationship, during the first week together, both Daniel and I said the three words that were taboo in gay relationships. Hell, taboo in any new relationship with the one possible exception being lesbians. He was young but not naive. I was nine years older but embarrassingly naive.

The relationship proved to be rocky from the start, and we disagreed on a lot of things. And although he had moved in with me at the one-month mark, my insecurities and depression issues effectively drove him away after fewer than three. He promptly moved back to Keegan's and ignored me despite our working in close proximity on two shows and my studio project. I was devastated and pushed hard to win him back.

Because, you see, pushing hard was what I did best. Every romantic relationship I'd ever had was forced. Ninety-eight percent of the time I was the one doing the forcing, urging the dating process along, hurrying me and whatever guy toward the idyllic white-picket fence scenario in my head that was never going to happen. It was a rare occasion that one of those relationships felt like it fell into place, natural and effortless. This one felt that way, and I was desperate to get that feeling back.

After the breakup, it was torturous to work alongside him in the workshop of an original musical called *Light Along the Cumberland.*

Daniel refused to speak to me with the exception of running lines backstage for our scenes together. I was miserable through the entire process and made no effort to hide my grief. The production told the riveting history of the Cumberland Presbyterians and was performed in a church gym. Exciting fare, I know, but I figured a credit was a credit. I didn't want to be there, but I also didn't want to be at home alone with my thoughts. I needed the distraction.

True to form for Daniel, his heart often changed on a whim. And during rehearsals for a production of *Oklahoma!* where I played Curly and he played second chorus cowboy from the left, another conversation occurred in a different parking lot. And with a bit of sugar-coated pleading and marginally cloaked desperation on my part, we reunited. My world once again shifted from dull-and-sad sepia to brilliant Technicolor.

And so, we loaded Daniel's belongings into his 1990 Chevrolet Cavalier (the Taurus had died a sad, duct-taped over, death) and moved him back into my house on Sunnymeade Drive.

Then, one romantic pizza-and-a-Blockbuster-rental evening at home led to casual, then serious talk, which culminated in an awkward, mutual marriage proposal worthy of a scene from a TV sitcom.

I was relieved, over the moon, and with my easily excitable mind on fire, I wasted no time making commitment ceremony plans, purchasing gold wedding bands, and funding the entire production on my credit cards since Daniel's main source of income was as a part-time waiter at a Mexican restaurant. And not even a good Mexican restaurant. *Así no hay mucho dinero trajo a casa.*

I had it bad for the elusive, impossible-in-the-real-world Disney fairy tale. While on a business trip at Walt Disney World, I ditched the work group on a free afternoon and ran like a banshee through the Magic Kingdom to find two miniature prince figures for the top of the castle-style cake. We had decided that I would be Prince Phillip from *Sleeping Beauty* and that Daniel, with his gorgeous dark brown hair, would be Prince Charming from *Cinderella*. And that's how we plopped them atop the three-tiered cake after the cake lady left (no doubt thinking she had just set up for a straight wedding), and we gave the stand-in Princess Aurora the boot, relegating her to a box of décor under the plastic-skirted cake table.

In fact, everything about the soon-approaching faux nuptials was a Disney storybook wedding brought to cheap and tacky life, with the ceremony at West Nashville's Darkhorse Theatre on its intimate stage and the reception in the former church's basement.

I think, to Daniel, the "marriage" was an outward affront or a sort of nose-thumbing at his estranged and devout Pentecostal upbringing. For me, it was the happiest day of my life, as well as a three-foot-thick smoke screen of denial. I thought that the ceremony and the convention of marriage (gay marriage was about fifteen years from becoming legal) would permanently cement Daniel and I together. Hiding behind this false wall of forced security, I wrongly believed I was safe, protected from ever again facing abandonment. Man, was I ever wrong. Aside from the biblical bugaboos posed by this flimsy charade of a non-legal union, both Daniel and I entered the relationship for equally wrong reasons. But I never quite figured out his angle or exactly what he expected from the faux marriage.

The wedding planning stage was brief, and December 18, 1999 arrived quickly. With two actors being the stars of this particular charade, we had all the right players in place: lighting designer, sound engineer, stage manager, and even a show director, Dan, who doubled as our lay minister and had all the power vested in him to pronounce us—well, nothing legal and definitely nothing binding. I think we both treated the wedding as if it were a show. I scripted the vows for both of us. Daniel contributed a few passages of scripture and the heterosexual tradition of the unity candle.

Wedding photos were taken, then the whole group retired to the Darkhorse basement that Daniel and I had decorated on a nickel. It looked like Party City had too much wedding punch and threw up. We also cooked the food ourselves to save money because by that point, I had made a dangerous dent in my savings and maxed out every credit card.

When it was time to embark for the honeymoon, we went out to find my Toyota truck covered with shaving cream and condoms as if it was the safe sex float in a Pride parade. I wanted to clean off the car, but Daniel insisted we let the wind do the job, a "blow job," he joked, while we drove the four hours east to the Smoky Mountains.

We sped away in the condom mobile for a glorious two-day honeymoon in Gatlinburg, Tennessee, just a "spit across the holler" from Pigeon Forge, home to Dollywood, quite possibly 300 pancake restaurants, and dinner shows performed by every has-been country singer imaginable.

I had located via the World Wide Web (as we called it in late 1999), a tacky bed and breakfast with themed rooms, most done in overwrought Victorian and a couple in ghastly Mondrian-modern. I selected for us a nice, secluded room, the Grizzly Hideaway, on the top floor in the back of the house where we could consummate our marriage in privacy. In typical tell-it-all Lewis fashion, when I checked in, and while Daniel waited in the truck, I asked casually if they did anything special for newlyweds.

"Newlyweds? Oh, well, my goodness. We have you two love-birds in the wrong room," the desk clerk drawled in her thick, sing-song east Tennessee twang.

I looked at my printed confirmation. "Ah, well, we're in the Grizzly Hideaway junior suite. In the back. Top floor."

"Oh, no sweetie," she continued. "You two lovebirds belong in the Love Nest! It's our special honeymoon cottage over yonder." She pointed outward, somewhere beyond the main building. (Every time she said "Love Nest," she sickeningly elongated the word "love.")

"Well, what's it like? Is it more expensive? I'm on a tight budget. Oh, and is it secluded?" Secluded was a big thing for me.

"Oh, it's just *precious*! It has a sunken living room, a kitchen-ette, a revolving round bed, and a heart-shaped Jacuzzi tub for two." The words flowed like a country aria from the innkeeper's mouth as she flapped her false lashes.

"But how much more for it? I mean, is it even available?" I asked.

"No extra charge. We at the Smoky Mountain Lodge would be *deeee-lighted* to have you and your lovely bride in the Love Nest."

I suspected she wouldn't be so "deeee-lighted" if she found out my lovely bride had a hairy chest and even hairier legs. Although, come to think of it, considering it *was* east Tennessee, it may not have been so unusual.

Their Southern hospitality still intact, the husband-and-wife team who owned and operated the lodge wanted to help the happy couple get settled into the Love Nest. I tried to politely decline but was told it was a bit of a hike down to the cabin, and they didn't want "Danielle" to twist an ankle.

"I hope she's not still in her wedding heels," the Innkeeper Wife joked as she fumbled for the keys to the Nest.

"Oh, I'll bet she's not," I said nervously.

Boy, were they ever surprised when they forced their way out to the truck to assist with the luggage and caught a glimpse of Danielle. The confused look on their faces was priceless. Had we been in the days of cell phones I might have warned Daniel to take cover (or wrap a makeshift burka over his head and face), but it was 1999, and we still only had pagers. Not that there was any signal on that Gatlinburg mountainside anyway.

After an awkward group hike, we were, I believe, reluctantly ushered into the Love Nest. I think the couple was secretly hoping they had misunderstood something and that the womenfolk had yet to arrive. The husband hightailed it back to the lodge, as the wife tersely led us on a quick tour of the suite, including a rushed lesson on how to turn on the rotation function for the bed and a quick demonstration of the heart-shaped Jacuzzi. I was red-faced and embarrassed beyond belief the entire time. Daniel, I think, was suppressing a huge laugh at the utter ridiculousness of the whole scene.

But once we were settled into the Love Nest, I was struck with the overwhelming feeling of "now what?" There was nothing to consummate, no family to plan. Rather, it was the familiar letdown of working hard for several intense weeks to mount a show, then after the final performance, there remained only the sudden absence of adrenaline and the inevitable deep dive into depression.

30

End of the World

Part two of our honeymoon was a trip home to my parents' house in Colorado where we had to take off our rings and hide them from my stepdad during our brief Christmas visit. It was awkward for all involved. Daniel and I needed to get out of the house and took Mom to a gay dive bar in Denver where she was cruised by an older lesbian. Mom was mortified, Daniel was amused, and I felt like a total dick for dragging her into an uncomfortable environment.

On New Year's Eve 1999, we hunkered down with a bunch of theater people at a party in Inglewood, a few blocks north of my house. It was the night that everyone was watching the clock with intense focus, as the Y2K computer glitch was feared to shut down the power grid and propel us all back to the Stone Age. Midnight came, the power stayed on, and we successfully crossed into the new millennium. News stations reported a collective sigh of relief across the globe, thankful that the world didn't end. At least not yet. At least not mine.

Daniel continued living as if he were single, often forgetting to wear or even know the whereabouts of his wedding ring. His world was divided among gay church, performing, and late nights at the bar without me. I tried attending the local gay church with him but was as uncomfortable as the night Loretta took me to her three-ring snakefest.

Daniel was the most religious, and at the same time, most anti-religious person I've ever encountered. I marveled at his faith, I guess. Or at least what appeared to be faith. Maybe it was all just for show. It's always been hard to say for sure with the hand-raising denominations. When we attended the gay church in West Nashville for a period after our commitment ceremony, I would often sneak a look at him during the seemingly endless praise choruses. His arms would be stretched to Heaven, eyes closed, body swaying. I wondered what he was feeling. Moreover, I wondered why I *wasn't* feeling anything. I could finally relate to the character Diana Morales' lament in *A Chorus Line*: "And I felt nothing; I'm feeling nothing."

I tried to emulate him and his confident, outward show of faith, but my attempts were all just empty and phony and stupid. It was yet another point in my life where I realized I had missed out on something important along the way. That there must have been some secret message decoding the mysteries of life behind those mindless Sunday-school activities of gluing pinto beans on paper crosses and pasting cotton balls on cardboard sheep. Back then, I had no clue what I was doing or why I was doing it. And now, once again, I was just as much out of place, even among a group of gays and lesbians who had always been shunned by the church. Somehow, even these people found solace in religion and worship and seemed to be better because of it. So why couldn't I?

As I was still struggling with my own belief system, Daniel's theology and attempts to immerse me in his smorgasbord of religious activities didn't help. Gay church, gay-church choir, gay-church fundraisers, gay-church bake sales, and of course, gay-church potlucks. Church was *that* word that I despised. As did the word gay. Gay, gay, gay. All gay, all day. Gay for breakfast, gay for lunch, well, you get it. It was simply living with too *much* gay, as if he were living out some perpetual Gay Pride fantasy. And despite wearing wedding rings and attending gay church, I knew the right-wing, hardcore Christian conservatives would say we were skipping merrily down a rainbow-colored path to *eternal damnation* (imagine heavy reverberation on those last two words).

So as much as I would grit my teeth with dread for Sundays, Tuesday nights—karaoke night at the Chute—were torturous. I had performed for 250,000 people in Phoenix but put me in front of 40 queens, and I would instantly choke and freeze, forgetting the words that were blinking at me from a monitor, my usually perfect studio pitch failing me.

But not Daniel. He was the king of karaoke. He would still be singing when the bar staff switched on the lights and flipped the last drunken drag queen upright from her slump over the bar.

One Tuesday night, I gave Daniel his space and stayed home. I was trying to make room for our varied interests in an effort to become a functioning couple in a healthy and balanced relationship. I felt proud of myself for being mature and brave and doing what I felt was the right thing.

"I'll be home early, honey," he promised.

I felt like we were finding rhythm as a couple. I poked at some design work for the next Euphoria! production and did a bit of light cleaning before going to bed. In the process, I found his ring on the fireplace mantel next to the side door we used as our main entrance. He must have slipped it off before heading out. The ring was so prominently placed that it seemed more than forgetfulness, but I shrugged it off. *Ah, the foolishness of youth,* I might have thought. Daniel was, after all, nine years younger than me. But why take off the wedding band he had worn for a little more than a month?

I went to bed but awoke in a panic around 3 a.m.—Daniel wasn't in bed. Maybe he didn't want to wake me and crashed on the couch. Nope. He wasn't home. I freaked. Had he been in an accident? Was he OK? Where was he? I threw on clothes and a ball cap and raced to the Chute to see if his car was there.

As I drove south on 8th Avenue, I could only see an empty lot, but as I turned the blind corner behind the bank (the bar shared parking with a Bank of America branch), I saw one remaining car: Daniel's.

So, he had been there.

I hoped it was simply that he'd had too much to drink and couldn't drive home. But why not be delivered to our home rather than sleeping on someone's couch? My mind raced and spun out a montage of possible scenarios, each more dire and devastating as the hours passed.

I drove around all night, smoking two packs, guzzling four Diet Cokes, and eating a box of Hostess chocolate donuts. I drove by every place I could think of, anything to pass the time. Or maybe to find a passed-out Daniel face down in someone's grass.

As the sun rose, I was too exhausted to drive any further. I went home and got ready for work. Still no Daniel. I was shaking from fear, too much caffeine, and a lack of sleep. Then, as I was pulling out of the driveway, the blue Cavalier crunched the gravel in the front parking spot.

"Before you say anything, I can explain," Daniel said. "I had too much to drink and went and stayed with Steve, you know, the guy who runs karaoke."

"Why didn't you just have them drop you off here? Not like we live that far from the Chute. And why didn't you call?"

"Well, I didn't want to wake you up. I know how hard it is for you to fall back asleep." Good move on his part; he just played the "Lewis's insomnia" card.

"Why didn't you wear your ring?"

No answer.

"I guess you didn't want to lose your ring, is that it?" I asked. I sensed my tone becoming parental.

"It's no big deal. I just forgot."

A larger conversation about rings and drinking and commitments needed to happen, but not then, not there on a Wednesday morning in front of my house with one partner exhausted and the other massively hungover. Instead, the conversation happened two days later on the crumbling concrete of my steep side steps. I paced and smoked; he had trouble making eye contact.

Daniel launched the first volley. "At some point, I may want to jump on a cruise ship for a year to perform, and I need a husband at home who's not going to fall apart when he doesn't hear from me for a month."

I tried to unpack everything in his declaration. "I know it's your dream to perform and travel. I just thought we would spend our first year growing into marriage, you know, with you staying local. But even so, if you went on tour or on a ship, wouldn't you want to talk to your new husband more than every so often, when the mood struck you? Certainly more often than once a month?"

I had made a major misstep.

"Whoa. That's not what I said or what I meant. On a ship, there's limited communication with land." Now, he was trying to lock eyes with me.

"Convenient excuse." I clearly didn't know when to shut my yap.

"You're way out of line. I should be able to be married to you *and* perform. It feels like you're forcing me into making a choice."

Yeah, it sure sounded that way. I didn't realize then how I was playing the role of the Butthole.

I started to cry. "I'm not forcing you into a decision. I just love you so much and want to be with you. Is that wrong?"

"We have the rest of our lives to be together. I don't want to be held back in my career."

We had come to an impasse. I went inside and feigned activity. Daniel got in his car and started the engine. I ran out to him. "Why are you leaving? Where are you going? Are you leaving me?" The verbal diarrhea of insecurities spilled out of me.

"I need some time alone." With that, he put the car in reverse and sped down Sunnymeade.

* * *

At the time, Daniel and I were starring in the small cast of Euphoria's new show, an obscure musical revue called *Personals,* that turned out to be a smash hit. That felt great after the utter flop of *Rosewater*. We couldn't add enough performances to meet demand, and the show ultimately ran for nearly three months.

I was doing the marketing, serving as properties master, and built a couple of specialty costumes for the show. Daniel half-heartedly agreed to assist me in gluing and sewing together a Mr. Potato Head costume for one of the show's sight gags. But as he would later tell me, it was too much togetherness for him, and he was feeling suffocated.

When two of the actresses couldn't stay with the show through the second extension, Daniel took that as his exit cue, and we were left recasting half of the six roles that comprised the small cast. He accepted a role at Chaffin's Barn Dinner Theatre in *State Fair* and unbeknownst to me at the time, began an accelerated exit from my life.

I didn't see much of Daniel due to my work and show schedule and his rehearsals. When we did speak, he was downright giddy about a new friend in the cast named Oscar.

"Does his bologna have a second name?" I asked, the joke landing flat.

"That's actually not funny," Daniel said. "He's a really sweet guy."

Why was he describing a fellow cast member as a "sweet guy"?

Monday, March 6, 2000. Something felt off when Daniel left for rehearsal and I left for work. I mean, really off. Foreboding. So much so that I left work around 12:30 p.m. and went home to see if Daniel was there. I just had a sick feeling in the pit of my gut that he was moving out. But he wasn't home nor had any of his things been removed. I chalked it up to yet another unnecessary panic attack.

I went to check my email in my home office. We had been sharing my lime-green iMac, and upon wiggling the mouse, I saw that Daniel was still logged into his Yahoo Mail. I could have just gone to the upper-right corner of the screen to log him out, but instead, I took a look. The first message in his inbox was titled "re: Not sure what to do." *Crap, this doesn't sound good.* I read the latest entry in an email thread between he and his best friend, and my heart fell to the hardwood floor with a nearly audible thud.

The email went into great detail about how Daniel was miserable in our relationship and wanted to get out, but there was the whole marriage thing. His friend reminded him that the commitment wasn't binding and urged Daniel to come stay with him while he sorted it out. Reading further down the thread, I learned that his friend had been urging him for about a week to leave me. Then, Daniel lamented about his greatest dilemma: "being in love with Oscar."

I raced across town to Chaffin's Barn, went inside, and saw Daniel on stage in rehearsal. I signaled that we needed to talk, and on the next break, Daniel reluctantly met me in the lobby.

"Is everything OK with us?" I asked, making the first volley into what would be an unpleasant conversation.

"Let's go sit in my car," he said. Once inside, Daniel would not look at me and simply stared straight ahead, gripping the dark blue steering wheel of his Cavalier. "Why are you here?"

"You left your email open, and I saw a disturbing message." I gave the high-level synopsis of what I'd read.

"Why were you reading my email? Never mind." With tears in his eyes, he fished his wedding ring out of his jeans, handed it to me, and said, "I don't love you anymore. I don't know if I ever loved you. I don't know anything, but I know I can't be your husband. And I'm in love with someone else."

I felt a thunder clap in my head, instantly triggering one of my trademark migraines. I cried and begged him to reconsider, reminding him of the vows we made in our little sham of a staged wedding. But Daniel was stone cold and muttered that he had to get back to rehearsal.

"Can't we talk about this? Please? Please? When can we talk?"

"I dunno. I don't think there's anything to talk about. I'll get my stuff this week."

So that was that. As easily as Daniel had jumped into our relationship and marriage, he just as easily slunk away. I was crushed. I truly believed when I made my vows that I would never be single again. How quickly life can come to bite one in the ass.

I went home, and after smashing a couple of our wedding gifts, I hit my knees, crying out desperately to God. "Why? Why can't I have someone? I deserve to be happy. Why? Whyyyyyyy?"

I attempted to pray, as I always did as a kid when I wanted Mom to come home from a date, or as an adult when I wanted a part in a show—the old "Dear God, dear Jesus, dear Whoever's up there, help me" Hail-Mary all-call for divine intervention.

My faith was as tiny as the proverbial mustard seed, entirely shaky and wholly uncertain. Still, I did my best to pray to the God I had never known, the God I had never made time for. Now, in my hour of desperate need, I felt incredibly alone. I didn't know the first thing about proper prayer or submitting to God's will. I prayed incessantly, begging over and over again for God to bring Daniel back, to restore us, to wake me from the nightmare that was destroying me. I felt that repetition would help my case, that the more times I repeated my pleas to God the better the odds of Him granting me favor.

I made empty promises to God, using every possible bargaining chip in my tedious pleas. Because I wasn't really a Christian—I believed in God but still didn't get the whole "Jesus" thing—I didn't know to pray that God's will be done, that His ways were higher than mine, and that whatever He deemed right for my life would ultimately be best for me.

Blinded by my tears, sleep deprived, and living on Diet Coke, Marlboro Lights, and chocolate donuts, my mind was far from being clear. Certainly nowhere clear enough to hear God's voice even if He had shouted in my ear with a megaphone. I think that is what I wanted, what I needed. I tried to listen for that still, small voice I had heard about in church, but the violent collision of scrambled thoughts only created a cacophony of noise.

Unable to sleep, work, or function, I was equally unable to be in my own home. As such, I took up residence on Jamey's futon in his spare bedroom. Jamey was gracious and welcomed the company, a welcome I quickly wore out by screaming and bawling during the night.

After two weeks, his wife Laura put her foot down and politely, but emphatically, asked me to leave. It was time for me to face my demons alone in my empty house that resembled a crime scene from my smashing every remaining souvenir of our relationship on the floors and against the walls. More than once, a co-worker took a day off to come to my house to listen to me cry and babble, talking me off the ledge as I made empty threats to kill myself.

Finally realizing that desperation wasn't attractive, I proceeded to Plan B, the plan to get Daniel back at any cost.

I went back to the gay church and joined the choir. Of course, I had ulterior motives. The choir was planning a trip to Atlanta to perform an Easter concert at a sister church. Since Daniel was in the choir, I figured this could be a good opportunity to talk. The hopeless and helpless romantic in me had concocted a chick-flick scene about us sharing a bus seat, reconciling, and snuggling close with all forgiven and restored. Not so much. Daniel wouldn't speak to me on the trip, and I had a miserable time. My heart wasn't in it, nor did I have any interest in going out clubbing with the combined gay choirs. I rented a car and drove back alone to Nashville in the rain, beating my fists on the steering wheel, fighting the desire to ram the car into a tree.

After this failed reconciliation attempt, I began what would be a series of irrational decisions. Talk of cutbacks to the contractor workforce at my steady job had me in a panic, and I took a graphic designer position at a boutique marketing firm near Music Row.

I was about three weeks into my new job when one weekday, at 5 a.m., my home phone rang.

"Um, hi. Uh. Hmm. This is Daniel."

"It's 5 a.m. What do you want?"

"Um, well, ah, I was wondering if I could be your husband again."

This time it was my jaw that hit the floor. I tried to play it off, play it cool, while inside, my heart was leaping. My next response avoided answering the question.

"Well, after you left, I pawned the rings at that place on Gallatin Road."

"Oh no. Can you get them back?"

"I can try. No guarantees. They may have been sold."

"They can't sell them without your permission."

"Honestly, I have no clue how pawn shops work. I never thought I would set foot in one."

"But can I be your husband again? I still love you. I was wrong and stupid."

I was overjoyed. "Yes, but there are some things we will need to talk about," I said calmly, still not fully awake and still not fully believing that this wasn't a dream.

"I know. I screwed up."

Oh yeah, you screwed up. I stood before God and all of our friends and made vows to you. If I wasn't such a low-self-esteem schmuck, I would hang up on you.

"We can fix this," he continued. "I'm going to leave my show and get back home in the next few days. I'll call you."

"Just not at 5 a.m., please."

Daniel had taken a summer job as a singer-dancer at a theme park in what was referred to as the Redneck Riviera—a tourist area between Georgia and Florida. I had my doubts he would actually walk away from a paid performing gig. The next day, Daniel called me at work and asked for money for airfare to get home to me as soon as possible. I asked about his plans for getting his car home, and he shrugged off the question. I booked a flight for him.

On the day he was supposed to fly home, Daniel called me at my new job.

"Good morning, Powell Creative. This is Lewis."

"Um, hi. This is Daniel. Do you have a minute?"

"I'm at work, but yeah, I can talk for a few. Your flight's this afternoon, don't forget."

"Um, well, that's why I'm calling."

OK, crap, here we go. "You don't have a way to get to the airport, right?"

"No, it's not that. I'm not coming home to Nashville. At least not right now and not to you. I've given it more thought, and I can't be your husband. I'm sorry."

With that, the phone clicked, and the dial tone burned my eardrum as my heart burst into a firestorm, consuming every hope, every positive thought, every dream, every wish, every desire.

I can't believe I fell for his bullshit again.

I couldn't breathe but tried to remain calm and keep working. Impossible. I had to take the rest of the day off. I figured I would go re-pawn the rings. But I just drove blindly around town, smoking three packs and crying uncontrollably.

But this time around, the sadness was quickly replaced with a rage of anger.

I should have known. I fell for it. I'm the idiot.

The domino formation began its chain reaction.

One week after Daniel called off the reunion, I was fired from the design firm. The female partner sat me down in her office and said my work wasn't "what they wanted," and I was told to pack my belongings and leave immediately. Another panic attack. Now I was single *and* unemployed. Perfect.

Through a contact at a printing shop, I was referred to a direct-mail marketing company that needed a graphic designer. With a much-needed stroke of luck, I was hired within three days, making more money than at the boutique firm. Good riddance.

Emboldened with a burst of renewed confidence, I traded in my paid-off Toyota truck and bought a black Mitsubishi Eclipse that I grew to hate within minutes of driving it off the lot. The doors were long and heavy and slammed against my left shin as I tried to exit the car, slipping on the over-polished leather seats.

I embarked on a total kitchen remodel costing $16,000.

I traded in the Eclipse, lost more money, and bought a black Toyota king-cab truck.

Next, I figured a dog would be a good thing for me and could be the remedy for my loneliness. Jamey and Laura had a black pug, so on Daniel's birthday—total coincidence—I fell in love with a black pug puppy at a breeder's place halfway to Memphis. Buzz, the tiny black pug who tugged at my shoelaces to pick him, came home with me. But I was unprepared for raising a puppy and nearly gave him away.

I continued to spin out of control until Jamey approached me and asked if I would join him in starting his own theater.

In October 2000, the Boiler Room Theatre (BRT) was born, opening its doors on March 16, 2001. Working as a managing director, actor, occasional show director, set designer, properties master, and chief toilet scrubber, I threw my heart, soul, and savings into the little 120-seat professional theater, and I eventually threw all remaining caution to the wind and left the direct-mail firm. Soon, I was working 100-hour weeks, living the dream.

Years later, Jamey told me he not only pulled me in as his theater partner for my marketing and creative expertise, but as a lifeline to save me from the pit of self-destruction into which I was rapidly sinking. The Boiler Room had saved my life, he said.

31

The Rabbit Hole Opens
NASHVILLE: 2002–2004

"What time are you available? Does now work?" I asked StraightGuy4Fun.

"Well, I'm not sure yet."

"Your profile said you were looking for 'now.'"

"I have to wait and see when my wife will be home."

"Oh—you're married. That's—"

"Hot, huh? A real, straight guy with a big, straight cock."

"Hot. So, what's your name?"

"I don't do names."

"Well, I don't do married guys. My moral compass may be broken but not so much that I'm willing to help you cheat on your wife."

"Fuck you, asshole."

~StraightGuy4Fun has left the chat~

* * *

Between my 100-hour work weeks at the Boiler Room Theatre and constant disappointment with trying to meet someone decent online, I opted for meeting those who were not decent. Especially since no nice, professional guy wanted me due to my baggage, work hours, broken-down car (I surrendered the truck in bankruptcy), and lack of expendable income.

So fine, I'll take the low road, I thought. *I've heard Hell is more fun anyway.*

In the year 2000, the Internet was an amazing digital frontier for porn and potential hook-ups. Hence, I began to master the art of the "trick." For years, I had sworn off the meaningless, mindless one-nighters in search of nobler connections. Now, it became a convenient way to get fifteen minutes of false validation. And usually it only took a couple of hours online to make the necessary arrangements. OK, maybe three hours on a slow night with a spotty dial-up connection. In short, it was a lot of prep for a seven-to-ten-minute thing, and it was rarely worth the time. It didn't take long before the occasional hook-up became a daily need to receive a false stroking of my fragile ego. Although I didn't yet know the term, I had become a sex addict.

Being the master of my own schedule and running the theater, I was able to carve out plenty of opportunities, at all hours of the day and night, to seek these selfish pleasures. A mid-morning drop-by at some unknown guy's house for a quick session. A lunchtime tryst with a straight married man in a restroom at the nearby mall or at the married man's house if the wife wasn't expected home. A midnight rendezvous with a confused young guy in the back of the theater. I'm ashamed of having no shame.

Already experienced with bathhouses and adult bookstores, I quickly discovered upon moving to Nashville that bathhouses and sex clubs were non-existent in the sexually-repressed South. But there was one place to haunt: a twenty-four-hour adult bookstore and video arcade just off of "Truckers' Curve," that is, where I-65 and I-40 dangerously intersect and merge. More thrilling than the mad dash across four, fast-moving lanes of traffic just to stay on one's particular freeway was the mad dash *off* the freeway, beating the red light at the underpass, then doing California stops at every stop sign *en route* to the bookstore. I'm not even sure it had a name, just a neon sign that flashed "Adult Books – 24 Hours," a fiendish beacon that cast a toxic green glow across the Cumberland River.

For the required minimum purchase of five bucks' worth of tokens, men of all shapes, sizes, and walks of life bought admission to the dimly lit, seedy, and sticky block of video booths. Signs clearly warned that loitering was forbidden, but if you played your cards right, ducking in and out of vacant booths and avoiding the security cameras, you could make a pocketful of tokens last all night. Or at least long enough to find someone interesting and interested in anonymous company.

In my early days of the nightly stop-off at the Bookstore (after all, it *was* on my way home), there were "glory holes" cut into the plywood partitions separating the private booths. Even better, in those days, the doors had locks, so a lot of nameless, faceless pleasure could be had from the comfort of your private, locked cubicle. A few Boiler Room actors also frequented the Bookstore. If we saw each other, it was silently understood that we would keep walking past each other, with maybe a "sup?" nod, but definitely no theater shop-talk in the hallways. Nothing killed a late-night quest for sex faster than a couple of queens in the hall discussing the latest Broadway show.

Later, the holes were covered with sheet metal, and the locks were removed, supposedly to appease the Nashville Police. But eventually, the Bookstore reverted to its sleazier version, and back-room business was once again booming.

I was never much of a drinker (except when nursing a broken heart) and had never tried any drugs, not even marijuana. But years prior, a flight attendant in Phoenix introduced me to a seemingly harmless drug. And so, holed up in my private booth, I would inhale generous hits of poppers, a slang term for the chemical class of alkyl nitrates, a liquid that came in an innocuous little brown bottle that took up residence in my jeans and jacket pockets. There was also a bottle in the glove box, one in my work bag, a bottle by the bed (when it wasn't buried under a pile of seventy-five gay porn magazines), and, as the sexual adventures grew wilder, bottles in the basement near the leather sling I had somehow managed to install myself.

Eventually, the Bookstore became tedious, and the online hook-ups mined from trolling gay.com seemed tame. Thanks to Mitchell, I had a weakness for dominant guys, especially those who used ropes and handcuffs. It's probably a good thing that I cut my teeth on S&M (sadomasochism) in a mild city like Nashville rather than jumping in head first in a larger, seedier market such as Los Angeles. Often, I was the instigator, creating and even "directing" the sadomasochistic scene to my particular fantasy *du jour*. This is what is known in gay circles as a "pushy bottom." Not a skill that anyone would list under "special skills" on their performance resume, unless, I suppose, they were auditioning for a porn film, and even then, it's probably not a marketable skill.

Because most of the local guys were also pushy bottoms (regardless of what their online profile stated), there was never any real danger, and the hook-ups left me feeling empty and unfulfilled. I did theater for a living, so acting out sex scenes wasn't too much of a thrill. Not that a hook-up ever resulted in any kind of fulfillment. Ten times out of ten, it left me feeling dirtier, sleazier, and emptier than before.

There's another reason that particular stretch of intersecting freeways in Nashville is called Truckers' Curve. Nashville is a major trucking route in and out of the South. And with trucks came truckers. Truckers were rougher than business-class corporate dudes who stayed at nice hotels. Truckers stayed at sleazy, fleabag motels along noisy interstates where a TV could be turned up loud to mask other sounds. Plus, there were no curious bellhops. And, truckers were able to carry some interesting bondage gear and sex toys because nothing had to pass through airport security metal detectors.

My "sexploration" meant living out fantasies that were increasingly risky. One of my hook-ups provided a too-real taste of danger. The guy was in from out of town, I guess, and was staying at the Comfort Inn on White Bridge Road in West Nashville. The bit of scripting I had supplied during our online conversation was ignored, as were my pre-set limits.

I knocked at his motel room door. "It's open," said the voice.

I pushed the door open and was quickly pulled inside. A pillowcase was placed over my head and secured with what felt like a belt. I was kicked over to the bed where I was handcuffed.

"Now you listen up, fucker," he said, as he hit me in the right ear with an object. Through the thin, white fabric I saw the outline of a pistol. I was having trouble breathing, but instead of loosening the belt, he took a knife and cut a hole over my mouth. I gasped for air, but the hole was filled with the barrel of the gun. "What's that you say, fucker?"

I started to panic and yelled as loudly as possible and must have made enough noise for him to be concerned. The gun slipped out of my mouth.

"What the fuck is your problem?"

"I can't breath!"

"Tough shit. Soon you won't be breathing at all."

I wailed as loud as I could, thankful for a powerful voice from years of singing. "Wait! Please…"

He had a tight hold on the belt, as he ripped the mouth hole further open. "What the fuck do you want? You have three seconds to make your case."

"I told the front desk clerk I was coming to your room and to come up in fifteen minutes," I lied.

He removed the belt around my neck and unlocked the handcuffs that had been cutting into my wrists. "Get the fuck out," he yelled, as pushed me toward the door, pillowcase still on my head. "Take that off after you're in the hallway. Any sooner, and I pull the trigger."

I had managed to escape what may or may not have been real danger. Chances are it was all a charade for the man's pleasure. I ran to my car and tried to compose myself enough to drive home.

The hook-up scared me so badly that I took a break from the S&M fantasies and went back to regular, old dating. But a part of me, deep down, held onto the thrill of the endorphin-releasing and intoxicating rush of the scene.

32

Go Back West, Middle-Aged Man
NASHVILLE: 2005-2006

"This lobby and your set design are just amazing," said the BRT season ticket holder. "I'm always blown away with your work. Why aren't you working for Disney?"

The guest was referring to my elaborate Haunted Lobby, complete with sound and visuals—thunder and lightning, a self-built animatronic talking head (a la Madame Leota at Disneyland), Pepper's ghost effects, and a self-rocking rocking chair.

I paused for a moment as I scooped his box of popcorn at the Boiler Room's concessions counter. "I don't know. I've thought about it a lot, but I doubt they would ever hire me."

"Seriously? I bet Disney could use someone with your design expertise and attention to detail. I always feel like I'm at Disneyland every time I come here."

A seed was planted. Or more aptly, an old seed was fertilized. Truth is, I had long been inspired by Walt Disney, and the Boiler Room brand reflected such.

I started to research jobs at Disney and soon discovered what a formidable and monumental task it was to get in with the company.

I also learned that for any decent position (i.e. pays a living wage) at Disney, applicants were required to have at least a bachelor's degree, except as a Jungle Cruiser Skipper or Haunted Mansion attraction host. Then, I learned those positions are the most coveted roles in the kingdom, that everyone wanted to be one, and that those positions were nearly impossible to secure, short of an Old Testament-style miracle.

Well, crap. And there the dream stops.

What an idiot I'd been. I should have stayed with pursuing my degree as I had in Phoenix, but at the one-course-per-semester rate that I could afford, it would have literally taken the rest of my life to finish.

Then, God knocked again. "See Me, find Me, come to Me," said the still, small voice.

The next night, as I was driving a detour route home from the theater, a light bulb of erratically blinking hope beckoned me from a billboard for Trevecca Nazarene University's degree completion program. "Finish your bachelor's degree in as little as thirteen months," the billboard in West Nashville screamed. I had some sense of the meaning of Nazarene, and upon further investigation, I learned that the school's curriculum was Christ-centered and biblically based.

Of course, there would be a catch; it's the old church crap again.

Upon reviewing the program information packet, I panicked. There were two required courses in Bible study. I soaked it in and allowed my mind to calm a bit. It's basically like literature classes, and I always excelled at those. *At least they don't require any algebra, just a course in statistics. I can do this.*

In May 2004, I began the grueling thirteen-month program that would yield an actual bachelor's degree. The program required about twenty hours of class and study time per week. I added that to my work docket at BRT, and my work weeks ratcheted up to 120 hours. I amped up my set designs, imagining each to be a Disneyland project that required the utmost attention to creative nuance. All the while, I was documenting every detail of every design for some sort of eventual pitch to the Mouse.

The degree completion program was exhausting, and after a few months into it, I was tempted to bail. But I had been too much of a quitter in too many pursuits, and this time, I mustered the renewed determination to slog through. The Bible study courses were as difficult as Russian lit with all the names and genealogies. Further, the instructor freely espoused his opinions, his doctrine, particularly that all gays are going to Hell. It was exactly what I didn't need to have crammed down my throat. This theme is evergreen among conservative, "Bible-thumping" Christians: "the gays" are the ones going to Hell. It only drove a bigger wedge between God and me.

Hearing the Gospel again during the Trevecca coursework, I had an intellectual understanding of Christ's redemptive work on the cross and how Jesus' death covers the sins of all sinners who accept the Lord. But apparently, the Trevecca faculty felt that gay people were exempt from His forgiveness. The struggle between being gay and being Christian began to make more sense. I imagined, just as I had since childhood, that Heaven was a boring place with one perpetual church service; the thought of Hell filled with fellow gay people seemed far more appealing.

* * *

In February 2006, I awoke one morning at 4:44 with a vision of the self-marketing package I needed to create to get hired by Disney. I felt an angelic presence, as I scribbled and sketched on a bedside notepad. Although my belief system was all over the map, I knew that this idea was from God. The vision showed me packaging the promo kit inside vintage Disney lunchboxes with a clever punchline. Essentially, each recipient of the package got a pretty awesome gift just by opening the shipping box. And each box contained a DVD with a seven-minute self-promotional film I wrote and produced in a fun, retro style, along with other themed goodies.

Prior to sending my promo boxes and at the suggestion of my best psychic friend, I began taking nightly salt baths to clear negative energy from my being.

I prayed constantly to the God I still didn't know.

I lit candles.

I burned sage and stared at the burning sticks without a clue what to do next.

I "Fenged" the "Shui" out of my house.

I learned enough rudimentary witchcraft to set up a beginner's spell circle in my basement. I bought spells online and witchy *accoutrements* at the local occult bookstore and attempted to cast them while prancing around naked, burning stinky incense that nearly caught the house on fire and chanting seemingly nonsensical words like a raving lunatic. If anyone had looked through one of the basement windows—with the apprentice witch set-up on one side and the leather sling on the other—they certainly would have thought I had lost it. And perhaps I had.

But my intentions were good. Always good. Just like those paver stones on that proverbial road to Hell. I just wanted a new life away from the memories of Daniel and the increasingly stressful and unhealthy environment at the theater.

One of the Witchcraft 101 books instructed that the novice witch has to be spot-on specific, incredibly detailed in his or her intentions when manifesting via spells. So, I was. My list of wants could have been a letter to Santa. I wanted a great, creative job at Disney that would allow me to work directly with Disneyland; a nice-looking, caring partner; a cozy little storybook cottage with diamond-paned windows and hardwood floors and a fenced-in yard for Buzz. And to be close to work. Oh, and a Porsche. Well, the book *did* say to be specific.

In the middle of May, with extra prayers, salt, and chanting for good measure, I shipped twenty-five of my lunchbox kits to key folks at Walt Disney Imagineering. All in, it was a $5,000 investment in a possible new future. Contrary to the teachings of *The Secret*, I never imagined receiving a single response.

On the contrary, I received overwhelming response, including a call from the senior assistant to a vice president (who was already well-known for the *Toy Story* and *Cars* films), who scheduled a full day of "meet-and-greets" with key decision makers.

The interviews went remarkably well. Each interviewer offered unspoken cues, as well as blatant rhetoric that there was, indeed, a promising future for me at Disney. But there were no job offers, just a vague array of possible work opportunities, coupled, of course, with the admonition that I needed to live *there* in order to be seriously considered. To be available when the work dictates. And since most

Imagineers start as consultants and contractors, being local and available were essential. I was told that had I been living there at the time of the interviews, they could have brought me on right away as a consultant. That same week.

I could barely contain myself on the flight home. "The spells and prayers and salt baths and candles worked!" I told myself. *Yeah, right.*

I returned to Nashville excited and scared. It took every ounce of guts to put my plan in motion. As I broke the news to my partners at the theater and to friends, I was met with mixed reactions. Some were genuinely happy for me going off to chase my next dream. Others were vocally skeptical, warning me that I was headed into shark-infested waters. And some were jealous of my opportunity and attempted to undermine my shaky confidence.

Ewan was a member of the jealous group. We had dated on and off since 2002; it was now 2006. He was Scottish by birth, somewhat worldly, and exotic in that certain way American boys are not. But Ewan was patently weird, and his stories of massive family wealth and multiple college degrees never quite lined up. I managed to avoid contact with him for a couple of years, but then, on a break from packing my stuff, I bumped into him online. I told him of my plans, and he seemed supportive. He said he wished I wouldn't leave Nashville but wanted to get together for one last "shag."

"You know, Lewis, I'm really going to miss you."

"We haven't gone out in more than two years. Why now? Why the sudden interest in me again? Last time we were together you said you could never be with someone who drove an old beater car like I have."

"I've changed. I'd like to be your husband."

Well, *that* was out of left field. It smacked of the 5 a.m. Daniel call a few years prior. Nope. Not falling for that again.

"Well, your timing sucks, for one. And plus, that's what I wanted when we were first together. But now—now is not the time. I have this big chance—OK, a long shot—to fulfill a lifelong dream of working for Disney. I can't stay here."

"I understand. But I want to make love to you one last time."

Soon, we were back in his feminine canopy bed doing the nasty. I usually avoided anything that wasn't strictly oral, and when I veered, I was typically the vigilant and responsible one, suiting up my suitors in latex. That night, Ewan said he had it taken care of. But something felt wrong.

"Hey! I thought we were being safe."

"We were. We are. I guess, perhaps, the prophylactic broke. But you know, I'm negative, so not a big deal. Anyway, it felt so good, didn't it? I wanted to share it with you one last time."

"Yeah, I guess you're right." I had been tested prior to the incident and was confident of my clean status and had no reason to believe Ewan was any different.

I returned home and resumed my packing, chiding myself for new fantasies of retiring with him to the Highlands and wondering if I could get an all-cotton kilt.

* * *

Thanks to the remodeling work I had done on my East Nashville house, it sold quickly. In fact, it never even went on the market; two friends from BRT made an immediate offer.

All of my possessions had already been loaded onto a fly-by-night trucking company's semi by three Russian guys who spoke little English. I honestly didn't know if I would see my things again. I slept my last night in the Sunnymeade house on a blanket on the bare, hardwood floor in the front bedroom that had always been my home office.

I awoke on July 10 ready to finish packing the 1999 red Ford Escort that a theater friend had generously gifted me. But as I tried to get up from the floor, my head felt like it was nailed to the hardwood. I didn't feel right. Hot eyes. Scratchy throat. Sick to my stomach.

Must be nerves. And just my luck, I would be sick for the 2000-mile drive to my new place in Pasadena.

But I had been pushing myself hard getting ready to leave—getting little sleep and smoking two packs a day.

Finally, I was headed west to California, eyes full of well-wished-upon stars and ears full of Disney music loaded in the Escort's CD player. The car was stuffed to the gills with my most treasured possessions, photos, yearbooks, those same Annette records, as well as my computer gear—just the irreplaceable items and the stuff I needed to work until the movers delivered my 8,000-pound load of crap. Buzz was crammed into the front passenger seat and, as always, was an extremely well-behaved canine traveler.

It was a grueling drive, as are most cross-country car trips. But halfway through the first day, my head started to throb—not my usual migraine pain—and I was so nauseated I couldn't even smoke. I stopped for 7UP and took my temperature at a rest stop: 101 degrees.

OK, I'm actually sick. Damn it.

Still, I forged ahead. I made it to a motel somewhere in Oklahoma, hauled in all the computer gear, luggage, and dog then collapsed on the bed.

On July 11, I awoke in the middle of the night drenched in sweat. Another thermometer reading revealed a 104-degree fever. There was no way I could drive further until the fever broke. So, for the next thirty-six hours, I was holed up in a hellhole of a trucker motel off Interstate 40. I called a nurse friend, and he supported my decision to stay put. This wasn't the way the dream was supposed to go.

The next morning, my temperature was down to 100 degrees. The illness spooked me, and I called my psychic friend, Gina, who assured me it was only a bumpy start due to mixed energies. Although I was weak, I got back on the road. Six hours into the day's driving, my temperature spiked to 102 degrees. Still, I pressed on.

By July 14, I made it to Pasadena and the little one-bedroom bungalow I would call home for the first four months. The moving company experienced a major delay, and as such, I had to wait three weeks until I had a bed. I made a palette on the bedroom floor out of two blankets from the Glendale Wal-Mart and there I laid, sick as a dog. I tried calling the Disney contacts who had interviewed me, but no one was responding.

Perfect.

I left the theater, sold my house, and although I made a $60,000 profit and had enough money in the bank to easily carry me over until I could be hired by Disney or some other company, I laid shivering, sweating, and panicking over my latest catastrophic life decision. Like arriving in both Phoenix and Nashville unemployed and without a local friend to my name, this time was far worse as I was horribly ill and couldn't shake whatever had a firm hold of me. I found a doctor in nearby Altadena, and he had no clue why I was so sick. He pumped me full of antibiotics, which didn't make a dent.

It took more than three weeks for my stuff to arrive via "Moose and Squirrel" Van Lines. As each damaged box came off the truck and was piled in the tiny front yard of the bungalow, it was a sad reminder of how much I had actually accumulated and felt necessary to bring to California, a good portion of which arrived broken.

Most days before my bed arrived, I just laid on an air mattress, fever relentlessly burning, listening to almost nightly gunshots in the alley. I could only keep down the number-seven combo (quesadilla and a taco) from Taco Bell. An occasional mint served as the balance of my diet. I had apparently moved to Hell. But the bungalow had powerful air conditioning, and I turned it to the highest setting to drown out the noise from my latest act of brilliance.

Eventually, the illness passed (HIV conversion illness I would later learn) and by August 25, I was working as a consultant art director for Disney Entertainment at Disneyland itself. It was a small miracle that I landed that role (God bless you, Mr. Dave Earick) and was able to parlay my first major design project into being hired as a salaried production manager. I got the job and even moved to Anaheim where I rented a house with diamond-paned windows. All that remained was to make friends, buy the Porsche, and find that ever-elusive life partner I so desperately desired.

I had crushes on several of the guys around me: a young producer who resembled Jim Carrey; a show director who was perfectly tanned, gorgeous, and way out of my league; an openly gay, fellow production manager.

The condemning voice in my head weighed in. *"Not one of these guys would be interested in you. Not even as a friend. You don't belong here. All of these people here are highly successful. They're talented. They're the best in their field. They belong here; they've earned it. You— you, Lewis—you don't belong here. It was a fluke. You're the same pathetic loser you've always been. Maybe you should just leave. Do California a favor, and go bang your head until it bleeds. Then leave."*

Not good enough. Not attractive enough. Not enough talent. It was the mantra of my life, the anti-motivational tape loop that ran day and night in my brain. But who exactly was the anti-motivational speaker? Dennis? Ruben? Dr. Fruitcake? Every guy from every relationship I'd ruined? An amalgamation of all of them, perhaps? It made getting through the day damn hard. This was the feeling of worthlessness that always drove me to overachieve, to work harder than anyone around me. Imagine for a moment living with that kind of little voice talking down to you your entire life. It's beyond significant. It changes a person for the worst.

The voice continued. *"You're not good enough. You'll always be alone. You'll never have any friends. You shouldn't be here. Why do you even bother getting out of bed? Maybe you should just lie down and die. No one will care, and maybe they'll find you in three weeks stinking up the place. Pathetic fucking loser."*

The voice was relentless.

33

Further Down the Rabbit Hole
LONG BEACH: 2007

In 1986, I published a GWM (gay white male) seeking GWM ad in the personals section of Denver's weekly arts paper *Westword*. It was clever. Perhaps a bit too clever. While it did receive the dubious honor of being named "Romance Bestseller of the Week," it yielded no promising responses whatsoever. Still, it was creative, if not smacking a bit of the plot from a Gordon Merrick novel.

◆ ◆ ◆

LEADING MAN

Their hands were intertwined as they strolled down the white sands of their Greek island hideaway. "I'm so glad you answered my *Westword* ad. I knew we'd find each other..." Needed: leading man to star opposite GWM, 22, in permanent romance. Like co-star, should be masculine, attractive, successful, and in shape. Contact MD at Romance Box 925. Let's write our own happy ending.

◆ ◆ ◆

It was a heartfelt attempt but full of shit. I was hardly successful or in shape (other than height-weight proportional) at that time. I wasn't twenty-two either; I was twenty. Funny how one adds years to their online age when he's young but subtracts as he gets older.

Years later in Nashville, I created an online ad with an equally sugary diatribe about "wanting what I deserve." I copied the Yahoo profile of a good-looking, muscular attorney in Kansas City who owned a small mansion and proclaimed that he had worked hard for everything he ever wanted and had obtained it all—everything except the partner. And by God, he felt he deserved one. Rather, he was owed one.

I could relate!

I not only had the audacity to lift the better part of his ad and tailor it to myself, but I also listed it on no fewer than ten dating sites. But according to the Nashville Church members I encountered every time I went to Kroger, what I really deserved was Hell and eternal damnation. But at the time, I identified with the nebulous descriptor "spiritual." Essentially, I was just a self-made amalgam of squishy spiritualism that threw in a little of everything for good measure. And I believed that I was, at my core, basically a good person and was therefore also owed a life partner. Didn't God and/or the Universe owe me that?

Right.

Turns out the Bible states nothing about special little Lewis deserving a partner so he could feel complete and validated.

I tried this same ad in Los Angeles but was admonished and reminded that I was in the hook-up capital of the world, and no one there wanted an old-fashioned, monogamous relationship. Gay guys in L.A. wanted open relationships, not to be yoked to the same dude.

As I realized that my idea of a monogamous gay relationship was as antiquated as slavery in the South, it didn't take long to start spinning this new way of thinking into more dangerous pursuits.

And so, I tumbled further down the rabbit hole.

With the tutelage of some older guys dabbling in sadomasochism, I was shown that I *could* "belong to," that is, be permanently "owned" by one guy, by one master. I didn't know what that would entail, but I was intrigued. The little negotiator inside my head said, *"Keep talking, keep talking."*

My research revealed that one master could choose to have several slaves, each for a different need. He, being the master, had all the control, and I, being one of his slaves, would have no control but *would* have the privilege of belonging to someone and the joy of feeling the satisfaction of fulfilling my life's purpose. Crap, is this what Dr. Fruitcake meant so many years ago?

Admittedly, it was a truly twisted way of thinking. But that same little voice told me that I was in uncharted territory where my misguided ideas of a gay relationship simply didn't fit. If I wanted male companionship, it would have to be on L.A.'s terms. (Some of this has since changed with the advent of legal gay marriage.)

This particular relationship model was a good fit with my life-long lack of self-esteem. Through online conversations with "dominants," I learned that I had these feelings of low self-worth because I was born to be a slave with the sole purpose of providing pleasure and service to one master. The lie sounded good, as lies from the enemy always do. And it seemed to make sense in my head.

I met Rick and Rob on Gay.com in February 2007. They lived in Long Beach, were into kinky sex, and were both dominant masters.

Being unequally yoked, they were looking for a second part-time slave to cater to their household and sexual needs.

(I'll mention here that in S&M, the master typically requires in written communication to have his title, "Master," spelled with a capital "M," and any subsequent pronouns, such as "He" or "His," to also be capitalized. The slave is always referred to with lowercase letters and only as "it." I will not be using this protocol in this book unless it fits within standard grammatical conventions.)

"OK, slave lewis. Sir Rob and Sir Rick are willing to give you a one-month trial. If you please us, you may be considered for a part-time slave position," said Sir Rick.

"So, what do I—"

"It will always wait for permission to speak. You may speak."

"So, what do I—"

"Uh uh uh, slave. It will always address the Masters as 'Sir.'"

Good grief. This was like a child's game of Simon Says.

"Sir, what do I—"

"Uh! Slave will always refer to itself as 'it.'"

At that point, I was ready to bail but stayed to see it through.

"Sir! What is expected of it as your trial slave, Sir!" I tried the military approach, complete with a salute, and was met with a disapproving head shake.

"Slave will not mock the Master/slave dynamic. First, slave will improve its body. It is badly out of shape and will be expected to work out daily and report daily via email to Sir Rick. Body fat will not be tolerated by Sir Rick."

Now he was referring to himself in third person. This was just plain stupid.

"Slave will be shaved from the neck down and will maintain a hairless body itself."

"And finally, slave will be locked in a chastity device to prevent unauthorized touching of its worthless penis."

The first item, improving my body, was probably the worst requirement. I've always despised working out because I never achieve any results.

The second requirement wasn't the traumatic experience that the guys probably intended. I've never had much body hair, so it was no big deal.

The last item, the chastity stipulation, was intriguing and strangely erotic. I was to have my genitalia locked in a plastic device to prevent me from pleasuring myself. The device was a commercially available little novelty made of molded plastic that scrunched one's penis into a short tube, and with the aid of some other plastic pieces and a padlock, semi-effectively kept a novice slave's hands off his master's "property." It appealed to my increasingly kinky side and kept me perpetually aroused, at least within the confines of the model CB-2000. The biggest challenge was keeping the device hidden under dress pants at work. That and peeing. (Ultimately, the plastic device couldn't withstand the constant stress of nighttime erections, and as such, I snapped the cage in half.)

The initial visits with the couple were lame. I would strip naked at the door, then sit on the floor as we casually chatted about work while waiting for a pizza. It was stupid.

One month into the trial run, both Rick and Rob were ready to take things to the next level. Part of that was the requirement to be tested for HIV every three months. Before I could see them again, I had to deliver proof positive of being HIV negative.

On Sundays, an HIV testing mobile (actually just a tricked-out RV) would park in front of the Long Beach location of the Out of the Closet thrift store on Pacific Coast Highway. Testing was anonymous, simple, and yielded results within twenty minutes. A simple mouth swab was performed, and I killed time inside the store looking at used combat boots. When time was up, I returned to the folding table by the RV, ready to get my negative status. If my sixteen-character identification number was highlighted in green, I was free to go. If I had a pretty pink triangle next to my number, I had to be seen inside the van by a nurse. I was taken to a private consultation room separated from the testing area by a pink plastic shower curtain hanging from three pink plastic hooks.

And there, I received the news: I was HIV positive.

My crappy life sort of flashed before my eyes, so to speak. The warnings from Darrell, the stupid Ayds diet pill commercials I laughed at in high school ("Why take diet pills when you can enjoy Ayds?"), the close call with Dexter, the AIDS quilt, being mean to the other Daryl, all the late-night trysts at adult bookstores, and visits to any remaining bathhouses.

"There's no way I'm positive," I said vehemently to the African-American male nurse.

"No need to cop an attitude, girl. Being positive is what you make it."

Fantastic. I was being seen by the black Norman Vincent Peale of Long Beach.

"I'm not a girl. I mean, I can't be positive. I never have butt sex. Only ever oral, and you can't get HIV from that."

"Oh, yes you can, honey. And it's called anal sex, sweetie."

"I know that. I was trying to be funny, I guess."

"AIDS is not a laughing matter, girl. Now make a fist. The blood draw will confirm the oral swab results."

"Still not a girl. And I don't want to confirm; I want to deny and disprove the result. Or prove that it was a glitch."

"Honey, I don't do glitches, just bitches." With that, he laughed at his own joke. "The oral-swab test is accurate something like ninety percent of the time."

Wonderful. My life is at stake, and all this particular queen can offer is "something like" statistics.

With the blood draw complete, I ripped open the shower curtain and started to bolt.

"Take a brochure, girl."

Not knowing who to call, I called Rick, told him of the preliminary result, and was promptly informed that he and Rob were no longer interested in me being their part-time slave. I could stop by for the chastity padlock key on my way home. I explained it wouldn't be necessary. They said I could keep the broken device but wanted fifty bucks for their trouble.

That was March 13, 2007.

Two weeks later, on my birthday—March 28—I received the call that confirmed the oral swab. My fate was sealed.

I'm officially damaged goods.

I doubted that anyone would want to be with me now, this broken soul, this human equivalent of a '78 Plymouth Duster in need of a new transmission trying to sputter its way onto a freeway of sleek, sexy cars. But you know, I felt this coming for years. Hadn't some psychic predicted this fate? I had often allowed my mind to play out the scenario of getting AIDS and how I would become super-religious on my deathbed, finally embracing the Bible and becoming a real Christian.

But I wasn't feeling that. Rather, I was just pissed at myself for becoming infected. I had always banked on the statistically low transmission rates via oral play. I wondered which Nashville bookstore trick had passed it to me through a hole in a video booth.

It wasn't until a couple of years later, when I ran into Scottish Ewan on Twitter, that I got my answer. His profile proudly proclaimed being HIV positive and had been since 2004. I called him on it, and he claimed we'd never dated. I reminded him that we slept together in 2006. Then he said he didn't know me before blocking me. At least I identified the probable source.

Still, I wasn't scared of dying as much as I was of being alone, of slipping into the great eternal unknown without a partner.

But there was something else: a surreal sense of relief. Now that the proverbial elephant in the room had made its large presence undeniably known, I figured I could be an adult, deal with it, treat it, and move on. Maybe it wasn't the end of the world.

Part Three

DEMONS APPROACH

34

Date with the Devil
ANAHEIM HILLS: 2008

After my diagnosis, I basically thumbed my nose at life and started to live recklessly. It was almost a sense of relief, a sick kind of license to pursue previously forbidden pleasures since AIDS appeared and effectively "ruined" unprotected sex. You see, the subset of my generation—those of us still in junior and senior high school when AIDS first emerged—got swept away, wrapped in latex from the backroom, free-for-all, Devil-may-care recreational sex our older counterparts had enjoyed so thoroughly. We were educated that the best way to not get AIDS was to not have sex; hand-holding and giving back rubs were preferable. Try getting that through the thick skull of a horny 18-year-old.

I wasn't even fully sure what being positive really meant. During one hookup at a sex club early after my diagnosis, the nameless top in the tiny cubicle asked in a gruff whisper, "Are you clean?"

"Of course," I replied. "I showered before I got here."

"Not what I meant, dude. I mean do you like it wrapped or bare?"

Bare. The word hung in the air. I hesitated, trying to formulate the correct answer. He answered for me, for both of us.

"Well, I only do bare. You cool with that?"

Yeah, I was cool with that. I mean, it was the ultimate forbidden, taboo pleasure. I was cool with anything.

* * *

When I tell my story about my introduction to the hard stuff, the general assumption is that Hollywood was to blame. I even started to believe that for a time. That is, until I rewound the warbled VHS tape inside my scrambled head and remembered that it happened in an upscale neighborhood in Orange County.

Honestly, I have no idea what I was thinking the night it happened. It was a typical Friday night for me: bored, lonely, and horny—a dangerous combination. With no prospects on the horizon in the dating realm, I wandered over to Craigslist to the now-defunct Men Seeking Men section of the personals. Living in Orange County, I figured that any trouble I could get myself into would be mild on the kinky-fun scale. It was, after all, Orange County. And all that nasty stuff happened about twenty-eight miles north via the Santa Ana and Hollywood freeways.

I was about one year or so into my submissive phase, seeking out dominant guys to engage in some seemingly harmless sexual role play. I was never much of a drinker; I didn't need alcohol for my overly creative mind to devise explicit and often elaborate scenarios. Fueled by cigarettes, Bud Light, and poppers, my fantasy life soared and swirled as my fingers flew across the keyboard seeking out the perfect Friday night fun.

A guy around my age in Fullerton who was a newbie? No

thanks. I'd just spend our short time together directing the scene.

A guy in his late 50s whose wife was out of town for the week-end? As much as I was attracted to straight guys, I still had no desire to help anyone cheat on his spouse.

Then, a listing that showed great promise. I won't attempt to recreate the ad's content. Suffice it to say, the guy fit the bill.

As agreed in our email exchanges, I packed a large gym bag full of brand-new bondage gear and adult toys, plus a fresh bottle of Pig Sweat—one of the stronger brands of inhalers—I'd bought at The Crypt in Long Beach. (On a side note, when your bank statements start showing purchases at places called "The Crypt," "The Pleasure Chest," or "Mister S Leather," you might want to take a closer look at your lifestyle.) And, as instructed, I stopped at a liquor store to buy the guy a bottle of vodka.

Robert lived in a large, expensive home in Anaheim Hills, overlooking an expanse of east Orange County. He said he owned a car dealership, so that explained the high-end abode. He ushered me to his bedroom, and we put one of my porn flicks in his DVD player. We both stripped down and had a cigarette while Robert knocked back a few shots of the vodka. As instructed, I laid out the contents of my gym bag for inspection.

The sexual play began as it typically does between men. But Robert didn't seem too interested and was constantly checking his phone, texting with someone who had captured his attention more than me. The fantasy scene in my head was already disintegrating, so I started to gather some of my things, deciding to salvage the night while it was still early enough to go to Hollywood.

Abruptly, Robert stopped texting and apologized for being

distracted. He explained he was chatting with one of his clients. Although it was going on 11 p.m., I figured he was wrapping up a used-car sale.

"You want to get high?" he asked.

"Um, no. No, thanks. I don't smoke pot," I answered.

"It's not pot."

"What is it?"

"It's Tina."

"As in Tina Turner? I've always liked her music," I blathered. The joke was lost on my host. "No, I don't know. I've never tried the hard stuff. I better not."

"Suit yourself," he said as he flicked a lighter and held it under a small, clear glass pipe. He took a drag from the pipe and exhaled a sweet-smelling cloud of white smoke. Whatever was in the pipe made things spring to life below his waistline. I watched with heightened interest.

"C'mon, try a little. That's an order from your Master, slave," he barked, finally picking up the semi-scripted scene we had outlined two hours earlier via email.

Tentatively, I reached out for the glass pipe, and stupidly, I grabbed it by the round, bulbous end.

"Shit! That's hot!" I yelped.

"You weren't supposed to touch it, slave, just put your fucking mouth on the end of it and inhale when I tell you to."

"Oh, OK. I mean, yes Sir."

Robert shook the lighter to redistribute the small bit of

remaining lighter fluid and finally produced a decent flame under the pipe. He instructed me to inhale slowly and deeply and to hold the smoke in my lungs until he told me to exhale. I did as I was instructed. Immediately, my head felt amazingly light, and my body felt alive and electrified as a strange tingling sensation enveloped my arms and legs.

"Oh, wow!" I said. "What is this stuff?"

"It's crystal. Have another hit."

I complied and took another, longer drag off this little glass pipe that seemed almost cute and relatively innocuous.

"Oh my God! I've never felt anything like this."

"Get busy, slave boy. Get down there and take care of me," he ordered.

"Yes, SIR!"

OK, now this was getting fun, I thought. I had no cares in the world, not a single thought in my head. I was totally in the moment, something I'd always struggled with as an actor, let alone in a scene from my own life. My head had always gone ninety miles per hour with thoughts careening and colliding around in my brain, each begging for attention.

"Hang on. I'll be right back." He disappeared into the adjoining bathroom. I waited in a precarious position on the bed for probably twenty minutes, then as my high started to subside and anxious thoughts came clattering back, I decided to check on Robert to see what was going on. Maybe he was taking a shower. I apparently caught him at a bad moment, and he barked viciously at me to go back to the bed. Several minutes later, he emerged from the bathroom, plopped down on the right side of the bed, and lit a cigarette. I inquired again about his activities in the bathroom, and he flatly stated he was "doing a point."

"Huh? A point? What's that?"

"A shot. A point. Man, you're a stupid asswipe."

"I'm sorry. I'm just new to all this, I guess. What's a point?" I asked, suddenly feeling very self-conscious sitting naked on the bed.

"Did you like the way it felt when you hit the pipe?"

"Yeah, it was great. Better than anything I've ever felt. So, what's a point?"

"I'll show you."

In a flash, Robert whisked us into the bathroom and roughly sat me on the edge of the tub. He spun the combination-lock dials on a stainless-steel briefcase and took out a small bag of white rocks, a tablespoon, and a medical syringe. He flipped some of the crystal out of the miniature Ziploc-style bag into the spoon, crushed it with the back end of a cigarette lighter, and then melted the white powder into liquid. He drew it up into the syringe through the cotton from a Q-Tip, held the syringe in his teeth, and wrapped a piece of rubber tubing around my right arm.

I watched him perform this action with equal parts excitement and fear. "Um, ah, I'm not sure I should. I mean, I've never—"

"Make a fist and pump your hand. You're going to do a point whether you want to or not. Now shut the fuck up, and do what you're told." He tapped the veins in my right arm and was clearly getting frustrated.

"You'll never find a vein in my right arm. Many nurses have

tried," I giggled. "It's like getting blood from a turnip."

Ever the helpful little submissive idiot, I directed Robert to the large vein on my left arm. I had already learned from the ongoing blood draws from HIV tests that it was the only spot from which nurses could extract blood. He pushed me to the toilet in the water closet.

"Shut your fucking mouth NOW," Robert yelled.

He grabbed my left arm so hard I thought he would tear it off.

Then, my life changed—inexplicably, irrevocably changed—as Robert drove the needle fast and deep into my vein.

"Now, when I say so, open your fist, take a deep breath, and keep your eyes on me. Now, your head is going to feel really warm, then you'll probably cough."

Exactly as he said, precisely on cue, my head felt like it was on fire and an irrepressible cough escaped from my throat.

"Oh shit, oh shit, oh dear God," I squeaked out. A million bizarre sensations were running through every nerve, every fiber, every cell of my body. An intense wave of panic shook me. I had a sudden urge to urinate and told Robert I was going to pee all over.

"You piss on my floor, and you're licking it up, slave."

"I'm dying. Oh shit, I'm dying! I'm dying!" Sweat was pouring off my forehead, as my legs started to shake uncontrollably.

"You're not dying, asshole. Just enjoy the ride."

"No, really, something's wrong. I can't breathe. I'm dying." With that, Robert muttered a string of obscenities, then reached up and knocked the light bulb out of its socket, sending shards falling on me. He then slammed and locked the door behind him, leaving me alone in the dark shaking, sweating, and freaking out.

Oh, dear Lord, dear God, what have I done? Please make this stop.

I bargained with God, promising I would do anything for the horrible sensations to stop. I was certain I was dying, and this jerk had left me alone without showing any concern.

My mouth was so dry I couldn't swallow, let alone cry out for help. I considered scooping some of the water out of the toilet bowl to rinse my shriveled tongue but couldn't manage to make my arms move. The shaking subsided, and I sat in the dark, motionless, naked, totally panicked on the toilet in some guy's house somewhere in Orange County. I tried desperately to pee, but my muscles had clamped down.

I'm not sure how long I sat on the toilet—it felt like at least an hour—before he knocked on the door and begrudgingly asked if I was OK. He was probably more concerned that he had an overdose on his hands rather than a scared guy who had never tried drugs before. Yes, that's right. With the exception of one puff of pot that caused me to vomit, I had never done drugs, let alone the hard stuff. Then, in one night, I went from an innocent hit on a crack pipe to shooting up a dose of crystal meth that could easily have killed me. Or a horse. Or me and a horse.

I told Robert I didn't feel well and was scared. He was pissed because I "just wasted sixty bucks of good shit" and spent the best part of the high acting like a frightened two-year-old. He tossed a wet washcloth at me and told me to cool down, chill out, and come out to the bed. After being frozen in place for another twenty minutes or so, I dragged myself out. I felt like I'd been hit by a truck. Rather, two eighteen-wheelers that had a head-on collision and flipped over on top of each other in a muddy ditch, causing a forty-car pile-up and shutting down a major freeway for several hours. Well, something like that. Point is, doing a "point" turned out to be a horrible experience. By the time I crawled onto the bed, any sexual desire had dissipated. I just wanted the whole mess to be over, and maybe I'd wake up to discover it had been a nasty dream.

"It's time for you to leave," Robert said.

"But I'm not sure I can drive."

"You'll be fine. Just drive slow."

Robert had little to say to me, as I started to dress and gather my stuff. He was catatonic, sucking on a cigarette and staring into space.

It's no small miracle that I made it home alive and without being arrested for driving under the influence of an illegal substance. The drive home was fuzzy. When I got home, I couldn't sleep and felt wired beyond any caffeine-induced state of alertness I'd ever experienced. I spent the next several hours—well into the next day—doing what I would later learn was tweaking. I was online looking at hook-up ads, repeatedly, frantically, until my right hand was rendered immobile on the mouse and my desk was covered with cigarette ashes from all the Marlboro Lights I let burn down to the filter in my left hand.

I tried to sleep but couldn't stop my mind from racing. I tried to put clothes on and take the dog downstairs for a much-needed walk, but I couldn't manage to complete the simple task of dressing myself.

Finally, around four in the afternoon on Saturday, I was starting to feel human again. I showered and finally got my incredibly patient pug outside. My cell phone beeped with a new text.

"You OK?" It was Robert.

Now here was one of those pivotal moments in life when a choice had been presented to me. I could delete the text, delete the emails from the night before, and vow to not try drugs again. Or I could respond to his text, which is exactly what I did.

Back in the years when I placed a lot of stock into quasi-spiritual hokum like horoscopes and carnival psychics, I would tell you that it was my nature as an Aries to not learn from my mistakes. You see, I'm the guy who would inevitably touch the hot stove, repeatedly, until finally, at some point (and after my hand was sufficiently scorched), I would get the message and stop touching the blasted stove. Because, the astrologers say, those born under the sign of Aries are headstrong, childlike, and too trusting. Or maybe I was just a hard-headed, dim-witted moron.

By ten that night, I was back at Robert's house, touching the stove.

Always the perfectionist, I said, "Let me try another point. Please? Please?!" I sounded like a pathetic little child.

"No way. You totally blew a perfectly good point last night 'cause you freaked out."

"I know. But now I know what to expect. Please? Let me try again. I'll even pay for the stuff. I'll prove to you I won't freak." Good grief. I was talking to Robert like he was my father.

"I said NO," Robert barked.

We smoked a little from the glass pipe, and it must have got him riled up. Soon, he disappeared into the bathroom, pulled out the aluminum briefcase, and started to prepare two points.

Following after him like a stupid puppy, I asked if one was for me.

"Get on the toilet, sit down, and keep your mouth shut. Not one fucking sound out of your mouth, or so help me, I will break your fucking arm and lock you in here all night to suffer," he said, gripping the orange cap of the insulin syringe. "Make a fist," he said, as he roughly tied the rubber tubing around my left arm. He jabbed the needle into my arm with greater expertise than any nurse I'd seen. Then, he slapped me hard across the face.

"Take that you fucking whore." He flipped off the light, locked the door to the water closet from the outside, and left me naked in the dark. I screamed for help but only heard him laugh maniacally as another door slammed shut.

Something is wrong. He must have made this one stronger.

After letting me sweat out and scream through my initial high, Robert came and unlocked the door. My clothes were in a pile outside.

"Get dressed, and get the fuck out."

Any sane person would never have allowed me to get behind the wheel of a car. I staggered out to my car, the black Chrysler PT Cruiser that had replaced my dream Porsche Boxster just a few months earlier. I backed ever so cautiously out of his driveway and drove like a senior citizen, winding my way slowly back to Fullerton. Three more miracles occurred that night: I didn't kill anyone, I didn't get pulled over, and I didn't get hauled to jail.

I spent all of Sunday in a horrible state of coming down from my introductory two nights of partying. I was casually seeing a poz guy from an HIV positive dating website. He called to check on me and, in hearing I didn't feel well, insisted on bringing over home-made chicken soup. A bit of conversation had me spilling my story and confessing my sins. Poor guy. His tone changed as he told me of his personal experience getting clean from meth and detailed the dangers of drug use. I wanted to throw the chicken soup in his sanctimonious face.

After standing him up for two coffee dates, my friend started to get the message loud and clear; I had found a more seductive suitor named Tina. But as is typical with the drug, Tina proved early on to be a bitch.

Monday, March 17, 2008—St. Patrick's Day—was not lucky for me. As I was getting ready for work, I felt awful. My chest was heavy, and my breathing was labored. I was extremely light-headed, and lying down just made the room spin worse than being drunk. I was nauseated and couldn't recall the last time I had food. I tried nibbling the corner of a Saltine, but my throat was so dry I couldn't swallow. I tried some orange juice, but it stuck in my throat like a hair clog in a backed-up bathroom sink.

Instead of getting ready for work, I threw on jeans, a T-shirt, and a ball cap to perform a test walk down the hallway of the third floor of my apartment complex. It didn't go so well. I couldn't walk a straight line, and with each step, I was increasingly fearful I was having a heart attack.

In my trademark "act before you think" mode, I decided I would drive myself to the emergency room. After all, it was probably nothing, and I couldn't afford the $200 co-pay let alone an ambulance ride. My eyes refused to focus. Nonetheless, I went swerving and speeding recklessly up Harbor Boulevard to St. Jude Medical

Center, ran inside like a madman, and announced I was having a heart attack. I was placed in a wheelchair, while vitals were taken and a brief medical history was extracted from my fried brain.

Then, nothing.

Why are they ignoring me like this? I'm dying, and they're letting me fester in this damn wheelchair. I have insurance, good insurance, Disney insurance, dammit.

I called Robert. "Thank God I reached you. I'm in the ER having a heart attack. Do you think it was from the stuff you gave me?"

Robert was quick to shush me. "Not on the phone. Don't say another word. Where are you?"

I told him my location, and he said he would come help. Three hours passed and still no Robert. I called his cell but only got his voicemail. I pleaded my case after the tone. "I'm dying. I know I am. I don't know what to do. No one will help me. They've parked me in this chair and are ignoring me. Why? Why?"

Another hour later. "Me again. I need your help. I think there was something wrong with the drugs you gave me."

Finally, I received a text message: "Chill out, ride it out. Not coming to save you. You're just a stupid fucking bottom who couldn't handle his party. Tough shit."

For some reason, I felt Robert owed me some level of aftercare. After all, he shot me up with *his* drugs. I couldn't see the reality that I had put myself in a bad situation, offered my veins, and then went back for seconds.

Another two hours passed, I gave up on the ER and walked out. I drove home feeling like over-cooked crap, managed to take the dog out, and collapsed into bed. I hadn't died. I'm sure it was all too clear to the hospital staff what was going on after they checked my vitals. "He's on a bad trip. Let him ride it out. Only way they learn," I imagined the attending physician telling the triage nurse.

By the weekend, I was craving the drug but had no idea how to find it. Robert wouldn't take my calls, so I knew I was now alone on this path of self-destruction. I was still feeling kind of wobbly and thought the old hair-of-the-dog remedy was what I needed.

For all the years of trying to be the good guy, trying to take the high road by frantically searching for a partner so I wouldn't end up old and alone, my time had finally come to let loose.

Screw the high road. I'll take the other "high" road, thank you very much. Who needs a relationship anyway?

And so, with a vengeance, this kid in a candy store all too soon became a messed-up bull in an already damaged china closet.

35

That Stuff Will Kill You
HOLLYWOOD: 2008

So, how did this seemingly good kid who grew up trying to do everything right to please others end up as a meth addict? I suppose the long-held desire to fit in, the desperate need for others' acceptance, and the bone-chilling fear of being alone helped propel me down this especially dark and slimy rabbit hole. Except I wasn't chasing the White Rabbit in *Alice in Wonderland*, I was chasing the elusive "first-time" high.

But what exactly *was* this high? What exactly was this white stuff that looked as harmless as salt or rock candy?

Crystal meth is a supercharged crystallized stimulant based on methamphetamine. It is entirely man-made and is usually manufactured in filthy, makeshift labs inside homes or storage units using various toxic and caustic household chemicals that are cooked down to a crystalline or powdered form.

Meth cooks combine legal, over-the-counter cold medicines containing pseudoephedrine with readily available but highly toxic ingredients, such as hydrochloric acid (chemical used to make plastic), lithium (highly corrosive chemical used in batteries), acetone (flammable liquid typically found in nail polish remover and paint thinners), sodium hydroxide (used to dissolve roadkill—yum!), and sulfuric acid (active ingredient in drain cleaners).

Meth has been around since the early 20th Century but was not a part of the American drug subculture until the 1980s, when it began to replace cocaine as the drug of choice among users, largely because of its availability, low cost, and long-lasting high. Gay men embraced this drug due to its ability to create a sense of euphoria, heighten sexual desire, and lower inhibitions.

Crystal meth is commonly known within the gay community as Tina, Christine, Chrissy, crank, party favors, ice, speed, and tweak. Other nicknames like "go fast" exist, but they're limited to heterosexual users. Meth can be snorted through the nose, smoked through a glass pipe, taken orally, injected intravenously, or shot up the rectum with a turkey baster. Happy Thanksgiving!

In short, crystal meth is nasty shit. It's highly addictive, highly destructive to the body, and inevitably catastrophic for relationships and careers.

And, if you're of a certain age group, you probably remember those old public-service commercials in which an egg is cracked into a hot skillet. "This is your brain (the egg). This is your brain on drugs (the sizzling egg)." With meth, now imagine that same egg in a microwave burned to smithereens then placed in a blender. Yeah, that's meth.

And what's this about chasing the high? One of the particularly cruel aspects of meth is that there is never a high as intense and exhilarating as the first one. Not ever. Each repeat use requires more of the drug in vain attempts to recreate that first libido-exploding high. And after a while of using, sometimes the high doesn't happen, and all you get is an episode of extreme paranoia and panic. Or, maybe a session of dry heaves. Or a staph infection. Or maybe pouring sweat until you pass out from dehydration. And like Forrest Gump's infamous box of chocolates, with meth, you truly never know what you're going to get.

But first, you had to get it; and for a newbie, there were no instructions online for procuring the drug or securing a dealer. It's not like you can go to Yelp and find a reputable dealer with a five-star rating just around the corner.

I discovered some sleazy hook-up sites and engaged in a chat with a hot guy. His profile stated he liked PnP. I knew other acronyms, such as GWM (gay white male) and BDSM (bondage and discipline and sadomasochism), so I figured it was something sexual.

"Do you like to party?" Hot Guy asked.

"Well, I'm kind of shy, so I tend to do better in small group settings," I answered, ever the oblivious idiot.

"No. *Party.*"

"Well, I like birthday parties, I guess, but I usually don't get invited."

"Dude. *Duuude.* Do you like Tina?"

"Tina Turner?" A lightbulb. "Oh. OH. I mean, yes. Yeah, I do. I love Tina."

"Hot," said Hot Guy, as he ended our chat. I kept trying to reconnect with him, but it became clear I wasn't the party for which he was looking.

So, I Googled "PnP" and discovered it stood for "party and play." And now, I knew that "party" was code for crystal meth. Awesome.

I was a quick learner and became adept at getting in the same room with the drug. I still didn't know how to buy my own baggie, but that would come.

* * *

After my third weekend of partying and experiencing the horrible low that followed, I was starting to think I just might have a problem smoldering. *You think?* Doing the drug was consuming my every thought, and I found concentrating on my job to be difficult.

I poked around online for more info about the drug and stumbled upon a site for Crystal Meth Anonymous (CMA). *Oh, crap. So, this was a thing. A thing that was enough of a problem to warrant its own twelve-step group.* It was a Wednesday, and there was a meeting that night in Long Beach. I didn't relish the idea of going, and assured myself that if I did go, it would simply be for the purpose of fact finding. Just research, really. You know, in case I ever did have a problem. *Yeah, right.*

Denial: Still not that river in Egypt.

I showed up in my business attire (to prove I wasn't one of *them*) and boldly shared my "first night out" story.

"Do you think I have a problem?" I asked.

Heads were nodding, as I received a chorus of resounding "oh yeahs" and "you better believe its."

"But don't you have to be addicted first?" I asked.

A skinny queen next to me placed his skeletal hand on my thigh. "Oh, honeeee, puh-lease."

I looked at the people in the room and knew I didn't belong with them. *I'm not like them. I can quit anytime. I'm not an addict; I would never let that happen.*

But here's another factoid: since meth withdrawal is extremely painful and difficult, most users relapse (up to ninety-three percent return to using meth).

There's a good reason why crystal meth is often referred to as "the Devil's drug." Not only in the way it hooks a person, but it hooks them fast and hooks them hard. As I learned from the group recitation at the top of CMA meetings, "one is too many, and a thousand is never enough." In the context of meth, it means that one hit/snort/slam is enough to make you an addict. And once you've had that hit/snort/slam, another one or one-hundred or 1,000 will never satisfy the body's craving for the drug.

And what of trying to give it up? Maybe just a little here and there, you know, for fun? The answer was the same. "One is never enough."

But I'll just have a quick hit from the pipe before work. No one has to know. Just enough to give me a boost to get through the day.

Until that quick hit turns into another sick day spent mindlessly slogging through online profiles and hook-up ads. I need to mention that I never went to work high—ever. Hungover and strung out, yes, but never under the influence.

An experienced addict offered to become my sponsor that first night, meaning he was willing to shepherd me through the process of getting and staying clean and working the famous twelve steps. But I found his rough looks irresistible. He was a bad boy, covered with tattoos, and although he had been in prison for a number of years, he had a surprisingly calming and nurturing nature. He had been a dealer, and shared stories of having a new batch of two pounds of meth on his coffee table and breaking it into smaller chunks before he would weigh and bag it. One time, a buddy was helping him (the buddy probably knew they weren't doing crafts) and broke off a huge rock and shoved it right up his own butt, right there in his living room. And, there, on the floor, my drug-dealer-turned-sponsor had his way with the buddy. Unbeknownst to my well-intentioned sponsor, he proved to be a strong trigger, and I could only think about getting high and having him rough me up.

I'm not ready for endless, mind-numbing meetings and daily reporting to a sponsor—however hot he might be.

I had barely dipped my toe in the crystal pool and wanted to take a much deeper dive. I wasn't ready to be clean. I quit CMA after two meetings.

36

The Right Kind of Trouble
EAST HOLLYWOOD: 2008

"Turn right on Western," Will said. "It's half a block up on the right. There—the Coral Sands."

[Ominous music swells.]

There was something oddly familiar about the motel, with its six concrete columns creating a once-quasi-regal entrance statement. The poorly aging 1950s-era colonial façade hinted at its seedier interior. It had actually been, in its heyday if there ever was one, the Colonial Motel, billing itself on postcards as "a picturesque Colonial setting in the heart of Hollywood. Excellently furnished. Guided tours. Television and radio in every room."

"I think I've been here," I said.

"Then you know how much fun it is."

* * *

In the summer of 2003, I took myself on a vacation to Disneyland. I thought I would soak up some local color and test an early inkling that working for the Mouse could be the logical next leg of my life journey. I also thought it would be cool to stay in Hollywood. Of course, the Hollywood I had in my head was comprised of black-and-white images of Lucy and Ricky hanging out at the long-since-defunct Brown Derby. Cooler still, I thought, would be staying in a gay area. Heck, I might even meet "the one." (Update, 2019: Still waiting to meet "the one," by the way.)

An online search coughed up a charming little motel hailed as being gay-friendly. I imagined an idyllic, lovely, and romantic hideaway, nestled in the Hollywood Hills and populated by lovely gay couples and beautiful single guys who all wanted to fall in love and live happily ever after. I was three years from working for Disney but had obviously already drank Mickey's Kool-Aid.

I checked into the Coral Sands Motel—it sounded so tropical, so charming, so old Hollywood—and was a bit surprised that I had to be buzzed in through a locked security door to get to my room. *It was 2003 Hollywood, after all. Best to be safe. They must be a safety-conscious establishment. Well, kudos to them.*

My "excellently furnished" room featured filthy green carpet, mismatched furniture, a stained and cigarette-burned purple bedspread, and a cardboard-core door without a deadbolt lock. I called the office to request a better room. All rooms were the same, all equally nice I was told. I didn't want to take a chance with my MacBook, so I took it with me in the rental car as I drove to Anaheim for an evening at the theme park. But I was tired from traveling and decided to turn in around midnight.

The clock on the room's thrift-store nightstand blipped off its digital minutes, as I tried desperately to fall asleep. By now, it was well after two in the morning, and there was a steady and increasing flow of foot traffic and chattering outside my door. *Damn late check-ins. How very rude.*

Around 3:30 a.m., I peeked outside to see why there still was so much traffic. Scantily clad guys and the occasional drag thing were roaming around the two-story courtyard surrounding a pool that had seen better days. *Oh great.* So, this wasn't the romantic, meet-the-love-of-your-life retreat I imagined. It was basically a bathhouse. And because in those days in 2003, my head was only into the lure of a Hollywood romance and a Disney career, I promptly moved to an actual, clean, respectable hotel room a few blocks south of Disneyland, losing the balance of my motel fare.

* * *

I met Will in 2007 at a Poz4Poz Los Angeles social gathering of exclusively HIV-positive men. We had one glorious, beautifully romantic, seemingly promising date that concluded with a sleepover in his bed. Then, he became one of the "unreachables." He wouldn't respond to my calls, texts, or emails. He broke my fragile heart quite badly. Will lived in east Hollywood, and although he had no desire for anything long term, we remained friends. In fact, he was my only Hollywood friend, save for a colleague who had also had his heart stomped by the unbelievably adorable Will.

But now, it was May 2008, and I wasn't quite the same person. As I was about to go north for a repeat hook-up with an unattractive guy who had what I had recently learned were "party favors," I called Will and let him know I would be in his neck of the woods. I hinted at my purpose, and he caught on right away. I explained that if all went as planned, I would be buying my first—such an exciting, Facebook-worthy moment—baggie of Tina. *Yay, me!* He was intrigued with this new side of Lewis and wanted in on the fun. He told me to call him once I had the drugs, but to be a bit more careful with what I said on future phone calls.

Unattractive Guy wanted to mess around while we waited for the delivery from "his guy." I played with him, reluctantly, I think, my only thought being scoring my stash and hightailing it to Will's apartment for some better-looking fun.

With the goods tucked in the glove box of the PT Cruiser, I called Will. We discovered through some verbal charades that neither of us had a pipe to smoke the crystal. But he knew that the proliferation of smoke shops on Hollywood Boulevard sold the little glass pipes—if I only knew how and what to ask for. These pipes weren't prominently displayed with all of the fancy pot pipes and crazy-straw bongs. As simple as the devices were, these little pipes were like gold. A plan was devised for me to pick him up, drop him off near one of the shops, and then pick him up again a block away. The plan worked, and soon, we had a five-dollar pipe to go with my eighty bucks of crystal tucked into an adorable little Ziploc-style bag. The thing was downright cute, and I couldn't wait to show Will what I'd just scored on my own.

"Damn. Don't wave that thing around," Will scolded, swatting the baggie onto the passenger floorboard. "Let's go get a room."

"Why not just go back to your place?" I asked.

"Don't you want to see who else is out there tonight? We could do a group thing."

Oh, Will. You had me at "group thing."

"Hot! But, where? I mean, where is it safe to *party*?" I spoke like I was an old pro, placing great emphasis on the word "party." I probably sounded more like Mary Catherine Gallagher from *Saturday*

Night Live.

We made a quick stop at Will's to get some gear for the night ahead. And there, on his kitchen floor, down on all fours, bare ass in the air, Will introduced me to the joys of a Tina booty bump. That is, a slimy mixture of crystal and water in a plastic syringe up my booty. It produced an immediate high, although nowhere as intense as slamming. Still different from smoking or snorting. A smooth kind of high. A high that made me feel more confident and more attractive than ever before.

Soon, we were back in my car on Hollywood Boulevard. I was behind the wheel—why?

"Turn right at Western. It's half a block up on the right. There—the Coral Sands."

"I think I've been here," I said.

"Then you know how much fun it is."

I pulled into the familiar, run-down, and crowded parking lot. But this time, I was no longer the proverbial babe in the sketchy woods; I was the semi-experienced party boy eager to check in. We got the last room on the second floor overlooking the pool that was, according to Will, the perfect vantage point for attracting the right kind of trouble.

Through a different pair of eyes, rather, from a new perspective, the motel was a wonderland of forbidden pleasures. Instinctively, I knew all of this was wrong, but somehow being there, doing this with Will, feeling like we were the best of friends, made all the difference. It was the grown-up version of the Scott and Denny sleepover that never was. It was fun, exciting, and mysterious under a bright white Hollywood moon that bounced playful reflections off the cen-ter-court pool. The night was alive, utterly magical, and infused with a million exciting electrical currents. The whole night was ahead of us, a delectable surprise package to unwrap. Anything could happen. I felt a twinge of regret for missing out on such fun by being a goody-goody for forty-two years.

Well, better late than never.

The night flew by, and like two diligent Tupperware ladies, we hosted at least three different parties—that is, group scenes—in our room until the favors began to wane. And when they did, I felt I should have had a deli tray. Will phoned a buddy to procure more drugs. Easy peasy lemon squeezy.

And so, Friday night slipped into Saturday morning. As they do.

I had a dog at home to feed and walk but didn't want the fun to end. Neither did Will. We went Dutch for another night at the former Colonial, and I sped back to Fullerton, rushed Buzz through eating and pooping, then raced back to Hollywood. Will proved that, at least in this non-romantic situation, he could be trusted and was waiting in the room as promised, casually stroking his ample mem-ber that looked larger-than-life on his five-foot-six, slender frame as he watched one of the three channels of round-the-clock porn play-ing on the room's battered and sperm-splattered TV.

But Saturday night wasn't as much fun as Friday. And the pool wasn't the magical lagoon it had appeared to be while on a fresh high. The guys were less attractive and not as plentiful. As I would learn, the second day—especially the second night—of a meth high isn't quite as grand. It seemed like no matter how much I smoked or snorted or shot up my ass, I just couldn't recreate the sensations or duplicate the Friday-night high. If someone had produced a syringe and the know-how, I probably would have tried *that* again. That was the pisser of crystal meth: the first high can never be recreated and the first high of a new "run"—that is, a two- to three-day partying cycle—would wear off with increasing speed (pun intended).

By Sunday around 5 a.m., Will decided to take a cab home after he couldn't pry me away from the room. I had been lying naked, ass-up on the bed waiting for someone, anyone.

"Come on. I'll buy you a McMuffin. You should eat."

I could barely grunt a response.

"Suit yourself," Will said.

By this hour, the place was a ghost town with only a handful of massively tweaked twinks roaming the outdoor hallways. I joined the small throng, one of the few walking skeletons still haunting the place. It was rare to see a fat meth head; food is never on a user's agenda.

After twenty or more laps, I went back to my room. Then, I saw a wide-open door where a somewhat attractive and sexually desperate guy was lying on his bed. I paused, wondering if I dared go in. I caught a glance in my room's wall-sized mirror and saw that the guy was me. As the sun peeked over the Hollywood Hills, I reluctantly closed my door, repacked my large gym bag full of sex toys and bondage gear, took one last hit for the road, and slunk back to Orange County feeling depressed and dirty. The coming down part, as I was quickly learning, was far worse than a tired kid being dragged away from the theme park—cotton candy-stained lips and a deflating Mickey balloon in tow but blissfully floating atop a sleepy, sugary cloud. There was nothing blissful about coming down.

I would have another Friday night with Will, but soon, he grew tired of me. I missed my newfound party buddy. Will made it all seem like harmless fun, like a late night, romantic spree with a new lover in New York City, not something that was rapidly turning into a nasty addiction.

When Will became bored with our handful of weekends at the Coral Sands, I started to fly solo; it's the only way that has ever worked for me. I discovered Slammer, a sleazy sex club on Beverly Boulevard about one mile from the leather bar Eagle L.A. They didn't make any attempts at theming. No semi-truck cabs, no waterfall pools. This wasn't a bathhouse of another era. Just a row of glory-hole booths, semi-private cubicles, a watersports room, three sling rooms, and an outdoor patio connected to another block of mini rooms and a dark maze. It was the epitome of raunchiness, and a nocturnal playground for the horny, the stoned, the buzzed, and the tweaked.

On one of many frustrating, lonely, horny, desperate (feel free to add your own adjective here) nights at Slammer, I became a voyeur, if only for a few minutes. In the back of the club, there was a long, black bench for sitting, or in this guy's case, standing and waving. Not waving his hand, but stroking and waving his hard dick. He had a porn star body; hell, he might have been one. He drew a crowd of maybe eight overweight, hairy men in some stage of undress that were cheering him on, slipping him tips, and begging for him to shoot into a birthday boy's mouth.

I stood off to the side, aroused by the impromptu show but disgusted by the whole scene. And I wondered, did this guy put on little shows like this frequently at different sex clubs? Did he get off on the adoration from unknown fans he wouldn't touch with his ten-inch pole? Did he ever go home feeling filthy and gross knowing that he could have spent a late night anywhere but there? I decided such questions probably didn't cross his stoned, buzzed, and/or tweaked mind.

But as I stood there watching, as I made endless circles through the club looking for action in the glory-hole booths, the three sling rooms, and the watersports room, God was frequently in the back of my mind. Although I had never been officially saved, God was there. The still, small voice I barely knew was there asking, "Is this the life you want? Is this really where you want to be? It gets much harder from here; you need to know that." I shooed the nagging voice away.

After a night at the Slammer, I usually left feeling like I didn't get my money's worth as I slunk back to OC as inconspicuously as possible. Living in the Fullerton apartment near the college, the majority of my neighbors also dragged in during the wee hours looking as haggard as me, so no eyebrows were ever raised. I did get the odd congratulatory fist bump and "way to go" from a couple of guys who saw me staggering, looking like death warmed over, pleased to see I had successfully "gotten my party on."

I was only three months into my addiction, and a pattern had developed, like a sort of mental game of musical chairs. At the beginning of each new party cycle, the first type of guy my brain landed on would be my laser-beam focus for the next, say, eighteen hours. I guessed that was the tweaking part I'd heard about at CMA. But for me, it wasn't disassembling things or stringing Christmas lights all over my apartment. Instead, it was me sitting immobile at my computer, flipping through the same ten profiles of guys who may or may not have been online on a hook-up site at nine on a weekday morning when the rest of the world—the responsible, working world—was where I should have been: at work, being responsible.

Worse still was being in a room (motel, my place, someone else's house) with a couple of guys who were also tweaking. More often than not, each of us would be transfixed by our own laptop, chasing after some fantasy that would never materialize. Even if one managed to find a guy that fit the fantasy, the scene never ever played out as imagined. This go-all-night party drug called Tina was a fucking liar; it made guys go all night but rarely together. And no one was getting off. The drug made sure of that. There was never a finish line, a demarcation that the party was over. Well, actually there was one: when the drugs ran out.

* * *

I tried to get clean on my own and failed. I found a prescribing psychiatrist to get something to help me sleep. Will had spoken so fondly of his "best friend" Ambien (the wonder drug for both insomnia and date rape), so I asked if I could have it prescribed. Embarrassed, I admitted the drug use to Dr. Woo.

"Yeah, well, Dennis, you really shouldn't be doing that, OK? OK, well, I'll see you in three months. Try to have a good day, OK, Dennis?"

Thankfully, he also gave me the miracle comedown drug, Ativan, that proved to be a lifesaver as much as it was an enabler. As long as I had my Lorazepam, I could party with confidence knowing there was a way to bring the balloon back to earth.

I began to live a dual life, secretly partying while I was bouncing in and out of the "rooms," that is, CMA and Narcotics Anonymous

(NA) meetings in Long Beach, desperately trying to feel what the others were feeling, much like church. At each meeting, I heard stories of addicts losing everything, who, once they hit their own respective rock bottoms, decided to get clean. But the meetings were boring, as was what I perceived to be the clean life: movie nights, picnics, group hikes, potlucks. Again, with the potlucks! Clean little people doing mindless clean-little-people activities. Fuck, this *was* church. I quit the meetings once again, leaving a decent support network behind.

Screw them. And screw all the confused guys out there who acted like they wanted relationships. And screw all of the holier-than-thou church people. And screw the goody-goody CMA people. Screw everyone. No more Mr. Nice Guy. I've waited my whole life to let loose. It's my party, and this time, I'm not gonna cry.

37

Ghost in the Window

Frank rummaged through the disaster zone of what once appeared to be a kitchen, searching for a screwdriver. His hilltop Los Feliz home was virtually empty except for several dozen dilapidated boxes spilling their contents, mostly clothes and random stuff, onto the stained, dirty, and once-white carpet. His story was that his wife had recently left him and took all the furniture, but he got to keep the house with the great view. OK. I didn't care. *Just find the damn screwdriver, Frank.*

Frank's dealer had come by, and only through Frank (I wasn't permitted to see the dealer), I funneled my $300 for an "eight-ball" of crystal. I was never good at fractions, so the weights and measures of drug use were lost on me. Basically, it was the equivalent of two "teeners" for a total of 3.5 grams.

This still makes little sense to me. I just knew that an eight-ball was a well-stuffed, miniature Ziploc-style bag that could, if I was prudent, get me through a month. That is, if I was extremely careful with how much I shared with tricks. I had quickly learned to never lay out my full stash on the coffee table lest my trick swipe it while he had me tied down.

Someone told me later that $300 was way too much to spend on an eight-ball, but considering I had yet to find my own dealer, I gladly paid any premium necessary to replenish my stock. And the money at Disney was good. Good enough, at least, to pay the high cost of California living and still allow for a drug habit.

I was panicked about transporting this amount of meth back to Fullerton, so Frank spent the better part of an hour examining my PT Cruiser, trying to determine the best hiding place in the event I was pulled over. He ruled out underneath the seat cushions: too obvious. He started to remove one of the molded-plastic interior door panels, but I protested, explaining I would never be able to get the thing back on and would only manage to break all the retaining clips. Finally, he decided to place the meth inside two layers of plastic bags and employed four layers of duct tape to secure the pouch to the back of my rear license plate.

But he needed a screwdriver to remove the plate.

I wasn't one to carry a bag of tools in the car. I did, however, tote around my adult toy collection that had grown to fill a medium, rolling Samsonite. Wrong kind of tools.

Frank was, no doubt, tweaking, as it took him nearly two hours to find the damn screwdriver. He kept checking his phone and running to his lower-level office to see who was online. He toggled between at least three different hook-up sites, as he trolled for a couple of guys to join us for a group scene.

"Just watch out for cops," Frank said, as he removed my license plate. "Act like we're fixing something on your car."

Umm, we are Frank. We are affixing *three-hundred bucks' worth of crystal meth to my car.*

The 3.5 grams were enough to garner me a felony conviction, cost me a $1,000 fine and thirty days in jail, plus three years' probation. It would have also cost me my job at Disney.

"Just hurry, please. I'm so nervous."

"Well, for God's sake, if you're going to be such a nervous nelly then maybe you shouldn't be doing this fucking stuff."

You think?

With the stash in place and the license plate reinstalled, we headed inside and online to find trouble. A marginally attractive Hispanic guy was all too eager to come over when he learned we were partying. Frank must have figured that would keep me occupied while he found something more to his taste; he wanted a young, barely legal jock type.

When I was high, my taste in tricks would vary depending on a variety of stimuli. Sometimes, it would be the memory of a guy I saw during the day, say, a rough-looking, tattooed guy at a convenience store. Or a rough-looking road repair foreman, slick with sweat under his orange safety vest. Or a rough-looking...well, you get the idea. The one constant seemed to be that the guy be rough-looking. And physically rough. But for now, I only had a tweaked top and a fellow bottom with whom to play.

"You guys ever smoked it from a water bong?" Frank asked us.

"No," Fellow Bottom said.

"Isn't a bong for pot?" I asked like the seasoned drug addict I was becoming.

"I made one myself that works with Tina," Frank said.

"Cool," said Fellow Bottom.

"Cool," I parroted back. At this point in my addiction, I was willing to try all possible delivery methods.

Frank loaded up the glass pipe that he had rigged to a huge bong. He instructed me on when to inhale, as he put a barbecue lighter under the contraption. It packed a wallop ten times stronger than a five-dollar pipe. It literally knocked me on my ass, and I rolled back on the floor laughing.

As was typical with meth use, after the first hit, all clothes were quickly torn off. Especially for me, there was just something about being naked once I was high. The three of us messed around a bit, with me trying to direct the scene, but they remained detached and largely disinterested.

"Have you guys ever eaten it?" Frank asked.

Another dumbfounded look from me and a vigorous head shaking from Fellow Bottom.

"Wouldn't it taste bad?" I asked, ever the knowing idiot. "I mean, do you just stick it in your mouth and chew it?"

"No. You won't taste it. It's just like taking a pill," Frank explained, as he produced three large and empty pill capsules. Carefully, he pulled the two halves apart and filled the first capsule with what seemed to be a lot of crystal meth. This one he handed to Fellow Bottom as he prepared mine.

I eagerly gulped my capsule and washed it down with someone's glass of lukewarm backwash and water. And piss. There was probably some of that in there too. I didn't care. I waited anxiously for something to happen. Frank could tell I was in my rookie season.

"You won't feel the high right away. It has to dissolve and get into your system. But when it does, you'll feel it for sure."

While we waited for the elusive high, Frank ushered down the stairs another guy he had picked up online. Apparently, Frank hadn't mentioned the two naked bottoms draped across his basement bed. New Guy took one look at us, shot an I-don't-think-so look at Frank, and bolted.

"It was me, wasn't it?" I asked, paranoia setting in. "I know I need to work out. Dammit. He was hot too. I always fuck things up."

"Shut it. He just wasn't expecting a group thing," Frank scolded.

That moment killed whatever mood we *didn't* have going, and I was the first to get dressed. I was still riding a significant high from the water bong and didn't want to waste it. I was ready to hit the town. I just didn't expect it to hit back.

I was hyper-alert, as I navigated the steep, narrow road down the Los Feliz hillside. I vaguely knew my whereabouts and was eager to get to the Faultline, a dependably sketchy "Levis and leather" bar in Silver Lake on the famed Melrose Avenue.

Around 1 a.m., as the high intensified, I decided to head to Slammer.

I was relieved to find a parking spot in the entrance lot that was surrounded by a tall, chain-link fence and manned by a security guard. I felt better knowing that my eight-ball would be unknowingly protected by a tall, rough-looking African-American dude with an unofficial badge.

I completed my initial circle tour of the club before it hit me: the high was more intense, yet different than others before. Because I had also ingested the drug, it made sense that it was adversely affecting my stomach. The bathroom was in use, so I ducked into a large, private booth and locked the door. I went into the back corner and doubled over, ready to vomit. I must not have eaten that day because all my stomach produced were some painful dry heaves.

Then, I had to pee. Badly.

I was too afraid and too paranoid to leave the booth, so I attempted to piss in the same back corner. I held onto a hook on the wall and tried to go, but my muscles had clamped down on my bladder, worse than after any surgery. There was an eighteen-inch gap between the door and the floor and at least two curious heads popped under for a peek.

The bladder pressure continued to intensify. My legs were shaking as if they were two strands of limp spaghetti. The room was spinning, and I was on the verge of blacking out.

Then once again. *Dear God, please don't let me die on the filthy floor of this nasty sex club. What would Mom think?*

After another hour of trying to piss in the corner of the booth, finally, a scant couple of drops came forth but provided no relief.

After two hours, I mustered the courage to leave the cubicle and made my way to the patio for some fresh air and a cigarette. The sick stomach finally gave way to the exceedingly horned-up feeling I was seeking. I saw a sketchy guy wearing a T-shirt that blatantly suggested he partied. I asked outright, and he nearly dragged me to another back-corner booth, the one complete with a sling.

The drug must have been doing the talking for us, or perhaps we had some drug-fueled telepathic connection. In a flash, my jeans and combat boots were off, and my T-shirt pulled over and behind my head as I positioned myself in the leather sling. A hand-soap dispenser on the wall hung by one screw. Conveniently, it was filled with a thick lubricant, and it wasn't long before his hand went somewhere it didn't belong.

Our nasty play session was interrupted by a full lights-on of the back area accompanied by a Slammer staffer shouting that the club was closed and we needed to leave—pronto. It was well after the 4 a.m. closing time, and this, apparently, had been our third warning, but we hadn't heard. Lost in the drugs, I'm sure. The worker stood watch as we dressed. Mr. Party T-Shirt was out in a flash. It took me longer, of course, because I had to pull on my jockstrap and jeans and lace up combat boots. My hands were shaking badly and barely worked as I spilled the contents of my jeans' pockets all over the disgusting floor, now refulgent with harsh, fluorescent work light.

I stumbled to my car and got behind the wheel. I was just beginning to realize the extent of this bad drug trip. As such, I just wanted to sit and chill for a few minutes, but the security officer hurried me out—mine was the last car in the lot—so he could close and lock the gate. I cautiously pulled out onto Beverly and tried to formulate a plan. I knew I was in no condition to be driving a motor vehicle, and at 4:30 a.m. on mostly quiet roads (even by Hollywood standards), I was a slowly moving target to be pulled over by a cop.

My goal was to get to the Coral Sands, get a room, and hole up for however long it might take for the drug trip to end. I knew if I could get there, I would be safe.

I made it as far as North Hoover Street, less than a block from the Eagle bar on Santa Monica. Since the bar and its parking lot were both closed, I needed to find a place to park and ride this out. I pulled down one of the residential streets where I had previously parked to go to the bar and managed to find a spot.

Maybe if I just recline the seat and rest a bit, I can make it home to Fullerton.

Reclining only gave me the feeling that the car was spinning wildly. I sat up and had two cigarettes. No better. The paranoia had returned and worsened. Maybe some air and a walk around the block would help.

I locked the car and started off on foot toward the Eagle. I at least wanted to get to a business area that might have a convenience store with a bathroom. I made it to a 7-11 at Sunset and Santa Monica, bought a large bottle of water, and prayed the clerk would allow me to use the restroom. No such luck. It was hard enough to find a public restroom at a fast-food joint during the daytime in L.A., let alone at 4:45 in the morning. I usually had no problem convincing store clerks to be lenient and allow me use of the facilities. But then, I usually had my car and looked like the clean-cut and mostly respectable guy I used to be.

That's alright. I'll just pee in an alley.

I tried calling Will for help. He would know what to do. He would come help me, I was sure. That is, if he would answer his home phone. I called at least a dozen times, leaving a series of pathetic messages begging for assistance. On the thirteenth (or so) try, I only got a busy signal and knew that avenue was closed. I knew no one else in L.A. and wasn't about to call a Disney co-worker.

And so, with a forty-eight-ounce bottle of Crystal Geyser in hand, I started walking without direction or purpose. Somewhere a step above walking aimlessly, I suppose. I figured if I just kept moving, I would (a) look like I had a purpose and (b) walk off the high. I didn't manage to accomplish either.

Roaming another residential area in the vicinity of Melrose and Vermont, my mission was to find a dumpster, an alley, a bush—anywhere to pee. Truth is I had likely passed several opportunity spots, but the paranoia was so great that I felt I had a million eyes watching me. I wanted to cry. I wanted to sleep. I wanted to lie down and die.

I was back walking along Vermont Avenue as the sun started to peek over the Hollywood Hills. I was horrified when I caught a glimpse of myself in the large-paned window of an abandoned storefront. As I studied myself, I jumped when I saw someone—a homeless person, an apparition—looking back at me. When I moved, it moved. When I turned away, it turned away. I looked back, and it was still there. Then, I realized the ghost in the window was me, wandering through my little corner of a self-imposed hell. My image was affright. Disheveled hair that refused to be tamed due to some sticky substance tangled in my cowlick. Clothes that were filthy. My navy-blue T-shirt had white stains down the front that would make Monica Lewinsky blush. My jeans were dirty, with wet knees and gross brown stains on the seat.

Dear Lord, no wonder the 7-11 clerk refused me access to his restroom.

I was a walking restroom myself with the ironic twist that I still desperately needed to pee.

It was a good thing I didn't try walking into the Denny's down the street. I looked like a homeless dude without a cardboard sign. What would it have said, anyway? "High out of my mind and have to pee. Help me." I was a deplorable, walking mess with a small bag of meth in my pocket, just begging for arrest. I decided it was best to return to my car before I was questioned by the police and definitely before my car was towed.

As I walked, too fast for whatever time it was (6 a.m. maybe?), I was now painfully aware of how I looked and how I probably smelled. I asked myself if this was what I really had in mind when I poured all my money into that promo kit for Disney. Was this the life I imagined? Or did something go wrong with the basement magic? How was it that within only two years I was a full-blown meth addict?

Exhausted in every possible way, I slunk behind the wheel, immediately locking the door and blasting the AC in my face. A wad of McDonald's napkins from the glove box and the last of my water provided a whore's bath in the front seat. Cautiously, tentatively, I pulled away from the curb and made a few practice laps around the residential streets as the neighborhood started to come to life. Normal people fetching their papers, walking their dogs, getting ready for work.

Dog? Oh, yeah. I had one that needed to be cared for.

Work? Oh crap. Better sober up enough to call in sick. What would it be this time? I asked myself. *Coming down with strep. Yes. That would be reason enough for my boss to tell me to stay far away for as long as necessary.*

Still, I needed to get somewhere. I started driving toward the Coral Sands wondering if they might have a room available.

Well, of course they would have a room available. It was a Tuesday morning. Only hardcore partiers had rooms during the week.

Then, as I was silently condemning those I considered beneath me, I realized that I *was* one of them. I had become a hardcore partier.

I drove north on Vermont, creeping along, watching the rear-view mirror more than keeping my eyes on the road. I was convinced that every car in my mirror was a cop. Although it was the middle of summer—July, I think—I threw on a sweatshirt to cover my sins and stopped at a Ralph's grocery store. I needed something to sober me up. Will had once said that liquid yogurt was effective, so I bought three and guzzled them in the parking lot. Then, I was back on the road in morning commute traffic, driving well below the speed limit in the desperate hope I wouldn't call attention to myself. As it turns out, driving below the speed limit is a dead giveaway that someone has something to hide.

As I approached Sunset Boulevard, I saw flashing red and blue lights in my rear-view. *Fuck, oh fuck, oh fuck. I'm going to jail.*

The lights were now beside me and behind me. Two cop cars. *Perfect. Just perfect.*

I'll just act normally and pull into this gas station and fill up. *Morning, officers. How are you doing this fine morning? Ever been to Disneyland? I can get you free passes...*

The flashing lights followed me into the Exxon/Mobil lot, and I started praying as fast as I could.

Bracing for the worst, I glanced behind me. Nothing. I looked out my side window. No cops. Had they vanished into proverbial thin air? Maybe they got called to something else.

Or maybe they were never there.

But you know that drug-induced paranoia? It only gets worse from here, kids.

38

Hollywood Fun House

2008

The building was tall, regal, mysterious, and oozing Old-Hollywood charm. Plus, it had a Disney attraction loosely based on it. How could I not want to live there? When I learned that a third-floor studio was available with a partial view of the "H" of the Hollywood sign from the living-room window, I knew it was time to graduate from tame Orange County to residing in the heart of my addiction at the Hollywood Tower.

Immediately after moving in there were issues: a nightmarish parking shortage, an excessive number of flies in the tiny dining area, a kitchen sink that burped up the "insinkeratored" foodstuff from the five floors above me, an intermittent supply of hot water, and a motel-style wall air conditioner that only managed to increase the humidity. I barely crammed all of my antique furniture and other assorted crap into what could have been a stunningly beautiful apartment. But I was there. In one single, brilliant stroke of brilliance, I was now living just steps away from trouble. Conveniently, the Coral Sands was just a few blocks over. Now, I had the option to get a room at the Hollywood fun house or simply stay home and let the party come to me.

I assure you, the latter was not a brilliant idea.

I didn't waste time and had a regularly appearing PnP hook-up ad on Craigslist. I would change a few words every couple of days or so to keep the ad top of the list. That ad, along with my profile on sites such as Recon.com (the "dating" site that catered to gay guys with sexual interests ranging from the mildly kinky to the seriously twisted), ensured I had plenty of rough and nasty trouble coming to my door.

It was a lot easier to buy meth in my new playground. I met a guy who was a rent boy whose side hustle was drug-dealing. When he couldn't be reached, I had to mine Craigslist and troll BarebackRT.com for tricks with treats. On one occasion, I connected with a twenty-something twink with tweak in his backpack, who promised to sell me half of his party favors—money up front, of course. I picked him up from a run-down neighborhood in downtown L.A. and rushed him back to the Tower. I was hoping that we would get naked and smoke, but as soon as we got to my apartment, he locked himself in the bathroom for an hour shooting up. I threatened to break down the door, to call the police—anything to get him and whatever remained of the drugs out. He finally emerged, but alas, the drugs were gone, and he had no interest in getting naked. And I had no interest in him hanging around. But he promised to get me drugs if I would drive him back home. He hopped out of the car and instructed me to circle the block a few times while he hooked up with his dealer. I never saw him or my $120 again.

* * *

One chilly day in early October 2008, I woke up extremely ill. I couldn't keep any food down. I called in to work and somehow got myself to a nearby walk-in clinic. Under the anonymity of the clinic, I offered my HIV status but failed to mention the rampant drug use. Blood was drawn, and a rush was placed on the lab order. I was down to 134 pounds and 214 t-cells. And on a 5'11" frame, that's not very much weight.

In lay terms, t-cells—technically known as CD4 T-lymphocytes—are a form of white blood cell that play a critical role in the function of the immune system. Healthy people have between 500 and 1,600 of them. Having fewer than 200 t-cells earns one the distinguished classification of having AIDS. A reflection of my crumbling life, my health was fourteen t-cells away from utter destruction.

The blood work showed, ironically, that I had a drug-resistant bacterial infection so serious it required me to be on an intravenous antibiotic drip through the use of an ambulatory (wearable) infusion pump. The pump actually delivered the medicine for thirty minutes at a time every hour during each twenty-four-hour period. A home-health nurse came to my apartment to hook me up and teach me how to change the bags and other parts. After three days at home, I was able to return to work but was required to wear the device for two weeks. Of course, that didn't stop me from getting high; it just meant smoking or snorting meth off the kitchen counter.

I had to change the gauze pads twice each night and haplessly discarded them in the bathroom trash can. One night, I was walking my beloved pug on Franklin Avenue. He was moving slowly, but then again, so was I. But then, he stopped cold and started vomiting stuff that looked like coffee grounds. His condition worsened over the next day, and I rushed him to a veterinary hospital. I was horribly depressed and worried sick, especially after the vet told me Buzz had only a thirty-percent chance of surviving surgery, reminding me via a signed release that all fees were non-refundable regardless of the pet's outcome. Meaning: a dead pet doesn't get you off the hook for charges.

Five days later, and after $3,000 of surgery, Buzz was ready to come home. A plastic bag was presented to me with the culprit that had blocked and shut down his digestive system: a wad of gauze and medical tape. He survived, but the fruits of my addiction nearly took his life.

Although this incident had me firing off my usual desperation prayers, once Buzz was well, I forgot to thank God and was back on my one-man party train.

But my illness weakened me, and after a soul-crushing, three-hour drive home in heavy rain on the day before Thanksgiving, I spent the holiday in bed eating two cherry Pop-Tarts. On Black Friday, I called my former landlord in Fullerton and leased another studio apartment. Within a week, I was out of the Hollywood Tower of terror and back in Orange County. And, for a while, I stayed clean.

39

It Wasn't Like This in Pretty Woman

"Hung, white, rough Top who knows how to have fun."

Topher's ad on RentBoy.com told me all I needed to know.

While I had managed to stay off meth through a lonely Christmas season and a bleak January, by Valentine's Day, I was feeling sorry for myself and needed a fix. Previous abandonments—namely Dennis, the father, and Daniel, the husband—as well as years of self-hatred were manifesting in increasingly dangerous manners.

A brief chat with Topher confirmed his interests, experience, and, of course, drug use. Better still, he had a reliable dealer who always slung "premium shit" and could hook us up with enough crystal to make for one hell of a night.

But Topher couldn't travel to Orange County. Of course.

So, I was back at the Coral Sands, checking into a secluded room in a back corner, waiting for the front desk to ring my room and alert me that my dream date (aka brother-in-law from out of town) had arrived. All my guy had to do was register with the front desk and leave his driver's license. Unfortunately, his license was missing in action, and I had to beg, plead, and slip the front desk clerk a tip to get Topher into the motel, concocting a cockamamie story about him being my brother-in-law whose fat bitch of a wife had run off with another fat bitch and left him holding the bag. Now broke, he needed to crash a night with me. The Pakistani desk clerk probably didn't buy it. Hell, I didn't even buy it.

So, $89 for the room, $50 for the desk clerk, $500 for Topher's services, and another $500 for the drugs with his "additional services" retail markup applied. It was one of my most expensive Friday nights yet, but I didn't give a damn. I had grown weary of online hook-ups that purported to be aggressive dominants who only turned out to be fellow tweakers wanting a hung top and party favors, which sounded a lot like my gig. I no longer had patience for the game and was willing to pay for a sure thing.

Of course, I had no experience hiring a hooker; everything I knew about prostitutes I had learned from *Risky Business* and *Pretty Woman*. So, in the back of my mind, I was hoping for a fairy-tale ending. An ending where the incredibly hot rent boy would see what a nice guy I was and fall head over heels with me, vowing to clean up his act and embrace a white-picket-fence reality. And hopefully not crack a Faberge egg in the process.

Topher was pretty well-tweaked when he arrived, and although he did fit his physical description, he was on the downside of a high and mostly in the mood to get my money and more drugs. After a bit of messing around in my room, Topher's burner cell phone rang. Turned out his guy no longer delivered to the Coral Sands, ostensibly because the queens at the front desk knew him too well. So instead of convenient delivery, we had to opt for carry-out.

Topher and I charged off into the night on a quest for crystal meth, and casual chat proved to be a buzz-kill. The fantasy was over, and we were simply two addicts in the heart of Hollywood searching for our next fix. We hit it off, and I started to fall for him. He said his real name was Christopher and explained that he had been laid off as a computer programmer. Unable to find a job, he resorted to selling his wares online to fat, old men. He admitted he had been pleasantly surprised when he saw me, and also felt an instant connection. While all of this sounds great and noble and redeeming, we were both liars. Tina, of course, was the biggest liar, just as she had always been.

We got our drugs and returned to the Coral Sands. We had a fun night, although it wasn't the fantasy I had purchased. Still, Chris felt like a kindred spirit, and I wanted to know him beyond the dirty walls of the drug motel.

In what had become a pattern for me, I booked another night and planned to rush home to take care of Buzz.

"Can I come with you?" Chris asked.

"Sure, yeah, I guess so. But honestly, I can't afford to pay you for another night."

"You don't need to pay me. Just let me hang out with you. Then, we can come back and have a better night. You know, the scene you were expecting."

It sounded like a win-win. We grabbed at bite at McDonald's, walked the dog, and hightailed it back to my room. Perhaps Chris knew the outcome all too well because that night we were more interested in cruising together than being sexual alone together. I had genuine feelings of affection for Chris and, as such, had lost the desire to have him abuse me in the ways I had laid out in our online conversation.

It was a slow Saturday night at the motel with few new faces, mostly just the same tired and tweaked ones left over from Friday night. Around 5 a.m., we parked ourselves in the hot tub.

"So, how did you end up doing this? I mean this line of work?" I sounded like an inexperienced human resources manager.

"Like I told you, I had a great job until the market started to crash, and I was fired."

"I thought you said, 'laid off.'"

"Same thing."

"Is it? I've heard that with layoffs there's a better chance of going back to work." This was February of 2009, and layoffs were happening all around me at Team Disney Anaheim (TDA). My co-workers speculated that we, the production managers, would be safe from the axe, but to some extent, we all had our collective heads up our respective asses. My coping method was to get lost in the partying. If I ignored it, maybe it would just go away.

"I don't know if there's a difference. I just know that I blew through any money I had left, lost my apartment, and was sofa surfing," Chris explained. "When you get down to nothing, you tend to use whatever resources you have to get by. I used my looks and my big cock."

I was imagining Chris living the semi-glamorous life of a well-to-do male prostitute, akin to Richard Gere in *American Gigolo*. I was a bit envious of the freedom Chris seemed to have, not being tied to corporate America.

"Do you have a place now?" I asked.

"Not really. I don't know where I'm going after you check out. I can't reach my buddy. He's probably sick of me on his couch. Do you think you could book your room another night and let me stay here? Just until I can work a few things out."

My high had worn off, and my thinking was less clouded. "I'm not comfortable with doing that, Chris. But I want to help, and I want to be your friend."

"Well, then let me stay here another night," he pleaded.

I just couldn't allow him to stay on my open credit-card tab.

"Come home with me," I said.

"Don't you live in Orange County? That's too far away from my business. My clients are mostly up here."

"I'll bet you can make good money in OC," I suggested, completely unsure of just what I was offering.

"Let me stay here. Come on, be my friend."

"I am your friend, but I can't leave you here. Just come home with me. Have a good meal, take a hot shower. I have clothes that will fit you." By this point in the weekend party cycle, he stunk, a unique and pungent odor that emanates from a meth user's skin, especially one who's a slammer (an intravenous user).

I convinced him to leave with me. Although I didn't have an end game in mind, at least I had extracted him from the Coral Sands and was able to close out my room charges. On more than one occasion, I "lost" a trick inside the motel. And until a paying guest got his visitor out, said guest could not check out. There's probably a "Hotel California" irony here, or *Motel* California, rather.

While Chris showered at my apartment, I peeked in his

toiletries bag on my bathroom counter. It was a kit cobbled together by a world-weary local traveler, a collection of bent and dirty needles, skin creams, and pancake makeup. Guessing from the dozens of abscesses on his arms, I assumed the makeup was an attempt to mask his battle wounds; too many years of injecting had collapsed his veins. His worn-out backpack held an assortment of dirty underwear, jock straps, T-shirts, and a couple of cell phones with cracked screens. I felt guilty for snooping but felt I had the right to know just what I was bringing into my apartment.

Sunday night, Chris was looking and smelling almost human again. We ordered a pizza and watched a movie from my collection. He told me how he was once Armistead Maupin's lover in San Francisco. Maupin was the author of the aforementioned *Tales of the City* books that Mitchell introduced me to in 1985. And I was weak for any connection to celebrity, however obscure. I was dreamy-eyed, as I imagined "taming" Chris and molding him into a respectable romantic partner in classic *Pygmalion* style.

Against my better judgment, I left Chris alone in my apartment when I went to work Monday morning. He was sacked out on the couch and said he was going to sleep all day. I dashed home at lunch and was relieved to find him still sleeping. Asleep, Chris looked so innocent, so in need of love and caring. Still, it was impossible to concentrate at work; all I could think of was the handsome hooker at home and wonder if my computer was still there.

That night, we went grocery shopping and, even for me, the whole situation felt a little too contrived, a little too *Leave it to Beaver*. When I came home from work on Tuesday, I found that Chris had eaten everything in my kitchen except the dishes. Further, he had piled all of the trash on the floor around the overflowing garbage can.

"Would it be too much to ask to have you take out the trash?" I scolded.

Man, this is weird. I'm such a nagging bitch. No wonder I'm single.

Chris barely grunted a response as he continued to flip channels.

I cut him some slack. He was damn sexy, and just to have him parked in my apartment made any inconvenience worth the trouble. At his request, I eagerly helped him update his resume on my iMac. I tried to make his sporadic work experience look marketable, but there were large gaps I couldn't hide with clever resume-speak. Then, Chris checked his RentBoy account and found he had missed three opportunities for work since Sunday night. His cell phone account was past due, and the phone had been shut down.

"Shit. That's my lifeline. I have to get this phone back on. Help me. I'll pay you back as soon as I can see a client."

"That's OK. I'm happy to help you get back on your feet. I mean, I'd want someone to do the same for me."

"You're an angel, really you are."

Oh, yeah, I'm a fucking angel. I selfishly brought home a rent boy, secretly hoping he would become my husband.

The week continued with a similar routine. Chris would sleep until I was off work, then I'd buy him dinner and drive him to Hollywood so he could turn a quick trick while I drove around. But by the beginning of the second week, the routine was wearing on me, especially as Chris offered no reimbursement for the cell phone bill, the gas, the groceries, nor the dozens of other non-party-favors I'd done for him. Not even the gesture of "here's a dollar, best I can do."

The second Monday night, he flipped out. Because he wanted us to "grow our friendship," he insisted we sleep separately. It wasn't quite what I had in mind, but I was thankful for the company and forced friendship nonetheless. Around 4 a.m., I heard bizarre noises in the living room. Chris was on the couch, naked, grabbing his ankles and rocking back and forth in a typical "bottom" sexual position.

"Hey. Are you OK?" I asked.

No response other than a string of gibberish, as he drooled and rocked.

"Really. Are you OK?"

Chris put his fingers to his mouth, rolling his lips and making gurgling, grunting *buhbah buhbah buhbah* baby sounds. His eyes rolled back in his head.

"Chris, you're scaring me. Are you dreaming? Wake up."

He stretched his legs straight toward the ceiling and started yelling incoherently.

"Man, it's four in the morning, and I have neighbors. Please stop. You gotta stop."

The volume increased as the rocking intensified. I assumed he was on some kind of bad trip as his shaving kit full of needles was spilled on the floor.

"You need to get dressed. Pick up your shit," I demanded, trying to put forth a commanding demeanor while I was shaking inside. I started to stuff his few belongings into his backpack. "Come on, you're gonna have to leave."

This statement brought him out of his trance-like state, and he started to dress. *Good. He's responding. Now to just get him out the door.*

"You can't do this to me. Where am I supposed to go? I have nowhere to go. No one," he pleaded as he gathered his used syringes.

"You're freaking me out. You need to leave."

"I thought you were my friend, Lewis."

"And I thought we were working on getting clean together. There's life beyond the party," I retorted with all the moxie of an CMA meeting chairman.

He grabbed his backpack, spilling the contents. In frustration or anger or both, he started to throw his clothes all over the floor. Poor Buzz was scared and tried to run for cover but got in Chris's path, as he delivered a swift kick that sent my pug flying.

"That's it. Get out! No one hurts my fucking dog." I managed to push Chris out the front door, tossing his backpack after him. I slammed and locked the door, panting and praying he would just go away. Instead, he just banged on the door screaming obscenities at me. I called apartment security and lied that a homeless guy was outside my door. I heard the scuffle as the guard removed him from the building.

I showered and dressed for work, afraid to take Buzz out for his morning walk. Chris was sitting on a set of steps on the north side of the apartment complex staring into space.

"Are you OK?" I asked tentatively.

"Please let me come back inside. I have no one, nowhere to go. I have nothing. Please help me."

"I tried to help you and thought you wanted off the drugs. Instead you shot up, freaked out, and kicked my dog. I can't do anything more for you."

"I understand," he said in defeat as if this scene had played out numerous times for him. "Will you at least try calling my mom?"

"What's the number?"

Chris recited an out-of-state number. I dialed, and a woman answered.

"Hi. Um, Mrs., well, I don't know your name. Chris needs help."

"I don't know a Chris," she snapped as the line went dead.

"What did she say? Try again, please," he asked.

I complied but only got a recorded error message; my number must have been blocked. "I don't know what else to do. I have to go to work."

"You're just going to leave me here? I'll end up on the streets or in jail or something."

Jail would probably do him good.

"I'm sorry."

At work, I plopped myself down inside a devout Christian co-worker's cubicle and asked if he would pray for my friend. He explained that I could do that myself but was happy to listen. I gave him the highly edited, noble version and broke down crying, hoping I wouldn't smear my carefully applied dark-circle concealer.

"I'm a horrible person for putting him out. That's not what God would want me to do, right?"

"God never wants His children to put themselves in harm's way. You did the right thing. Put your friend in His hands now."

40

Limited Time Engagement

LOS ANGELES AND PARIS: 2009–2010

I was high on meth the night I found Stuart's profile on Recon. com. Stuart's profile was different from the others. He claimed to enjoy cowboy boots, light bondage, and everything Disney. He was attractive in an odd sort of way. He didn't smile in any of the photos, and as it turns out, neither did he in person. He wasn't seeking a hook-up or a slave, or even a Dom-sub relationship. So what *was* he seeking? I've yet to formulate an answer. My profile clearly stated I was into PnP, but he never asked about it, and my guess was he didn't know what it meant.

A week later on December 5, 2009, we met in the Disney Esplanade—an open expanse that separated Disneyland from its then ugly stepsister park, Disney California Adventure. I had just finished a high-profile marketing event and was in full suit and tie. We went to a nearby Chili's where we ate and talked, and I tried to decide if I found Stuart attractive in person. Things looked up when he said he was born in Germany, immediately promoting him to "mysterious, exotic, and probably uncircumcised" status. I explained that I wasn't the person I claimed to be in my Recon profile. He stated that he *was* everything he professed to be.

I was seeing relationship potential, and against my better judgment (actually I had virtually no reasonable judgment skills left at this point in my drug career), he followed me home to my Fullerton apartment where we attempted to mess around. He was the awkward one, so much so that I questioned if he'd been sexual with another guy. The answer to this question, along with a whole host of others, would remain elusive.

Two dates later, we had an awkward, mostly one-sided (mine) conversation, as most of our conversations would prove to be.

"I like you," Stuart said.

"Well, I like you too."

"I think maybe I more than like you," he continued.

"I think maybe I more than like you too."

We had effectively skirted the dreaded "L" word in favor of the less threatening, lowercase "l" word. And so, it remained until Christmas when we traded up. He was even OK with my health status.

OK, he's the one.

We turned the corner into 2010, and Stuart announced that he made an annual trip home to Germany at the end of every January for his mother's birthday. I was feeling particularly co-dependent, but he assuaged my anxiety stating he would only be gone for a few days. But after some prodding, he admitted he would actually be gone for eighteen days. It felt like a devastating blow to our fragile new relationship. Yet it also afforded me some alone time I had been missing—a chance to take another brief spin on the party-go-round. Stuart was detached, aloof, and didn't act as though he would miss me anyway.

Stuart returned in February with a suitcase full of German chocolate and trinkets for our first Valentine's Day. While I had gotten high when he was gone, and although I did a lot of online chatting about it, I didn't hook up with anyone. But unwittingly, I had chatted with one of his dominant buddies on Recon, and Stuart had received an earful from the guy.

On February 18, he confronted me in my kitchen. His eyes were full of tears, as he leaned against the white stove. "I got an email from a friend named Mike. Master Mike. Ring any bells?"

"Uh, no. Should it?" I answered with a gut full of panic.

"You've been emailing him about becoming his slave. Is that what you want?"

"No, that's not what I want. I don't even remember talking to anyone named Mike. Or Master Mike. Even if I did, I love you. I want to be with you and you only." I was tap-dancing as fast as I could. Truth was there were *a lot* of Master Mikes on Recon, and I'd probably emailed a few of them.

"Well, I have copies right here of your emails. Would you like me to read them to you?"

Now I was crying. "I'd rather you didn't. Whatever I may have said, it was just talk. I was confused and lonely while you were away, and it didn't help that I barely heard from you."

"I care about you more than you know. So, I need to know, have you been faithful to me?"

"Yes, absolutely." It felt good to be able to answer honestly.

We hugged and somehow survived this initial hiccup.

* * *

We celebrated Stuart's birthday with a trip to see his mother and a two-day side trip for us to visit Paris. On his birthday night, May 7, we exchanged two six-euro stainless-steel rings atop the Eiffel Tower. Although we had purchased (I purchased, to be accurate) the rings that afternoon at some store on the Champs-Elysees, by the time we reached the top of the tower, Stuart had already forgotten, and I had to orchestrate the exchange. The rings were to be inexpensive placeholders until we found something more permanent. For cheap rings, they would prove hardier than our relationship.

All was well and good, and because I had pushed hard for a commitment with rings, I felt relieved to have it locked in with Stuart. It was basically the Daniel routine but without a ceremony. But 2010 had other ideas for us.

Stuart gradually began to move some clothes and toiletries to my place. I bought him a nightstand and a dresser, which were mostly filled with the silly gifts I frequently bought him.

Despite having a cheap ring on my left hand, and despite the feeling that I had finally found my life partner and was hopefully spared from being alone, Tina's allure still proved to be far more potent.

I was assigned to a four-city marketing tour for a new show at Disney California Adventure park. I had been part of the site-survey team in February and hoped that the tour would be funded so I could finally have a decent project that might yield a show jacket. The first leg of the tour was one week in San Francisco. I'd never held a job that included business travel, let alone staying at a four-star hotel. I told my producer that I intended to drive—on my own time and dime—up the coast so I would have access to a car while in the city, you know, to help the team. The producer said we could rent an extra car if we needed it. But I persisted, and he acquiesced, reminding me that there would be little down time and we would be working long hours setting up our elaborate marketing stunt at the Palace of the Legion of Honor. My real reason for driving was to haul a baggie of crystal and not one, but two suitcases stuffed with sex toys and bondage gear for the extracurricular fun I was hell-bent to find.

No need to go into detail about the week in S.F., other than to say that I probably didn't sleep a single hour. How could I? There were my work responsibilities, then there was a whole sketchy city to be explored. Hook-ups were easy to secure, much easier than in self-absorbed, plastic L.A. It seemed that most of San Francisco was either HIV positive or simply didn't care. And from a porn movie standpoint, it was the bareback capital of the world. Meth and those who slammed it were also easy to locate.

Stuart came to visit for the marketing stunt and stayed for a weekend. I was exhausted and still tweaking, but he didn't notice. He knew I hadn't had much time for sleep and believed my lie that I had been surviving solely on Rockstar energy drinks. "That stuff will kill you, honey," he would say. *Yeah, no shit.*

The remaining three cities—Sacramento, San Diego, and Los Angeles—were largely uneventful. I had to miss Sacramento due to my standing in as a producer at a park event. By the time we mounted the final stunt in L.A. at the Walt Disney Concert Hall, things were seriously strained with Stuart. I couldn't put my finger on it but remained convinced he had no awareness of my drug habit.

Stuart was eerily silent, even for him. Something was up; something was wrong. His work schedule was demanding, and we spent a decreasing amount of time together. On his days off, he would go to Disneyland or Knott's Berry Farm to ride rides. When he was in my area, we would grab lunch as we did on Thursday, August 12, 2010. We met at the Long John Silver's restaurant in Anaheim.

"Did you hear the news today?" I asked.

"You know I don't listen to the news. What happened?"

"Last week. A federal judge ruled that Prop Eight is unconstitutional." California had been in a multi-year battle to pass Proposition Eight, an amendment to the state constitution that would deem marriage to be solely between one man and one woman.

"Oh, that's great," Stuart said, unimpressed.

"They had a big celebration rally in West Hollywood last week. You realize what this means?"

No response.

"It means we can get legally married. We've got the rings on our hands. What do you say? Want to set a date?"

"Sure. Let's talk about it this weekend. I know you have to get back to work."

With that, Stuart sped away in his silver BMW convertible. We had plans for that night, but Stuart said he needed to go in to work. Since he worked as a manager for a retail chain, I didn't question it. He promised we would get together the next night to catch a movie; *Eat, Pray, Love* was opening at the Hollywood ArcLight. He was looking forward to seeing it.

I couldn't reach Stuart on Friday, August 13.

Friday the 13th, I thought. *Figures. Everything always gets wonky on Friday the 13th.*

I was about to find out just how wonky things could get.

41

Pay to Pray
MALIBU: 2010

Stuart wasn't at his condo, wasn't at work, and his cell phone went immediately to voicemail. I was concerned. Typically, when he got sick, he would hole up in his bed for two days, sleeping and ignoring the world. But he wasn't home. So, where was he?

I finally got him to respond to a text.

"I need some time to think. I can't get together tonight."

That, of course, spurred a flurry of panic texts from me. "Why not? What's wrong? Did I do something wrong? Are you mad at me? Can we at least talk? Please, honey, answer your phone. I don't understand what's going on."

Nothing but deafening digital silence.

I knew that Stuart would frequently retreat to the nearest beach to think. Since he lived in Glendale, the nearest was Santa Monica State Beach. I sped down Pacific Coast Highway (PCH), frantic to find him, talk to him, see his face. I paid ten bucks to enter the large parking lot and drove around twice looking for his car. Nothing. I tried to get my money back from the parking attendant in the cashier shack, but he wouldn't budge.

There were smaller parking areas further down PCH, and I scoured each one. With tear-blurred vision, I wended my way down the winding highway toward Malibu. Still, no silver 2005 BMW 325Ci convertible—at least not Stuart's—anywhere to be found. Finally, I parked at the Malibu Pier and started walking as the rain began to fall.

About a half mile on foot down PCH, I was soaked, but at least the rain masked my tears.

Why, exactly, am I in such a panic? He needs a night to himself to think. It doesn't mean the end of the world.

My behavior was irrational, but then, the two years of meth use had probably fried portions of my brain, at least enough to heighten my already-vivid and out-of-control imagination. Still, deep down in my gut, deep down in that sometimes-psychic and often psychically accurate area of myself, I knew something wasn't right. Or as Stuart would say when he was sick, "I just feel off."

A flashing purple neon palm shone in a storefront window on the ocean side of the highway, beckoning me to come closer. Akin to the palm silhouettes in neighbors' windows when I was kid, maybe here I could find help. Maybe herein lied answers.

The heavy glass door slammed behind me, as a cluster of little bells tinkled and smashed against the door frame, alerting the inhabitant (and probably the dead) of my presence. The pitiful waiting room had an assortment of New Age paraphernalia: a rickety shelf of geode crystals, a wagon-wheel coffee table with a tarot card motif mantel scarf haphazardly draped across its glass top, a dog-eared copy of *The Tarot and You*, and an ornate brass bowl filled with stinky-feet-smelling incense. A dead floor plant with a string of blinking Christmas lights dangling from its crusty limbs seemed to flash a warning: "Get OUT. Get OUT. Get OUT."

Soon, an interior door opened, and a female voice said sternly, "I'll be with you as soon as I can. Wait there. Don't leave." The sound of a television blaring *Wheel of Fortune* could be heard from some nether region of what must have been an apartment.

I paced nervously in the tiny lobby, tempted to leave but scared to go back out into the rain without answers. Soon, the female psychic slipped out the apartment door dressed in a shimmery caftan. She made no sound, as her outstretched left arm directed me to a small room behind a thick and dusty velvet drape.

"Sit. Don't tell me your name."

"But…"

"No, no, no. Don't say a word."

What the hell was this? The scene from *Back to the Future* where the 1955 Doc Brown pulls Marty inside his house to read his mind?

"You have come to the right place. I can help you. I'm Sandera."

"Sandra? Like Sandra Dee?" It seemed an unlikely name for a psychic, although, we were at the beach, and frankly I didn't care if her name had been Gidget.

"No. San-DER-ahhh. Sandera," she said with a sweep of her arm punctuating the middle syllable. "How can I help you?"

And here I thought she was the know-it-all, see-it-all mystic visionary who told me to remain quiet.

"I thought you said—"

"I know why you are here. What do you want to happen?"

I broke down in pitiful sobs. "I want him back. I've lost him. Have I lost him? Oh my God, I've lost him, haven't I?" This was some real pathetic drivel I was spewing.

"It's unclear," she replied, with an answer as generic as one side of the twenty-sided polyhedron inside a Magic Eight Ball.

"Why is it unclear?"

"It all depends on you. How much are you willing to give up?"

Oh, great. Here comes the money part.

"You mean how much money?"

"Don't insult me! This is about you surrendering. Of course, there will be a cost attached."

I looked around the tiny consulting room. To my right was a gas fireplace with a carved mantel strewn with a representative object from every known faith including a cross, a figurine of the Virgin Mary, a Buddha statue, the six-sided Jewish star of David on a stick resting casually next to a Satanic pentagram, and the Hindu "Aum" symbol painted on a ceramic tile. She had every religious base covered. If you were Jewish, BAM! She was a Jewish priestess. If you were Catholic, she was a nun. If you were a blubbering mess like me, she was a mystic goddess with an open palm waiting to be filled with money.

"How much?"

"I can get him to come back to you, but it won't be easy. Or cheap."

Come on, lady, spill the magic beans. I was ready to empty an ATM to get Stuart back.

"Fifty dollars today. Tomorrow, you will return with more."

The "more" scared me. "How much more?"

"Seven hundred."

"I can't afford that."

"Yes, you can. You can easily afford it. But this isn't about money. Do you want to risk losing the one true love of your life?"

"No. Do you take cards? I mean, other than tarot?" I laughed nervously at my own lame joke.

"This is nothing to joke about. Of course, I take cards—but only when the situation warrants."

Had I been in a different mental state I might have asked if that included Diner's Club.

From beneath a table draped with an Indian scarf, she produced a credit card machine and expertly zipped my card. She sold herself as she swiped. "I have helped many, many people. Stars, celebrities."

Cool. "Now, can I ask you questions?"

"Tomorrow, you may ask. Tonight, I must pray. Now you need to leave."

With thermal-paper receipt in hand, I left with a shred of hope and an appointment to return the next day at 4 p.m.

42

No Time to Waste
MALIBU: 2010

I finally fell asleep around 7 a.m. and awoke in a panic at eleven. Maybe it had just been a horrific nightmare, some kind of cosmic wake-up call. I half expected Stuart to be lying beside me.

The sting of reality bit me. Exhaustion washed over me in waves. I parked myself at my desk and was tempted to smoke some meth, inevitably losing myself scouring the Web for sex. Instead, I lit up a Marlboro Light and stared zombie-like at my screen. I nearly fell out of my desk chair when my Mac startled me with a Yahoo email alert.

◆ ◆ ◆

Saturday, August 14, 2010 – 11:14 a.m.

Subject: Saturday

Hi Honey,

I needed to be alone to clear my mind last night. Sitting at the beach is maybe my way of yoga. Sitting there for a few hours, it helped me… Also, another thing really became clear to me. I do love you very much, which made me realize especially after the last week that I am not the man you need as your partner. I do need my own time to deal with things. I only wanted to be alone to clear my mind about work… Sorry I cannot be that man to have to look at everything I am doing twice. Further, I cannot and do not want to put my current work stress on you, which clearly adds in a major way to your stress… Sorry I cannot be the man you need.

Stuart

◆ ◆ ◆

I doubled over as if I had been kicked in the gut and called the psychic but only got her voicemail. I left no fewer than five panicked messages, blubbering and trying to explain the email. I asked to see her sooner. She told me to get in the car immediately—don't shower, don't do anything. Well, except to be sure to stop at the ATM.

I soon learned that I had a $500 daily withdrawal limit. I hoped Sandera would take a non-tarot card for the balance.

Once I was back inside the multi-religion consulting room, I showed Sandera a copy of the email.

Sandera's face became ashen. "It's worse than I feared. Did you bring the money? There's no time to waste."

Her nod toward my jeans was a subtle prompt to dig out my wallet. I forked over five hundred bucks in cash and asked to put the rest on my Visa debit card.

"You really need to bring me cash. Charging my fees to a card tells the Universe you have a less-vested interest in bringing about change. I'll accept it this time only," she scolded as she swiped.

I wondered if she had had problems with clients disputing credit card charges when the desired results weren't achieved. "The Universe should understand daily limits."

Sandera gave me a chilling look of disapproval. "So. The email. Did you reply? I really hope not."

"No, I didn't reply. I didn't know what to say. I was hoping you would guide me."

"You did the right thing by not replying." She made big, sweeping motions over her head. "But you've already shifted the energies away from you. What did you do when you got home last night?"

"I went to bed."

"Before that. What did you do?" the psychic pried.

You mean before or after I jacked off?

"I threw all the stuff I'd given Stuart into a corner."

"What's on your forehead?"

"Nothing."

"There's a mark on your forehead. What happened?"

"I banged my head out of frustration. It's just something I do."

"Lewis, Lewis, Lewis. I told you *not* to touch anything, *do* anything. You've made it worse. Quick, you need to leave now immediately. I have to get my ladies to start praying. There's no time to waste. Call me tomorrow." The whole no-time-to-waste thing seemed to be her go-to line.

As instructed, I called Sandera first thing the next day, around nine Sunday morning. There was, of course, "no time to waste," so I sped to Malibu.

"The situation is much, much worse than I thought," she said in her unidentifiable Mumbai-meets-Mexico accent. "And because you did not follow my instructions—exactly to the T—it's going to take a lot more work. And a lot more money," she scolded.

Let me guess. There's no time to waste?

"But I can't afford—"

Sandera cut me off with a wave of billowy caftan. My guides tell me you can afford it."

"How much?" I prayed it would only be another couple hundred at worse.

"You—not following my instructions. You—moving Stuart's stuff when I very distinguishedly (I think she meant distinctly) told you not to. You and your lack of faith will cost you…$7,000."

I gasped audibly before literally falling out of my chair. "You've got to be kidding."

"I don't kid. Ever." She was as stern and as crotchety as an old Catholic school nun wielding her trusty ruler.

"But why so much more? I mean, I can't afford this."

Sandera leaned toward me, showing her best I'm-here-to-help-you face. "Lewis. We've already discussed this. You can afford it. The question is, do you want Stuart back or not?"

"Of course, I want him back. Would I be here right now?"

"You have a point. So. I must ask you to go get the money—cash only—so I can have my ladies start praying."

I thought they had already been praying.

"And due to the gravity of this crisis, I will have to try to find more ladies. I don't know if I can."

I don't know how she sourced her praying ladies, but since it was Sunday, I figured she could go scoop some up from some random church.

A realization. "It's Sunday. I can't pull that much cash out of an ATM."

"Then you'll do it first thing tomorrow, Monday morning. Before you go to work. You come here and bring me the $7,000. Cash, remember? Now, go home. I have a lot of work to do."

"Wait. Do I put Stuart's things back where they were or would moving them again screw with the energies? It's hard for me to see the things I gave him laying out."

She pondered for a moment. "Umm. Don't put everything back out, just a few special items. Now, go. No—wait! I have some things that will help you."

Sandera slipped back into the nether regions of her abode and returned with what appeared to be random stuff she simply grabbed from tables and shelves.

"Here's what I want you to do. And you must do it every night starting tonight in the exact order I'm telling you."

I scribbled as quickly as I could in the notebook I kept with me.

She handed me a cheap Catholic bargain-basement medallion of some saint. "Put this under your pillow every night and carry it in your pocket every day. Put everything back where it belongs. Light this incense on Stuart's side of bed for the next five nights. And write down your dreams."

She dashed into the waiting room and grabbed an enormous crystal geode that must have weighed thirty pounds and plopped it into my lap. "Place this crystal on his nightstand facing his pillow." I hoped his nightstand could support the rock's heft.

Next, she handed me seven vials of what appeared to be food coloring. "Anoint yourself with these essential oils and wear them while you sleep. One drop on your forehead, your throat, your heart, your solar plexus, below your naval, and behind each ear. You must anoint at the same time every night."

"Wait—which oil goes where?"

"It doesn't matter."

It doesn't matter. Oh, fine. I'm paying seven grand for "it doesn't matter."

"Here's the routine you must follow. Write this down. First, light the incense and wave the smoke from the head to the foot of bed on Stuart's side only. Second, read this card with the Jesus prayer on it." She handed me a fifty-cent devotional card with the serenity prayer that is used religiously at You-Name-It-Anonymous meetings. I later discovered that the prayer wasn't in the Bible nor did Jesus even speak those words.

"Third, anoint self. Fourth, place the Jesus card by the crystal geode. And last, you must wear all white to bed."

The only things she missed were for me to throw salt over my left shoulder and to jump down, spin around, and pick a bale of cotton.

"Do you have any questions?" she asked, as she started to push me toward the exit.

Yeah. Am I going to be on Candid Camera *while I do these ridiculous things?*

"No. No questions. I guess."

"Good. You be here tomorrow with the money."

Monday morning arrived, and I did as I was instructed. Blindly, stupidly, I pulled $7,000 out of my savings and drove as fast as I could—at least as fast as anyone could on the 405 on a Monday morning—and got to Malibu around ten. I delivered what felt like a ransom payment and was once again rushed out the door. No time to waste, of course. I went to work but found it impossible to focus on anything but the big chunk of change I had just forked over.

One day passed—no word from the psychic. Two days—nothing. Feeling like I was the butt of some cosmic joke, I followed through with the nightly routine, adding my own "Dear whoever's listening" prayer for good measure.

43

The Vision

CALIFORNIA STATE ROUTE 91,
WESTBOUND TOWARD SOUTH BAY: 2010

Wednesday, August 18, 2010. It was late in the afternoon, and I had spent the day working myself into a familiar state of panic; I hadn't heard from Sandera since dropping the cash into her magic bowl.

Unable to place any trust, however misguided, in anyone or anything, I bolted out of my office and toward South Bay, thinking I might find Stuart somewhere. Maybe at Floyd's Barbershop. Or at his favorite restaurant, the Rocky Cola Café on PCH. Or maybe—hell, I didn't know. It was just me being me, unable to be still, unable to still my mind, just filling the hours with activity, any activity, until I could legally drug myself to sleep. Of course, the drive included the requisite Hostess mini-donuts and lots of cigarettes.

As if it was scripted, the rain began to fall and traffic jammed. Mad at myself, mad at the world, I banged my head on my steering wheel over and over until my vision blurred.

The condemning voice was back, right on cue. *"You're a fucking loser. You screwed up your last chance for love. Drive faster. Just kill yourself. No one will care, and no one will even notice you're gone.*

You'd be better off dead. Do it now, and find peace."

The road opened up a bit, and I waged a private war of road rage, cutting off other cars as I zigzagged down the final westbound stretch of the 91 freeway that transitioned onto Artesia Boulevard. Skidding and sliding, I continued my suicidal drive through Gardena, running red lights and hoping I would just crash and die. If I was going to be alone for the rest of my life, then I didn't want to live.

The downpour intensified until I couldn't see through the rain pummeling the windshield. Even still, I kept my foot on the gas. I prayed I would die but spare any others who might be in what was about to be a twenty-five-car pileup.

Then, everything stopped. It felt as if the car had been lifted off the pavement. Kind of that feeling of weightlessness when you're in an automated car wash. Then, a blinding white light. A white-robed figure appeared to float mid-air in front of the car.

Oh crap. I really did it. Oh shit, oh shit. I'm dead.

I didn't hear a voice, rather sensed words in my head, kind of like seeing them on a giant teleprompter screen in my head. "Stop, Lewis. Stop now. You don't want to do this."

Just then, an incredible sense of peace washed over me, as what felt like an invisible hand gently brought my car to the side of the road and into the parking lot of a Ralph's grocery store. Weight upon heavy weight fell from my heart, from somewhere deep inside me. I sobbed. I breathed and wiped my tears.

Everything is going to be OK.

For a few unspeakably peaceful minutes, I was still. Stillness like I had never experienced.

I knew, without a doubt, that the vision of the white-robed figure was Jesus Christ. But I didn't know if the vision meant I was saved, condemned, or was even still alive. And like at least a dozen other terrifying drives in that stupid PT Cruiser, I looked around and was shocked that there were no flashing red and blue lights, no accident scene, no handcuffs waiting to haul me off to prison for reckless driving or worse. I cautiously got out of the car and started walking through the rain.

Why was I always walking through rain?

Another flashing neon hand beckoned.

44

Here's to the Ladies Who Pray
MALIBU: 2010

As the hamster in the wheel of my brain resumed running at breakneck speed, generating a tsunami of doubts, I found myself with my hand on the doorknob of yet another psychic's shop. I know. Hot stove will always be hot. Hot stove will always yield a burn. Hot stove must be avoided.

Hot stoves be damned. I stepped inside.

It was mildly hysterical how much Madame Karen's parlor looked nearly identical to Sandera's Malibu joint. There were withering plants and a Buddha statue reclining casually next to a bust of the Blessed Mother Mary on a long, narrow table draped with a ratty, found-it-at-Goodwill, bead-trimmed cloth. A plastic fish bowl was partially filled with an assortment of business cards behind a handwritten sign: "Drop your card in the bowl, and you may win a free introductory *physic* [sic] reading!"

Fantastic. Another magic bowl into which cards and dollars never return. And shouldn't one know how to spell the name of her own occupation? At least there was a chance I might win a refresher on quantum mechanics.

A heavy woman in a flowery caftan popped her bulbous head out from a side door, releasing a palpable odor of stinky incense.

"Take a seat. I'll be with you shortly," said the woman who I surmised was Madame Karen. Or Madame "Let Me Take More of Your Money." Same difference.

Not only did these psychics all use the same interior decorator, they all operated from the same tired playbook. So again, I waited. As I locked eyes with the Mary statue and sensed her disapproval, I was reminded of my vision and reassured myself that I had been led to this place. For validation? For verification of what I thought I saw? For the possibility of a free physics lesson?

I can look back now with pristine hindsight and identify some of the major moments in which God was trying to capture my attention. I had just had one of those life-changing, earth-shattering moments. Now, I see what a momentous and glorious occasion it was to have a larger-than-life vision of God's only Son appear to me during one of my most self-destructive moments. You would think that that sort of religious experience—as cliché as it may sound—should have been a bit more eye-opening.

Soon, I was taken into a consultation room that had all of *its* religious bases covered.

Holy schnikes. These people are all the same. Maybe it's a franchise.

"Why have you come here?" asked Madame Karen.

Um, you're the psychic. You tell me.

"I don't know. Well, I guess maybe you can tell me if the psychic I've been seeing in Malibu is for real."

"I see. What is her name?"

"Sandera. Like Sandra. Well, kind of."

"Did you see my sign? I charge seventy-five dollars per half hour."

I hadn't seen the sign, but yeah, whatever. "Sure. Yes, I saw it."

I proceeded to spill my beans about Stuart leaving me, about being led to Sandera, about the more than seven grand I'd dropped in her magic bowl. She proceeded to tell me how she did not like to comment on another psychic's work but that I could trust Sandera implicitly. And for seventy-five bucks, there I had it: concrete proof that I had thrown a good chunk of my savings down the New-Age drain.

This time, I didn't have to wait long for a response from Sandera. She called the next morning livid and demanding I get to Malibu immediately. I was producing an in-house cast event that day and tried to explain that I couldn't simply walk away. Sandera asked what was of greater import: (a) my job or (b) my desire to be with Stuart. My answer should have been "(a) my job." Instead, I dumped the responsibility of the event on my production assistant stating I had a family emergency.

"What did you do last night?" Sandera asked with the tone of a suspicious stepfather.

"I worked my event and then went for a drive."

"Why did you doubt me? Why did you doubt my work? You saw another psychic."

She's better than I thought.

"I, uh, well, I don't know." I sounded like a cheating spouse caught in a lie.

"My guides told me you consulted another psychic about me. Why, Lewis, why? Didn't you trust me? Why did you do this?"

My gut was that Sandera probably knew Madame Karen, and the latter called the former on her little pink psychic princess phone.

She continued. "I am so hurt by what you have done that I want to dismiss you as my client."

"I'm sorry. If you'll just give me my money back, I'll go away, and we can pretend like this never happened," I said.

"You know, Lewis, you do not understand how things work. How can I give you a refund? My ladies have already been paid. They've been praying around the clock for you and Stuart to get back together. So, no. No refunds."

"Well, again, I'm sorry. Has there been any progress on Stuart coming back?"

"Progress? Let me tell you about progress. Any progress that was made you undid. You destroyed my work and the work of my ladies. I really should just tell you to leave."

She saw the desperation in my face. And I saw it in hers; the Bank of Lewis was about to close its Malibu branch.

"I prayed all night about your situation, and after much prayer, God told me to not give up on you. So, I am here for you. But now, we have to start over. We have to undo the damage you did with your lack of faith."

"I'm not sure. I mean, I don't know what…"

"No, you do not know. This will cost you because I now have to bring in more ladies." She blathered on about how every minute of work that her prayer team (here's to the ladies who pray…) "had invested in my case" had been blown to smithereens by my act of cheating on her, my cowardice, and my deplorable lack of faith for seeking a second opinion.

"I'm afraid to ask, but how much more money are we talking about?"

"Seventeen thousand."

What the frack? I was under duress. There's no way I heard her correctly. "Seventeen THOUSAND—"

"Dollars. Yes, Lewis. That is what it will cost to start over and fix the mess you have made."

"No way. There's no way I can afford that."

"My guides tell me you can."

I've always wondered if, from that first swipe of my debit card, I had unwittingly given Sandera access to my Bank of America account information. It had to be that. I was convinced she wasn't much of a psychic.

"That will empty my savings account," I bluffed. Truth be told, I still had a decent chunk in the bank from the profit on my Nashville house sale.

"Lewis. Listen to me. This is very, very important. If you do not do this, if you do not continue this work with me..." her voice trailed off. "You need to trust me, Lewis. When I'm done and you have Stuart back, you will be amazed and wonder how I did it."

Oh, I'm sure the high price tag will have helped.

She continued with an ominous warning. "You need to have your life together by the end of 2012 as that's when a new cycle starts and locks in for the next ten to fifteen years. If you're in a negative cycle, it will lock in, and there will be no way out. Ever."

Clearly, I had no choice. "When do you need the—oh my God—seventeen thousand dollars?" The amount stuck in my throat.

"Today. Now. There's no time to waste. There's a Bank of America just a half mile down PCH. You need to go now."

I couldn't begin to fathom what I was doing. I pulled into the parking lot of the cozy, seaside-themed strip mall in which the bank branch was located. Was I so desperate for companionship, so afraid of being alone that I would fork over a huge sum to a psychic? I had already played out this scene in 2007 after Will dumped me after one date. (Yeah, I know. I'm the idiot.) But that time, it was a psychic in West Hollywood, and that time, it only cost me $500. But it was the same damn fear that I would grow old alone and never find love, that I would be the pathetic old queen in the corner of the bar, going home alone.

Stupid me. I always screw up every relationship. Well, this time will be different.

My palms were soaked, and my right hand tremor was at the top of its game as I approached the teller and asked to withdraw $17,000 from my savings. You'd think I was robbing the bank because, within moments, three employees in suits appeared wearing suspicious frowns and carrying handfuls of forms.

"I don't understand. It's my money. Why can't I withdraw at any time? It's a regular savings account, not one with penalties like a CD or IRA."

"It's not that you *can't* withdraw from your account, Mr., ah, is it Kemp-ster? Kemp-her?" Snivelly Suit #1 said, as he led me away from the counter to a semi-secluded spot.

"It's the amount that we're questioning," interjected Uptight Suit #2.

"And the purpose for which it's intended," chimed in Pompous Suit #3.

"But it's my money! It's my money!" Good grief. I was suddenly an angry customer, mobbing the Bedford Falls Building and Loan for my $242. "I don't understand why you need to know what I'm buying. It's, ah, a surprise for my wife. I'm buying a used car from a lady down the street."

Tap dancing was never my strongest suit.

The trio of suits uttered a throat-clearing "ahem" in unison. Uptight Suit #2 stepped forward and shoved a form at me. Turns out that withdrawing more than ten grand in cash on a single day has to be reported to the Internal Revenue Service as they might decide an investigation is warranted. Perhaps money laundering was afoot, an activity I never understood but always assumed had to do with an old wringer washer and a box of Tide.

I signed my life away, and within thirty minutes, I was leaving with a wad of cash. Had I been more prepared, I would have brought an aluminum briefcase with me. Had I possessed a brain, I would have run as fast I could away from Malibu, leaving my savings account largely intact, save for the first $7,000. Well, $7,700. OK, $7,750.

What the hell am I doing? I'm not even high. Why am I about to give all this money to a psychic?

I wrestled with a barrage of conflicting thoughts as I pulled onto PCH.

It was about what my life had always been about: the bone-chilling fear of being alone. In every relationship, I always felt the desperation for it to work, to grow, to last. Sure, it's easier to be coupled, to have a help mate. And it certainly makes for better "look at me, I have somebody" Instagram posts. But what was so horrifically awful about being single that had me draining my savings for a psychic with highly questionable talent and suspect motivation? One to a box, right? We come into this world alone and leave the same way, right?

I drove slowly. Went past the psychic's place, then pulled over to think some more. My phone rang.

"Where are you? When will you be here with the money? I cancelled my next appointment so I can meet with you."

Oh, chill out, woman.

I heard the desperation in her voice; there were ladies to pay.

"On my way."

And so, I dumped $17,000 in cash into the magic Tibetan singing bowl. Mentally and physically exhausted, I was ready to walk away in defeat.

Keep the friggin' money. I no longer care.

45

Back to the Beach

MALIBU: 2010

The streets were flooded, and my PT Cruiser struggled through knee-deep waters. The lesbian in my back seat—who just happened to be a dry cleaner—was anxious and telling me to drive faster. Then, the car stalled. I waded into a McDonald's bathroom and stared in the scratched mirror, as I started to peel layer after layer of skin from my face. I looked down at the leather harness I was wearing on my chest. It was heavy, making my neck and shoulders ache. I felt silly wearing it but assumed only I could see it. Apparently, I was wrong, as I got a disturbed "um, let's get out of here" look from a father taking his young son in to pee. I stripped off the wet leather and left it in the single stall.

That's all I could remember from the dream I had the night I gave Sandera half of my life savings. She had instructed me to keep a dream journal, to pay close attention to details, and to relay the dreams as accurately as possible to her.

"Good. That dream means we're making progress."

Lesbian dry cleaners and leather harnesses equal progress? Who knew?

400

Sandera continued. "And my guides have told me that Stuart is starting to really wonder why he hasn't heard from you. He's thinking about you. This is very good news!"

Well, it had better be good news for the hefty price tag.

"Do you think I'll get him back?"

Sandera's excitement faded. "That remains unclear and largely up to you."

"Wait. I paid you to bring him back."

"You paid me to *attempt* to get him back. I never made any promises. I never make any promises. That's not what I do," she explained with the precision of a corporate attorney. "But as I told you the first time you came to see me, I can't do this work alone. If you hadn't doubted me and gone behind my back to another psychic, you'd have him back by now."

Yeah, I know, I know. I'm the idiot.

"You must remain positive and focused on your desired outcome."

"What do I do next?"

"Keep doing your nightly routine, keep writing down your dreams, bring another photo of Stuart. And also bring the big crystal back to me tomorrow."

"Do you also want the broomstick of the Wicked Witch of the West?" I chuckled to myself. The joke was totally lost on Sandera.

* * *

Next day. August 25, 2010.

"The dream I remember from last night was quite disturbing. I was being chased, hunted by some extremely negative and scary guys. They marked me on the forehead with red ink from some kind of a gun. Then, I was hiding in a small, dark room. Drugs were involved."

"And what else?" Sandera asked.

"Nothing. That's all I can recall. Oh, yesterday was August 24th. My first husband Daniel's birthday. It was his birthday yesterday. Does that mean anything?"

Apparently not.

"Did you bring me the crystal?"

I did a mental double take, then realized she meant the big geode. I went to retrieve it from my car. I hadn't noticed before, but the innards of the crystal geode that had been a lovely purplish, ame-thyst-y shade was now a dingy gray. "I distinctly remember it being purple," I said.

"It was, it was!" Sandera clapped her hands to her cheeks in the classic *Home Alone* stance. It was as though she had surprised herself with her own parlor magic. "It's turned dark because it has soaked up a great deal of your negativity. You're doing so much better, Lewis. Keep at it. Quick! Put that one down." She hefted another large geode into my arms. "Take this one home. I have to recharge the energies of the first one. It may not be possible, and it may have to be destroyed."

I did a mental eye roll.

Um, gee, sorry about your rock, lady. Maybe you can get some sparkly gravel out of it for your dead plant.

The whole mess just seemed fruitier and sillier with every pass-ing day. Still, I lugged another heavy rock to my car, feeling ever more the stupid, lonely dude who put all his trust in psychics.

As I drove back to Orange County, I couldn't stop thinking about the little card with the illustration of Jesus and the serenity prayer. I skipped going home and went to a humble little storefront I had passed countless times: The Bible House of Orange County. I found myself drawn to the store and wondered if therein lied better, maybe different, answers to my quagmire. I stared dumbly at two walls of Bibles with unfamiliar acronyms: ESV, NKJV, NIV, HCSB, NLT, MSG. *No, can't do MSG,* I quipped silently, *gives me migraines.* It felt wrong to be cracking word-play jokes in my head inside a place with at least two dozen versions of God's Word. To a new seeker like me, the shelf tags looked worse than an eye chart.

Still, I knew I wanted a Bible. But in language I could comprehend, unlike the King James Version (KJV) I was given as a child. Having flunked the Shakespeare module of Advanced Lit in high school, I was tripped up by the formal thees and thous and thines. The New Living Translation (NLT) looked user-friendly. I selected one a little smaller than a paperback novel. It had a beautiful burgundy leather cover.

This feels right. I figured I might as well cover all *my* bases. Couldn't hurt to place a little more trust in God while I was still praying something good would come of the $24,750 I had spent in Malibu.

The night I purchased my first Bible, I had a vivid dream, one that felt too precious, too private to share with Sandera. I didn't want her psychic hands on it, dissecting and extracting meaning.

It was the morning of August 26. I woke at 4:37 a.m. with an overpowering feeling that, no matter what happened, I was going to be fine. I didn't have to strain to remember the details of the dream.

I had a vision of myself, possibly in a past life, fishing with Jesus. I sensed I was Judas Iscariot and felt deep remorse for betraying Jesus for financial gain. I was seeing this as if it was on a screen on my forehead. Then, a smoke screen descended, and I could no longer see the vision.

I knew the story from playing Jesus in *Cotton Patch Gospel*. Judas was one of Jesus' disciples, the one who betrayed Him for thirty pieces of silver. I located the information in my Bible, finding it first within the Gospel of Matthew. Fascinating. But I couldn't decipher the dream's meaning or significance.

It also took time before I came to the conclusion that past lives were probably a bunch of hokum, a fictional mechanism for explaining away phobias and getting a comforting "there, there" pat on the shoulder for present-life problems. It was a coping device I had relied upon far too often.

Having trouble with romance in this life? Well, of course. It's just some old emotional pain from a past life. Hating yourself? Well, no wonder. You killed yourself in three past lives. Nothing you can do about these missteps of the past.

At least that was the horseshit that had been peddled to me for more than two decades.

I was finally ready to make real changes. Positive changes. In *this* life. Here and now.

I quit smoking cigarettes cold turkey.

I bought a brand new, dark green Jeep Patriot that was fresh and clean and didn't reek of smoke nor was riddled with memories of swinging through Hollywood with Tina.

I got some much-needed sun on my face and got a military haircut.

I went back to the Bible store and bought a masculine cross on a simple black cord to wear.

I changed my radio station to 95.9 "The Fish" and started listening only to Christian music.

On my third trip to the Bible store, I bought a stack of Christian CDs, three Christian self-help books, a "Jesus fish" sticker for my Jeep, and a sack full of Christian *tchotchkes*. Did I mention that I tend to overdo things?

I prayed and asked to be saved but doubted I did it the right way.

Perhaps more importantly, I started to own my mistakes, own my life choices, and, with or without Stuart, decided to move forward.

During what were starting to feel like counseling sessions, albeit quite expensive counseling sessions, I shared my progress with Sandera. Coincidentally, miraculously, she had had a vision that *very* morning. "Stuart wants you to change from A to Z."

"Holy shit. Sorry," I half-apologized in the direction of the multi-religion mantel. "That's a phrase he uses constantly: from A to Z."

"He needs to see drastic changes in you, more enthusiastic about work, to take better care of yourself. He wants to trust you but does not trust you at present. You need to work very hard on your trustworthiness and self-confidence. You must believe in yourself."

Well, crap. There it was again. That same old, worn-out axiom that had been shoved at me my whole life. Believe in yourself. How in the world do I do that?

"How much does he know? I mean, do you think he knows about the drug use? I feel like I'm being watched or followed." I had yet to plumb the depths of methamphetamine paranoia.

"He has no proof of your meth use. If you admit this to him, rebuilding trust will be very difficult if not impossible. But to answer your questions, he has not been to your apartment. He has not hired a private investigator. Contact will occur within the next seven days. But before he contacts you, he needs to see changes in you."

How was I going to show positive change when he refused to correspond with me, wouldn't acknowledge nor respond to texts, and rarely checked in on Facebook? Still, I've never been afraid of a challenge, and the spate of new activity that accompanied the new project was a welcome time-suck for my overactive mind.

I staged a series of self-improvement selfies at several of his favorite places. Touching a stingray at the Aquarium of the Pacific. Taking in the view of L.A. at Griffith Observatory. Shopping for used CDs at Amoeba Records on Sunset. Eating pretzels and wieners at Alpine Village. In each photo, I made a point to show I was still wearing my ring. And each photo was texted to him with an upbeat "Thinking about you today," or "Hope you're having a great day," or something to that effect.

But I had no way to know if Stuart was getting the photos. He didn't have an iPhone as I did, so I didn't get the false comfort of status messages, such as "delivered" and "read." So, just in case he was looking, I posted the pictures on Facebook. And there, I saw that he had changed his profile picture. And in the new photo he was showing his left hand, sans a ring.

Of course, I panicked.

I called Sandera and left my usual litany of "There's no hope, is there" and "It's hopeless; what do I do now" voice messages. No response. It was as though everyone had taken their phone off the hooks.

I struggled to sleep, then awakened at 3 a.m. with a clear vision, much like the lunchbox one a few years earlier. I was to write a book for him. Not a novel, but something highly personal and deeply apologetic. I knew the title should be *From A to Z*. I knew that I should, letter by letter of the alphabet, detail the changes I was making and those I would continue to make. For example: A is for attitude (have a better one). Anxiety (have less). Appreciation (show more). For each word, I was to write a short paragraph. Further, the book needed to be completely handwritten and handcrafted. And finally, I sensed an instruction—*give the book to Stuart on September 13*—exactly one month after he walked out.

And so, because I instinctively knew that no off-the-shelf greeting card was going to win him back, I wrote him a book.

And I didn't just write a book, I meticulously handcrafted an entire book: binding, end sheets, cover art—all of it. The money came from finally cashing in the two gold wedding bands from the failed marriage with Daniel. There had been a part of me still clinging to that tired and shattered dream, and I knew it bothered Stuart. On the day he vacated my apartment, he took all of his personal items, leaving only the gifts I had given him, but he also left me a symbolic message. In my library cabinet, I had displayed the Prince Philip and Prince Charming figurines that had sat atop the 1999 wedding cake. On this occasion, on this latest hasty exit by a loved one, I found that the Prince Charming figure (who I always said personified Daniel) had been overturned.

Post haste, I smashed the two figurines in the third-floor trash room, trash room number 3B, at the Pinnacle at Fullerton Luxury Apartments. Sandera would later say the destructive act was a bad move. For the energies and such. Of course. For the energies.

With the $90 from the sale of the gold rings, I purchased all of the supplies to make and bind the custom book, which cost precisely $89.67. If the $24,750 to the psychic didn't do the trick, I prayed my little book would.

Despite Sandera's vision and prediction, contact from Stuart did not happen within seven days. By this point, it was ten days without a peep, and I couldn't stand the silence.

It was a Thursday night, and I boldly got through the security gate at his Glendale condo. I knocked and waited, then knocked some more. I heard muffled voices inside so clearly someone was home. Finally, Stuart's housemate—owner of the condo, also named Stewart (with a different spelling)—opened the door.

"Is he here? Please, I just want to talk to him for a minute," I pleaded as the door was closing in my face.

"My" Stuart appeared in the doorway.

"Please. Can we talk? Please?"

Stuart #1 dismissed Stewart #2. Teary-eyed, Stuart #1 hugged me and said that, yes, we could talk.

"Can we go get coffee or something?"

"Yes, we can," he replied.

I offered to drive. We walked two blocks to where I had parked the new Jeep.

"Where's your car?" he asked.

I clicked my remote, and the Jeep answered with two chirps and a cheerful flash of its taillights. Stuart shot me a confused grin. I played it off as nonchalantly as possible with a "you mean, this old thing" gleam in my eye.

The impromptu coffee date was short but successful. He had to work early the next day, so we planned a longer visit on Saturday. When he suggested we meet in Malibu, I nearly lost it. Did he know about Sandera? And what was it about Malibu?

* * *

Saturday, September 11, 2010. We met at the Getty Museum and awkwardly perused its collection of ancient art. By the time we grabbed a bite at their café, I was certain I had blown it. I had been intensely aware of every word Stuart uttered, every body gesture, every eye movement, anything that could provide a minute-by-minute gauge of my success-to-failure ratio. We strolled out to the parking lot where I was absolutely sure I would hear "Well, we tried. Thanks for buying lunch. See ya." Instead the offer came to spend more time together, go walk the pier, the one they had used in one of my favorite movies, Annette Funicello's 1987 comeback film, *Back to the Beach*.

He remembered the movie.

I took it as a good sign.

Eventually, we ended up at a beautiful botanic garden overlooking the ocean. I had been carrying the book in a gift bag since the pier. We sat silently, peacefully on an ornate bench.

"I wrote this for you," I said, as I tentatively handed the book to Stuart. "I *made* this for you." He flipped through the book as tears filled his eyes. "Can we start over?" I asked. His response was an affirmative bear hug.

We walked down PCH to an expensive-looking seafood restaurant. Knowing Stuart's love for everything ocean, I willed myself to eat fish. We dined at a table on the sand just a couple hundred feet from the water.

Over an enormous margarita glass of calamari, I choked down a piece of the squid then said to Stuart, "I more than like you, you know."

"I more than like you too."

We shared a double order of key lime cheesecake, as a picture-perfect, Malibu sunset bathed the ocean with brilliant orange light. It was… perfect. Maybe too perfect.

46

Immaculate Deception
REDONDO BEACH: 2011

I'm not sure how we got from reconciliation to co-habitation in the course of two weeks, but nevertheless it happened, and I was delighted. Stuart wanted to live near a beach and most definitely not in Orange County. I loathed the idea of another commute to Anaheim, especially after the Hollywood Tower fiasco. I wasn't surprised when he wanted to look at apartments in Redondo Beach. As was always the challenge in SoCal, finding a reasonably affordable apartment with reserved parking, air conditioning, and a washer and dryer in the unit at a property that allowed dogs was quite a tall order. I hadn't told Stuart anything about Sandera but privately wondered if she could locate a place for us.

Now that Stuart was back in my life, Sandera's services were considered rendered. Which was fine by me. I never again wanted to set foot in her place nor drop another dime into her magic bowl.

Around the beginning of October, we signed a lease for a tiny, albeit charming, one-bedroom apartment above the Redondo Pier. Stuart's search efforts yielded two reserved parking spots, a stacking washer-dryer unit in a hacked-up coat closet, and an incredible view of the Pacific. Buzz was welcome after I paid a hefty pet deposit. I lost the battle of the air conditioning.

"Who needs AC when you have all that fresh ocean air?" Stuart asked.

Well, me, frankly, because I had grown increasingly intolerant to heat and humidity.

Stuart was truly in his element living steps from the beach. He beamed with happiness, and I was happy for him, for me, for *us*. On the day we took possession of our top-floor unit, Stuart had prepared a little beach-themed, welcome home display on the kitchen counter.

And things were good for a time. Maybe too good. Because hanging over my head was always the unnerving, foreboding sense of the spell wearing off, the magic losing its mojo, the coach turning back into… well, you get the idea.

We had a picture-perfect, beach-themed Christmas and sailed into 2011 as if the separation had never happened.

We spent months combining our storage units into one, enjoying trips to In-N-Out Burger for Double-Doubles and "animal-style" fries in between the exhausting work.

There were trips to SeaWorld and getting in the water with a dolphin.

There were trips to the Aquarium in Long Beach and a private encounter with a sea lion.

Stuart put his finishing touches on the balcony and deemed it the most romantic place in South Bay. It was pretty special. Mom came for a visit, and she fell in love with the beach. I thought we'd have to pry her off the balcony so she could make her flight back to Colorado.

So, yes, there were these magical moments of joy, of bonding, and of making a home together. Still, I couldn't ignore that ominous feeling and the little voice reminding me it was all just a $24,750 magic spell, and that spells always lose their power—read any fairy tale.v The feeling was worse than the invisible dark cloud that had hung over me since, well, since Dennis shamed me in the Mad Hatter shop, denying me a $4 pair of Mouse ears.

As summer began to bear down on Southern California, driving up the heat and humidity, Buzz got sick again, vomiting uncontrollably and peeing all over the once-new carpet. My memory flashed back to his stomach surgery in 2008, the three thousand bucks to save his life, and the rest of that awful time in the Hollywood Tower. This time, however, Buzz hadn't ingested a piece of a toy or a wad of gauze; he had a malignant, inoperable tumor on his belly. Hard times and difficult decisions were ahead.

Then, that summer, Stuart's aunt in Germany died, and he went back for her funeral. That was when Tina decided it was time to stir up trouble in the inimitable way that only Tina can, finding just the right loophole to slip through.

Somehow, all of my Christian-music-filled commutes and weekly Bible studies weren't enough to keep me from being triggered. I had figured that my newfound faith would shield me from using again, that winning Stuart back was monumental enough to keep me away from the party. That's probably the point at which fellow addicts would scold me for not sticking with CMA. But as I've said, attending Crystal Meth Anonymous in and of itself was one huge trigger, as attendees spoke in detail about their drug use.

It seemed to have happened early in the summer during an

overnight test of watercraft on the Rivers of America for the show *Fantasmic!* I was with my production team at Disneyland's man-made river several sultry late nights in a row. Maybe it was a rough-looking tech or a co-worker whose demeanor hinted a penchant for partying. I never found out, but nevertheless, I was triggered. I wanted to use more than anything else, to get high and wild, and escape my relative normalcy for a while.

I had been clean for about nine months, I think, but I had been careful to keep the contact info for my dealer who I'll call Chad. He operated from, and ostensibly lived in, Long Beach, which was not only a hotbed for crystal meth activity but was also where the vast majority of CMA meetings were held. Depending on his delivery route on any given day, making the connection with Chad could be there or in Anaheim or halfway to Huntington Beach in front of a certain Radio Shack. He only dealt during bankers' hours and always requested several hours' notice. I made nearly all my connections in business casual with a Disney badge swinging from my hip on really long lunch hours.

I had the hardest part, the "what" covered. However, this time around the party-go-round, the problem was finding the "where." I was cultivating a small circle of partying buddies close to work. Typically, I would find a reason to leave work early and head to one of these buddies' houses. One regular was a straight guy who didn't care what I smoked, snorted, or otherwise put in my body as long as I provided oral service while he watched nasty straight porn and smoked a ton of weed, courtesy of me. Things were different from the previous years' romps through Hollywood and San Francisco. The highs weren't *that* high any longer. I stopped lugging all those sex toys around in the suitcase. It had officially become all about the drugs. I just wanted to be in a secluded room, doing my thing.

So much for that Jesus vision less than a year prior. So much for giving half my life savings to a psychic to win back my partner. So much for everything.

But there was a change brewing in me, an overpowering sense of guilt. For doing drugs, for cheating on Stuart, for not being as present at work as I could have. At every PnP session, I would make a point to not only remove my ring but to also remove the cross necklace. I had the correct sense that God was watching my actions. I would shake my head with disgust for myself, then whisper up toward God, "I know. I know. I'm sorry. Please forgive me." But I didn't go as far as saying "help me quit."

With my party revival going full speed, especially as I would come dragging in around five or six in the morning, I needed alibis. So, I started to weave a flimsy fabric of lies for Stuart. Fortunately, I had other projects that occasionally required overnight shifts.

"Remember those eels in *Fantasmic!*? Yeah, well, we've got to try more options. I'll be gone all night," or "We're installing a new exhibit at Innoventions, and I'll probably just sleep there." In my head, it was a plausible ruse. Innoventions was essentially a ragtag collection of corporate-sponsor displays with technical components of questionable interest for park guests. The whole mess was contained in the infamous, rotating building in Tomorrowland that had once housed the classic audio-animatronic show *Carousel of Progress*, as well as the short-lived bicentennial extravaganza *America Sings* that paid animatronic homage to 200 years of American music. The show—and the building—closed prematurely after a female cast member got crunched between two of the revolving seating sections, sometime between "My Old Kentucky Home" and "Pop! Goes the Weasel." Or, rather, splat goes the attraction hostess.

In the fairly creepy basement of the building was the Corporate Sponsor Lounge, complete with small offices, a conference room, and a comfortable seating area with one ridiculously long and curvy sofa. And that's where I told Stuart I slept on several occasions when I was actually tweaking with my new Orange County party buds. When one of them wasn't available, I would get a motel room at Harbor Boulevard and the 91. While I might have attracted more interesting guests had I gone to Hollywood or Long Beach, I figured staying close to work gave me a sense of justification that I was at work or close to it. Nearby, you know, in case I was needed to update a budget.

By this point, the addiction had a vise-grip on me. I was using on a daily basis; it was the only way I could survive. I'd smoke meth simply to wake up—it was only as mildly effective as coffee, and there was no high—then Ambien myself to sleep every night. It was a classic recipe for disaster; ask Judy Garland or any addict caught on the hamster wheel of uppers by day and downers by night.

Soon, the lies grew to fictional weekend trips to see a former colleague in Palm Springs. See him I did. But he also saw me a few times in weekend-long, unflattering positions in leather slings at sleazy leather sex "resorts." When I was too tweaked to talk or think or walk a straight line, Eric would bring me Chicken McNuggets, trying to get me to take some nourishment, however greasy.

Online, I met a kinky gay couple who lived up the coast in Santa Barbara or Santa Cruz or Santa Somewhere. A weekend-long play session yielded telltale red marks on my butt and my chest, evidence of intense Dom-sub play. Or Dom-Dom-sub. Kind of like a twisted game of "Duck, Duck, Goose." Two-on-one was one of my favorite configurations.

Through all this, I was convinced that Stuart had no clue. The weekend after being in Santa Wherever, I stopped at Walgreens to buy a tacky beach trinket that I lied and said was a souvenir I picked up over the weekend. Nothing says "I love you, and I'm so glad you're back in my life" like a $5.99 plastic snow globe purchased at the drugstore down the street.

Four years later when he left for good, he would finally mention the red marks and admitted his hurt and his knowledge that I had been cheating. But in my meth-twisted brain, I never thought of these Master/slave play sessions as cheating. I told myself they were a form of therapy, sessions during which I was working out issues that had plagued me since childhood.

But hadn't I already been the abused, pummeled by Mom's second husband? Wouldn't it make more sense to turn the tables and be the dominant one?

I'm working through it. It's a process, I told myself.

47

Bad Boys, Bad Boys
REDONDO BEACH: 2011

Then Stuart's mother came for Christmas and stayed six weeks. I had already met her, and she was a perfectly nice German woman. But the three of us—four with Buzz—in the tiny, cramped, humid beach apartment was too much. Because we only had one bedroom, we set up a futon in the living room for her, and she kind of just took over that area of the apartment. Stuart and I had already been bumping into each other among way too much furniture. I had insisted on shoving a full mid-century sectional from Salvation Army in the apartment. And then, there was Buzz, completely deaf and blind by this point, bumping into everything like a wayward pinball and leaving a chem trail of smelly cancer urine.

Then, with it being the holidays, Stuart was working uber-long shifts at the Park (he had, with my financial assistance returned to working at Disneyland in 2011), and with it being the holidays, my projects were already up and running for the season. As such, I didn't have much to do at the office. So, German mother and I would stare awkwardly at each other, doing an endless game of charades in an attempt to communicate. Her English consisted of "hello" and "chicken"; my German vocabulary was "ausfahrt" (freeway exit) and "schildkröte" (turtle). So basically, it was a conversation of "hello, my turtle would like your chicken to exit the freeway."

She couldn't sleep due to terrible arthritis. I couldn't sleep because I was smoking meth just to function. Stuart's mother and I had a spate of awkward, middle-of-the-night encounters during which she was sitting with her nightie open wide, legs spread for comfort, sans panties, on the futon. I pictured Marlene Dietrich. Or Madeline Kahn as Marlene Dietrich a la *Blazing Saddles. Where the hell are her panties?* Oh yeah. She had washed them, and they were air drying on the handles of our beach bikes. Well, nothing like the refreshing aroma of the salty Pacific.

It was far too much closeness for proverbial comfort. I white-knuckled it through Christmas then was blessedly busy with overnight rehearsals for Disneyland New Year's Eve 2012. On January 3, I decided (in the middle of the night, of course) to start disposing of my extraneous belongings in the name of simplification, of feeling the need to pare down. Hell, I was just trying to carve out a few square feet of my own. I shoved three-quarters of my clothes in our storage unit and donated my beloved Victorian gentleman's chair to Out of the Closet in Long Beach (the same location where I learned I had HIV). Later, I was heartsick over giving away the chair that had appeared on my set of *Angel Street* at the Boiler Room. So, dear, sweet, kind, forgiving Stuart paid sixty bucks to retrieve the chair and hauled it back home in the BMW with the convertible top down, undoubtedly getting strange looks on the 405.

I thanked him by locking myself in the bathroom with porn on my iPad and meth in the pipe. Seems I, too, was having "arthritic bouts" that required long, as in two-hour-long, soaks in the tub.

Once I was sufficiently drugged, I'd hide my stash and my pipe in the back of a bathroom drawer and head out for a sleazy encounter in a restroom on the pier or see what rough trade might be lurking along fisherman's wharf.

If I wasn't too tweaked, I'd head out in the Jeep to the one adult bookstore in Hermosa Beach. On one occasion, I snorted more crystal while inside a video booth. Then, the bright fluorescents came on and, from an overhead speaker, an announcement was made that the store was closed.

Why am I always closing down these nasty places?

A familiar scenario ensued of being too high to drive at three in the morning with not a clue of what to do next. So, once again, I started walking. There was a long strip of greenway below PCH with lots of mature trees and bushes, plenty of places to hunker down and ride it out. When that didn't work, I resumed walking and ended up in a restroom stall on Hermosa Beach. The beachfront clubs had just closed, and there was plenty of commotion from drunken revelers.

Good. The cops will be busy with that scene for a while.

In yet another brilliant move, I pulled the still-loaded pipe out of my sock and lit up.

Yeah, that's better. I think I can get back now. I think. Just another hit to be sure.

The closing-time commotion of the nearby bars had waned, and I could hear the crashing of the waves, the creak of the playground swings in the breeze, the squawk of a lone seagull. Then, the jarring, "scare the living crap out of you" pounding on the stall door next to mine.

It was the cops.

Soon, they were extricating my next-stall-neighbor, a belligerent homeless dude. With the drunken, incoherent yelling as my cover, and as carefully and quietly as I could manage, I got up on the toilet, so my legs weren't visible beneath the door. I didn't dare to breathe.

Fuck. I'm next.

My mind played a highlights reel from *Cops.* You know, where the often-shirtless perp is busted, cuffed, and sat on the ground while drugs and paraphernalia are pulled from the perp's pockets. *Lowlife drug addicts*, I used to think as I would shake my head in disgust.

How could anyone screw up his life so badly?

The reflection in the shiny metal plate mounted to the stall door ahead of me offered a visual hint.

Then, the cops were gone, and I had again narrowly escaped being caught and arrested. I walked as swiftly and nonchalantly as possible to my car, avoided driving on PCH, bolted up the side steps to my third-floor apartment, and hopped in the shower. Stuart was an unusually sound sleeper. He didn't even know I'd never come to bed.

48

Chasing the High
LOS ANGELES: 2012

When you've come to the end of yourself—the end of your rope—and you know rock bottom can't be much further away, meth tricks you, seduces you. Back into the game, back on the roller coaster. Except each ride on the coaster is different. The highs aren't that high. But the dips, the steep drops, are more intense and frightening. Each valley lowers you deeper into your own mire and muck, illuminating and amplifying every dark, repressed desire.

* * *

Buzz's health problems exacerbated shortly after the move to Redondo. A fellow dog walker blamed the water treatment plant leaking poison into our water. As such, I put Buzz strictly on bottled water. But, in addition to his growing tumor, he had, at some point during his eleven years, become diabetic. Thankfully, pet insurance covered the insulin and syringes. Our Redondo vet closely monitored Buzz and his tumor. As long as she felt he wasn't suffering, she'd continue to treat him. And that was good news for me, as I couldn't bear losing my pug-baby. Also because I couldn't bear losing access to the syringes.

By this time in my meth addiction—more than four years since the fateful first night out—I had to smoke a ton of crystal to get high. And even then, it was only akin to the quick jolt of an afternoon cup of coffee to stave off drowsiness. My drug of choice, methamphetamine, as I imagine with most illicit, highly-addictive drugs, quickly loses its potency with frequent use. It's that age-old dilemma of chasing the high. I had to go hardcore to get enough of it in my system to feel anything. I had squirreled away a couple of dull, used needles obtained from my dealer (it's a miracle I didn't catch hepatitis) and had become adept at finding my own vein, although all the hunting for a vein often produced nasty bruising of my left arm. I had heard about collapsed veins and was afraid that was beginning to happen. Not for fear of health consequences, but a dire fear of losing my precious drug-delivery routes.

In addition to my own kit of makeup and a battalion of bruise- and scar-reducing creams that resembled Topher's, I also had a large variety of hair conditioners, creams, moistening masks, and itch sprays. Perhaps it was a different variety of meth from a different "cook," or from using dirty pipes, but my scalp became covered with little red bumps that begged to be picked open. Speed bumps, I guess they were called. And they seemed to be getting worse the longer I was on the stuff. I read that addicts would often pick at their skin, trying to dig out bugs that weren't there. While I didn't experience that particular paranoia, I nevertheless picked until my fingers were bloody. Worse yet, I would do this at work at my desk, staring at my PC screen in a picking trance. I always wondered if others noticed, but no one said a word; everyone seemed to have their own cubicle quirk: nail trimming, snot snorting, gum smacking, bracelet jingling, desk tapping. Scalp picking was mine.

I had to carefully ration Buzz's syringes and reuse them as many times as possible before the needle became so dull it was like trying to drive a nail into my vein without a hammer. More than once, the syringes ran out before the insulin, and I had to beg a pharmacist to allow an early purchase, for my poor dog's sake, of course.

As my veins began to close up shop, I researched alternate injection sites. I learned online (isn't Google a wondrous thing?) that, if I was careful, I could use the vein on the back of my hand but faced the new challenge of the vein "rolling," that is, essentially running away from the needle—something I should have done after that first bad night.

The internet also taught me that I could inject in my foot between the big toe and the second toe and achieve a high, although not as grand as a true slam. Seems there's a million tiny veins running between the toes, and like shooting fish in a barrel, all I had to do was stick and go. The main advantage? A handy location to use when trying to hide evidence of using.

Not only was I trying to hide my addiction from Stuart, but from God as well. The vision of Jesus haunted me when I was using. I grappled mightily with the faith component; however, I knew I had become the worst, most pathetic version of a hypocrite, worse than any person I had ever labeled as such, as I eschewed all things church and religion. On my way to a hook-up and usually on the way to buy drugs, I would consciously tune the radio to something other than Christian talk or Christian music. When I hooked up, the cross (and the once-cherished ring from Paris) got slipped deep into my work bag, down with the lint, the forgotten pack of gum, and the powdery traces of meth. I was compelled to shove these tangible symbols of a clean life where no one, especially me, could see them and ruin the party. But I knew God could see my sin. No canvas messenger bag was a shield from an omniscient God.

49

Fearless Faggot
PALM SPRINGS AND PASADENA: 2012

Before the end of Stuart's mother's interminable visit, I could take no more and fled to the desert where I had booked a three-day stay at All Worlds Resort, a clothing-optional sex motel in Palm Springs. But it was mid-January, and for Californians, a nighttime low of forty-seven degrees was too cold for most horny gay dudes, but not me. Although I wasn't bold enough to walk around naked, I wore only a pair of boxer briefs and combat boots, with a towel draped around my neck as if I was going for a moonlight swim. Add to the image the fact that I was beyond tweaked; I was shooting up in my room about every four hours in an attempt to stay high and horned-up.

While usually effective in L.A., my PnP ad on Craigslist didn't produce much action. Judging by the sounds coming through the wall, it seemed all the Dom-sub fun had missed me by several feet. In briefs and boots, I knocked on the guys' door with the hopes I might be invited to play. I was ignored after a quick flip of the blinds accompanied by an emphatic flip of the bird. Dejected, I went and planted myself in the sling in the video room where it was me and one lonely television playing a tired old Jeff Stryker video. The whole scene was pathetic.

By the end of the third day, I was fucked up beyond recognition. Isn't that what the Millennials call fubarred? My fried brain couldn't figure it out. My hands shook. Greasy from lube, I couldn't work my phone or laptop to search for the term. Then, I got the feeling I was being watched. I packed up everything and shoved it into the small closet, me included, and hunkered down in the dark, not knowing what to do next. Eric rescued me again with McNuggets and apple pies and helped me pack. Stuart was preoccupied with entertaining his mother before taking her back to the old country and never bothered to text me.

* * *

With Stuart out of the country, I went wild. Thanks to one of my online profiles on hook-up sites, I met Alex. Hispanic, tats, rough exterior, but with a kind heart. We hit it off immediately in a romantic sense, if that was even possible for two meth heads. Together, we cruised the video booths at his favorite dirty bookstore in Asuza or Alhambra. Doesn't matter. In fact, we hit it off so well that I invited him to stay with me in Redondo where we shared Stuart's prized Tempur-Pedic.

I bought him meals and paid for the drugs. He wanted to be adventurous and hang out naked on the balcony. I was hesitant, hoping no one would see us. Alex didn't give a crap. I complied.

We were physically compatible, and he showed a tenderness I hadn't experienced in a long time. Alex suggested I leave Stuart and run off with him. And I seriously considered it. But once the drugs ran out, and neither of us could reach our dealers, the magic evaporated, and he went back to Asuza. Or Alhambra. Or Altadena. Or wherever. I probably paid his cab fare.

With Stuart still away, I just continued to shoot up. There would always be the reliable, out-of-control sex drive that had me posting the same old, anonymous hook-up ads on Craigslist, trolling the usual websites, and pulling every toy out of the suitcase.

But, there was something else.

Shortly after the initial high, panic would strike.

What if Stuart gets back sooner than planned?

It had never happened before, so there was no logical reason to believe this time would be any different, but that's the twisted logic of crystal meth. It knocks down inhibitions and amps up fears.

I looked around the apartment and could see evidence of my misbehavior: a stain on the sofa cushion, a burn mark on the carpet, a greasy white film on the coffee table. And so, I would begin mad fits of cleaning. I guess that was how I tweaked.

With Buzz's complete loss of bladder control, there was always a legitimate need to clean the carpet. I bought a Hoover steam vacuum and cleaned the carpet daily. Sometimes twice in one day. It was the frantic, desperate need to atone for the revolting, disgusting, dirty creature I had become.

After I cleaned until my fingertips split and bled, I shifted focus to my usually impeccable personal hygiene. There was something about using the drug intravenously that made me stink. My skin was greasier than a day-old chicken nugget, and my scalp was worse than ever. I bathed in scalding-hot water murky with mixtures of bleach and homeopathic soaps and body washes from Whole Foods. I was told that Dr. Bronner's peppermint liquid soap worked miracles for potheads. Too bad it only intensified the meth smell. I tried deep-pore cleaning masks, abrasive scrubs, organic black tar Castile soaps, coconut milk, coconut oil, olive oil, and coconut-milk-and-olive-oil shampoos. It was all a futile quest to rid my body of the stink of sin.

I knew the answer to the whole conundrum. I put God out of sight when I was partying, but when paranoia took over, I became religious and prayed my prayers of desperation. Always sorry, always filled with repentance, but lacking in willpower to quit crystal meth.

Still, I used.

I must have struck a pocket of partiers, as the next guy lived in Pasadena, which was in Alex's territory. I found him on Craigslist, of course. And he was an actual gang member. He never gave me a name, rather just told me to call him God. Even high I couldn't do that and told him so. Not even a "little-g" god. As an alternative, he told me to simply call him Sir Fag Basher (FB).

Have I mentioned that meth makes one fearless? I paid him to rough me up, requesting he leave no marks on my face. You know, because of work. Ever the creative one, I staged scenes where he was the (guess the adjective) rough gang member, and I was the faggot he finds cruising the restroom on fisherman's wharf. He would threaten me and take me to the ATM then up to my apartment. As long as I had the drugs and money for his "tribute" (or as he also called it, his faggot fee), Sir FB played along. Except it wasn't mere role play. As he would remind me in text messages and phone calls, "he owned me," making it clear that he knew where I worked, where I lived, who I lived with, and would make my life a living hell if I didn't pay him whenever and whatever he demanded. My life had been a living hell for some time, so the threat carried little weight.

On one occasion when he didn't have access to a vehicle, I was ordered to get a specific room at a certain motel in Pasadena. The plump, old lady at the front desk smelled a rat, but I spewed a lie stating I had stayed in that particular room before, and it held special memories. What a load of BS.

I laid out, as instructed, a spool of rope and a roll of duct tape. Three hours late, he showed up, and we shot up. I forgot to bring the Magnums, so he improvised by tearing off a piece of the plastic trash bag from the room's wastepaper basket and using it as a condom. Yeah, that was one of my lowest moments.

I kept peeking through the drapes, convinced I saw a cop car in the parking lot. I threw my stuff into my suitcase, resetting the room as best possible. But I needed to shower badly. And Sir FB wasn't leaving without me as he needed a ride. Although he assured me he "had my back," I still took my suitcase and computer bag into the bathroom, locked the door, and attempted to shower. The paranoia was so intense that I left the shower curtain open so I could keep an eye on my stuff and another on the door.

I met up with Sir FB several more times. He would call, and I would ask "how much?" When he managed to come to my apartment, I was so freaked that Stuart would walk in, I couldn't enjoy his company. It didn't make a difference to him. He got what he wanted, his high and my cash, usually $300 per visit.

Was I really so pathetic, so lonely, and so depressed that I would willingly shove fistfuls of cash into the hands of thugs and psychics? Did I really hate myself that much? I was running out of money, as I covered Stuart's half of the bills, the escorts, and my daily addiction. I blocked Sir FB's number and went on Recon looking for S&M guys who didn't want money.

50

No Way Out

For my long, Independence Day weekend, I told Stuart I was going back up the coast to see my friends in Santa Cruz. He had to work most of the weekend but could still manage to take care of Buzz, the dog. In the meantime, I would be taking care of buzz, the addiction. Stuart wished me a safe trip, told me to drive the speed limit, and reminded me to eat. Thanks, Aunt Bee.

Truth is I had found exactly what I was seeking, right there on Recon. Same place I'd met Stuart. Only this time, in a chem-fueled state of mind, I was ready to become someone's slave. For real. Job, partner, and messed-up life be damned.

Not surprisingly, he never provided a name; I'll call him Master Pain, or MP for short. I arrived at MP's run-down house somewhere between South Bay and Santa Fe Springs. It was in a creepy, graffiti-riddled neighborhood, the kind of place people go for one thing. I went with my own supply that fit well into the meth-crafted submission scene I had in my head. *Nice boys don't go to these neighborhoods*, I half-reminded myself, as I pulled my car through an eight-foot-tall chain-link fence obscured with once-decorative metal slats that were now intertwined with weeds.

But I was no longer a nice boy.

Once my car was in, I was instructed to close the gate, place my wallet, cell phone, and keys in a provided Walmart bag, strip naked, and assume the position. That is, on my knees, hands behind head, head bowed. The one item I was to keep in my hands was the enormous dose of meth pre-loaded in a syringe.

"Does it understand that the worthless slave is now my property?"

"Yes, Sir," I said, the scene unfolding as I intended.

"Crawl to the garage. Now."

It was an approximate 50-foot crawl to the garage over sharp rocks. "Can I walk? I don't want to skin my knees," I asked.

"Did I give it permission to speak?"

"Um, no."

"No, WHAT?"

"No, Sir."

"Damn right I didn't give it permission. It will, from now on, remain silent. I will tell it when it may use the bathroom. When and what and if it eats and drinks, even when it may fart. Failure to comply will result in a harsh punishment the slave may not be able to endure."

Cool. He's good at this role-playing thing.

"Now, start crawling before I knock the living shit out of you."

I silently showed MP the needle with a shrug of "what do I do with this?"

"It will carry the fucking thing in its teeth and start crawling. It may not even have teeth by the time I'm through with it, so it should use them while it can."

I was hoping MP would allow me to shoot up as soon as possible, as it would make the scene more fun for me. Because in pushy-bottom world, that's all that mattered.

As I crawled into the cinder-block garage, I saw a full wall of medieval-looking bondage and torture implements.

Awesome! This guy really gets into it. This is gonna be so great!

To my left was a primitive bondage bench, to my right was a large metal dog cage, and in a far back corner stood an iron-barred prison cell with its thick bars secured deep into the concrete floor.

"Did it tell anyone where it was going?" MP asked.

"No, Sir."

"Did I give it permission to speak?" With that, I received a slap across my mouth so hard my lip bled, and I feared teeth were loosened.

"No, Sir," I squeaked. A fist to the mouth this time. I was clearly the loser in this twisted game of Simon Says. I shook my head "no."

"Good. And where is its partner? Slave may answer the question."

"Sir, he thinks I'm, I mean, he thinks it's up the coast in Santa…"

A hard smack to my right ear, my bad ear. "Too many fucking words, slave. Lay on the bench face up."

MP attached rusty and dirty iron fetters to my ankles and shackles to my wrists. With equally rusted lengths of thick-gauge chain, my legs were pulled painfully under the table and locked in place with padlocks.

"Stick that in your arm," he said, referring to the syringe. After it was in my vein and dangling, my arms were pulled above my head so hard I thought my shoulders would dislocate. Duct tape was placed over my mouth. "Is it ready? Doesn't matter if it is." He pushed the plunger down hard and the familiar sensations washed over me.

With my mouth taped and my nose in its typically plugged state, I had trouble breathing. I panicked and thrashed around as best I could within my tight bonds.

"Oh, is it having trouble breathing?" He placed his large, stinky palm over my nose. "Tough shit, slave. Suffocate. You think I care?"

I was on the verge of passing out when the hand allowed me to gasp for air.

I don't know how long it lasted, but MP used a whip all over the front of my body. I felt blood trickling somewhere but couldn't figure out where.

How dare he ruin my high like this.

Using meth gives the user a notoriously dried mouth. Injecting it makes your mouth feel like you licked a litter box in the middle of the Sahara. I made wild eye movements, prompting MP to rip the tape from my mouth. I tried mouthing the word "water."

Oh, is it thirsty? Well I can take care of that." He unzipped. "Gag on that, you worthless piece of shit."

I started to cry and received a fist to my other ear. "I didn't give it permission to cry."

The shackles remained in place, and the chains rearranged as MP pushed me into the jail cell. My arms were locked behind me as the iron door slammed shut.

"Fuck you, you worthless faggot. Oh, and you can scream all

you want; I built this garage to be soundproof. No one will ever hear you." I heard the side door through which we had entered being bolted from the outside. There was little light remaining in the garage.

Something had gone "off script" I was sure. Surely this man didn't think I was serious in our online chats about being abducted and enslaved. It was the drugs talking. He must have known that. Then I remembered a bit of advice I received from an experienced Master who taught safety courses to the S&M community: "Always tell someone where you're going."

My mind raced over the events of the previous twenty-four hours. I hadn't told a soul where I was going. I guess I must have wanted, deep down, to disappear for real.

I sat shivering in the cage, wet from peeing on myself. I figured if MP ever returned, I'd have to pay for that. It was afternoon when I arrived, and there was sunlight seeping into the garage through a cracked window. Now, there was no light. The high was long gone, the concrete cold and uncomfortable.

I flashed on those idyllic, wistful, almost romantic first nights using, soothed by the warmth of the Coral Sands' hot tub under an enormous Hollywood moon.

I thought of Mom and how this would kill her. *Should have thought of that sooner*, I scolded myself.

I started to hyperventilate.

So, this is how it ends. What an idiot I am. I deserve everything bad that happens.

The next day MP returned and moved me to the dog cage where I was locked into a painful position. I said I was thirsty. Again,

MP relieved himself all over me through the bars and left.

But there was another Master in the house. A handsome man in a leather harness and tight 501 jeans slipped through the garage door.

"Slave. Do you want to serve Master Pain, or would you rather serve me? He'll be back soon, so you need to decide. I left you two alone until now, but I had to step in. He's planning to put you in his van and take you to Phoenix. Do you want to be with me?"

Master Tim (MT) was an angel in leather, and from what I could tell, had probably bathed recently. MP stunk so badly it made my eyes water.

With parched throat and mouth, I managed to squeak out "You, Sir."

MT unlocked my cage, unfastened my fetters, and helped me stand on weak legs. He helped me into the clothes I had relinquished on the day I arrived. Was it yesterday? The day before?

I was too scared to evaluate the decision I had just made. Would Master Tim be less cruel? We slipped out of the house and into my car, all while MP was passed out somewhere inside. Since I was in no condition to be behind a steering wheel, MT drove.

"It's not his house, you know. He's just renting it for the summer," MT offered as he drove me back to Redondo. "How long will it take you to shower and pack a bag?"

"Look, I desperately need to shower, but I can't walk away from my life. Not this way. Not right now."

"I thought you wanted to be a slave—my slave?"

"I do. I mean, I really do. Just let me get my affairs in order first. Can I give you money for a cab and just call you tomorrow, please?

I feel really sick."

I put Master Tim in a cab and went upstairs, locked the bathroom door, and sat in the tub under a scalding shower, weeping. I never contacted either of them again.

If Stuart had noticed my fat, bruised lips he never said a word. I slept for two days.

51

Demons at the Door

As frightening as the close call of the July 4th weekend enslavement was, it still wasn't enough to scare me to quit; I just became a partying recluse. Staying at home where it was "safer," I spun my elaborate scenes from the perceived safety of my desk.

I was beyond exhausted, and sleep came only in fitful, violent naps plagued with nightmares that would rival any horror movie. A handsome blonde man seemed to be present in all the dreams. He was beautiful. His name was Lucifer.

I spent hours searching online for images of and references to Lucifer, learning that he fit into the Christian reality as the Devil himself. I was obsessed. I wanted to know everything about the fallen angel.

Was he really that bad? But he's so good looking, I reasoned with all the logic of a twelve-year-old schoolgirl.

I joined Satanic chat groups and started to write to Satanic masters on Recon. Suffering from a severe inability to learn my lesson, I nearly chucked it all and booked a flight to Spain (Spain!) to be permanently enslaved, mutilated, and eventually killed. I was too exhausted and loathed myself far too much to care.

I found Satanic chants and prayers online.

How can this stuff even be out there?

I discovered that, if I truly wanted to follow the evil one and have his so-called protection, I would have to relinquish all ties to God by writing a vow in blood.

I drew some blood from the battlefield that was once my left arm. I only managed a couple of drops and tried using a ballpoint pen like a quill, dipping it in the blood to write. I was too high, hands too shaky to produce more than the letter "I." Good thing, actually.

Frustrated by the failed writing exercise, I shot up another time. I placed multiple ads inviting the roughest, meanest guys to come to the apartment and take out their frustrations. I laid out every sex toy, every implement of pain, every bondage device for the elaborate scenes I had staged in my thoroughly fried brain. I pre-shackled my wrists and ankles with the leather cuffs that were, by this time, well worn. By the time the first guy arrived, I was too tweaked and too freaked to do anything and told him to leave. Even when I knew that Stuart would be at work for several hours, I still imagined him walking in and telling me it was over. I was living the worst lie imaginable.

With the trick out of the apartment, I scooped up all the sex gear and shoved it back in the suitcase. I made sure all lights were off and that all blinds and drapes were closed as tightly as possible.

Just then, an audible whoosh of black, shadowy figures like bats seemed to surround me. I'd seen these apparitions before at the Coral Sands.

I peered out the peephole, absolutely sure there were cops in the hall (there weren't). The demonic shadow figures appeared to be swirling on the other side of my door like a flock of vultures ready for the feast.

I piled heavy boxes and furniture in front of the door. I contorted myself until I was severely cramped, all for trying to get a look at nothing in the hallway. I was frozen in place for three, maybe four hours. I had to pee. My mouth was too dry to swallow. Still, I kept watch. Finally, the high subsided. I dismantled the barricade, scrubbed the apartment, cleaned the carpet, and attempted to soak off my stink. Stuart would be home soon.

* * *

Buzz's tumor had grown to the size of a small orange. To keep it from dragging on the ground and bursting open, the Redondo vet fit him into a baby's onesie. He seemed to take comfort in his new attire and enjoyed showing off his new clothes during his short walks around the apartment building. He certainly garnered a lot of attention with women cooing at him.

But we were at the two-yard line with only seconds left on the clock.

I got up on Saturday morning, August 11, 2012 to find that Buzz's tumor had sprung a leak, and his onesie was soaked with blood. This was the day the vet had warned us about. Within thirty minutes, he was on her stainless-steel exam table. Her eyes filled with tears as she shook her head.

The vet left us alone in the room with Buzz to say our goodbyes.

Stuart nodded the go-ahead and an assistant peeled off Buzz's onesie and placed him in a white burial gown on a little white pillow.

The vet tied off one of his front legs and inserted his last syringe. In seconds, it was over, and Buzz was gone.

52

Persistent Knocking

I was sobbing out of control—sobbing, screaming, and pacing the apartment like a caged animal. Crying so hard I couldn't breathe and was choking on snot. Shaking my fists toward Heaven asking "Why? Why? Why?" I hated myself in every possible way. My body was an exhausted wasteland, my brain numb, my emotions annihilated.

I stumbled into the bedroom and got on my knees to pray.

No, on my knees isn't enough this time.

I lied prostate—that is, face down—on the floor with my head buried in Buzz's bed.

God could have taken my job or my relationship with Stuart or my Mom or my possessions, or even my freedom, to finally get through to me. Instead, He used my dog.

I thought of the thousands of dollars I'd spent to save Buzz only to later leave him alone for days while I partied in Hollywood. I thought of the wad of gauze I left carelessly within reach that Buzz ingested and got lodged in his intestines that marked the beginning of his health issues. I remembered the drive to California when I had a 104-degree fever, and Buzz sat calmly in the passenger seat, resting a reassuring paw on my right arm. Memories of Buzz appearing on stage at my theater, ever the well-behaved dog. This dog had been such an enormous part of my life, and now, he was gone.

I knew no amount of crying would bring my dog back. But God had me where He wanted me: face down, completely broken, and ready to finally give Him my life, all of it, especially the parts I always hoped He couldn't see. Although I had asked for salvation two years prior, it was on this day, August 11, 2012, that the Holy Spirit convicted me.

I sputtered through a laundry list of horrific sins, begging for forgiveness. I cried out to Jesus, begging Him to step in, to take over my life, to get me off the drugs.

I had been lying on the floor for an hour, maybe two, when a sense of peace washed over me, a peace that surpassed all understanding, just as the Bible describes in Philippians 4:7.

I stood, wiped my eyes, brushed the pug hair off my face, and started filling black trash bags with every sex toy, every leather restraint, every porn DVD, every remaining syringe, every dirty pipe, and every hidden stash of crystal meth. I tripled bagged the mess, and with a vengeance, wound duct tape around it as if I were binding up the Devil himself.

I logged into every hook-up site and deleted my accounts.

I deleted every bookmarked link to porn websites.

I wiped twenty-four gigs' worth of porn from my Mac. All of it, every photo, every video.

Then, I pulled back the drapes, allowing the sunlight to flood the apartment. I opened the sliding patio door and drew in deep, cleansing draughts of salty ocean air. Looking out to the ocean, peace and stillness washed over me.

It's going to be OK, I told myself. I'd spent my life so petrified of ending up alone that I'd pushed away everyone who had ever dared to come close, especially Stuart. But God was persistent. He never stopped knocking on the door of my heart. He had always been there, patiently waiting for me to allow Him in.

I quit meth cold turkey the day Buzz died, the day I finally submitted to God and His perfect will. I slept for three days, the sleep of a battle-weary soldier, the sleep of an addict who was ready to leave it all behind.

I didn't go through withdrawals. I didn't relapse or fall off the so-called wagon. I also didn't go back to Crystal Meth Anonymous, although their teachings stayed top of mind. They taught that each addict must place his or her trust in a higher power or God of their understanding.

There was a great amount I didn't understand about my God, but I was eager to learn.

Turns out that the God of my understanding was the same God who was the baby in the manger and the God-man on the cross.

He is the God who saved my life the day I was thrown into the Pacific and nearly drowned, and He is the God who brought me through the near-overdoses when I was drowning in my own vomit.

He is the God who saved me from getting DUIs and citations for reckless driving, and the God who prevented me from going to federal prison for drug possession.

He is the God who had always been there, knocking on the door of my heart, waiting patiently for me to call on Him.

God is Jesus and the "...or Whoever's Up There" in a lifetime of prayers.

God had always been there, and He won.

Epilogue

It caught my eye immediately, a little Ziploc-style bag with a bit of what I knew was meth. It was laying on the sidewalk as I was taking Marty, my third pug, on a walk to the nearby pond. I stopped and looked at it and my first thought was, "I wonder if there's enough to get high." Then the usually still, small God voice spoke rather loudly, "Don't even think about it." My next thought was to pick it up and save a dog or a child from sticking it in its mouth, or to prevent a fellow addict from sticking it wherever. I kicked the pouch into a storm drain. Good riddance.

So, yes, I'm an addict. I've been clean since August 2012, but it's insane how the urge to use can sneak up on a guy. Even during something as innocent as a dog walk. Lest I ever boast about the years I've been sober, it's little moments like this that remind me how close I always am to losing all that time being clean.

As much as I'd like to end this book with me looking out over the ocean (that did happen) while everything falls into place, quite the opposite occurred.

I have no doubts that God saved me the moment I cried out to Him. After all, isn't that what the Bible promises? The real miracle was that I had no cravings, no withdrawal symptoms (other than

446

exhaustion), and didn't relapse.

I'm still shocked at how seemingly well I held things together at work—how I was never questioned, never subjected to a drug test, and never brought into a meeting with HR to discuss drug use. Honestly, I don't think drug use was ever suspected. That's not how it's supposed to go, right?

I'm often asked if Stuart knew about my addiction. The answer is, I have no clue. If he knew, he never asked about it or confronted me. Even after I got clean, he never mentioned a thing. Surely, my behavior had been erratic enough to notice.

Then, everything hit the fan.

In January 2014, my half-brother Jay attempted to murder my parents prior to killing himself in their house. They survived, but Jim was permanently disabled in the shooting and has used a wheelchair ever since.

I took two months of FMLA leave to help my parents, only to return to work to find I had been shoved into an equal production manager role with inferior projects. I'm talking a Mickey appearance and three balloons in a hotel ballroom. I turned that situation into lemonade and was approved to write creative treatments for many large events. Disney production managers usually did not write creative; they only put budget to it. But having been a writer and theater owner, I was able to bring together exciting creative events that delighted my corporate clients.

Through all this, I stayed clean. Again, praise Jesus!

And then…

Stuart walked out on Thanksgiving weekend of 2015, taking

our rescue pug Bailey. It came on the heels of my brilliant idea to move to Hollywood, promising I could handle the commute to work at Disneyland. I couldn't. We stayed there less than five months, and it cost me more than three grand in round-trip moving expenses. (We moved to and from Orange County.)

But it also cost me my partner of nearly six years. Stuart was so excited to live in Hollywood, and I took that dream away from him. We would have celebrated our six-year milestone on December 5, 2015, but Stuart bailed one week in advance of having to buy an anniversary gift (smart financial move on his part). This time, there were no psychics and no reconciliation. I knew he was gone for good, and he left several visual clues for me to find. He took everything from his bathroom except for a wooden countertop organizer I hated. In addition to taking the dog, he took all of Bailey's toys and the dog food container that held a month's worth of food. He also took all of his clothes and all of his prized possessions. As he had done in 2010, gifts from me were left in conspicuous places.

Stuart's walk-out also came after nearly four years of pretty serious head hitting. I can't claim that behavior as a meth withdrawal symptom because I'd been doing it since I was four. I know the behavior scared him, scared the dog, and quite frankly, scared me as well. Stuart was probably afraid he'd wind up with a vegetable were I to hit myself hard enough.

I'd also become one of those annoying "baby believers" and listened only to Christian music, read the Bible, and attended Bible studies once or twice weekly. This, too, was a driver for Stuart leaving.

And although Stuart and I had only ever been mildly intimate, when I became clean, I also became celibate.

And finally...

Due to a combination of all of the above, my parents urged me to leave Disney and move back to Colorado to heal, to write, and to help them as their mobility continued to decline. I'd like to say that the move to Colorado in February 2016 fixed everything—not by a long shot.

So, let's see: half-brother's suicide, father becoming disabled, me being diagnosed with PTSD, reduced scope of work projects and negative perception, partner bailed, and I left Disney to sell the dead brother's crap on eBay in Colorado. Then, add in a whirlwind romance and marriage engagement in Colorado that knocked the wind out of me when I was dumped. I certainly have plenty more to tell in a second memoir! It even has a working title, *And Now for My Next Act of Brilliance: Another Memoir.*

My faith has gone from wobbly to firm to wobbly more times than I can count. I try to lean on God and Jesus to carry me through each day, so that part is working most of the time. I've tried church but still cannot reconcile the negative feelings about it that formed so many years ago. I'm working on it as best I can.

Most days, it's damn hard, but I try to forgive myself a little more every day and acknowledge those little successes that make all the difference, like walking away from a bag of meth on the sidewalk.

Acknowledgements

All my love and gratitude to Mom and Jim for helping make this book possible.

Heartfelt thanks to my beta readers extraordinaire: Dave Earick, Flynn Falcone, Jennie Lee Frank, Connie Gohata, Connie Landeck, John Kazlauskas, Mike Martinez, and especially Stephanie Moazami.

Immeasurable gratitude to Gina Griffiths, the Guides, the CW, and Spirit Shadow. Love you all bunches.

Gratitude to Pastor Bill Hoganson at Calvary Chapel Anaheim.

Humble respect and thanks to Martin Moran for 33 years of inspiration.

Kudos to Kenny Holcomb for cover design, LeeAnne Carmack for line editing, Lyric Taylor for copyediting, and Karen Maneely for bringing all the pieces together.

Thanks also to Ray Robinson, Regina Brooks, Mary Negrete, and University of California San Diego Extension.

My deepest apologies to those I hurt while I was trapped in addiction.